BEYOND
CULTURAL IMPERIALISM

COMMUNICATION AND HUMAN VALUES

Series editors

Robert A. White, Editor, Centre for the Study of Communication and Culture, London, UK
Michael Traber, Associate Editor, World Association for Christian Communication, London, UK

International editorial advisory board

Also in this series

BEYOND CULTURAL IMPERIALISM

Globalization, Communication and the New International Order

EDITED BY

Peter Golding

and

Phil Harris

SAGE Publications
London • Thousand Oaks • New Delhi

Editorial selection and matter, and Introduction, Peter Golding
and Phil Harris © 1997
Chapter 1 © Samir Amin, 1997
Chapter 2 © Tony Barnett, 1997
Chapter 3 © Annabelle Sreberny-Mohammadi, 1997
Chapter 4 © Cees Hamelink, 1997
Chapter 5 © Colleen Roach, 1997
Chapter 6 © Mohammed Musa, 1997
Chapter 7 © Phil Harris, 1997
Chapter 8 © Pradip N. Thomas, 1997
Chapter 9 © Richard C. Vincent, 1997
Glossary © Phil Harris, 1997

P96
.I5
B48
1997x

First published in 1997

SAGE Publications Ltd
6 Bonhill Street
London EC2A 4PU

SAGE Publications Inc.
2455 Teller Road
Thousand Oaks, California 91320

SAGE Publications India Pvt Ltd
32, M-Block Market
Greater Kailash – I
New Delhi 110 048

British Library Cataloguing in Publication data

A catalogue record for this book is available
from the British Library.

ISBN 0 7619 5330 2
ISBN 0 7619 5331 0 (pbk)

Library of Congress catalog record available

Typeset by Mayhew Typesetting, Rhayader, Powys
Printed in Great Britain by Biddles Ltd, Guildford, Surrey

To the memory of Barry Troyna,
good friend and comrade
from barricades to terraces.

Contents

List of contributors

Samir Amin is Director of the Third World Forum in Dakar. In 1957, he graduated with a PhD in Economics in Paris, and became Research Officer in the Planning Administration of Egypt until 1960. He has been a Technical Adviser to the Government of Mali for Planning, Professor of Planning in various countries and Director of the African Institute for Economic Development and Planning in Dakar. He is the author of numerous books on Third World economics.

Tony Barnett is Professor of Development Studies at the School of Development Studies, University of East Anglia, Norwich. He has carried out research on development issues in many parts of the world, including Sudan, Papua New Guinea, Eritrea, Gambia, Zambia, Jordan, India and Malaysia. Since 1988, he has been working on the socio-economic impact of AIDS in Africa. Recent books include *Sociology and Development* (1988), *Sudan: State, Capital and Transformation* (1988), *Sudan: The Gezira Scheme and Agricultural Transition* (1991), the latter two with Abbas Abdelkarim, and *AIDS in Africa: its Present and Future Impact* (1992), with Piers Blaikie.

Peter Golding is Professor of Sociology and Head of the Department of Social Sciences at the University of Loughborough, where he is also Co-Director of the Communication Research Centre. He is co-editor of the *European Journal of Communication*. He has written widely on media and social policy issues. His books include *The Mass Media* (1974), *Making The News* (1979), *Images of Welfare* (with Sue Middleton, 1982), *Taxation and Representation* (with David Deacon, 1994).

Cees J. Hamelink is Professor of International Communication at the University of Amsterdam and was President of the International Association for Mass Communication Research (IAMCR) from 1990 to 1994. He is the author of more than ten books on international communication, culture and technology, including *Cultural Autonomy in Global Communications* (1983).

Phil Harris is Adviser on Communication Policy and Strategy to Inter Press Service (IPS) and Editor of *Terra Viva*, the IPS newspaper. He graduated with an M.Phil. degree from the Centre for Mass Communication Research, University of Leicester, specializing in international news flow and North–South issues. He has extensively studied the problem of dependence in international communication, and is the author of a major report for UNESCO on 'News Dependence: The Case for a New World Information Order'. For the last fifteen years he has helped train journalists from Africa and Asia in news agency journalism.

Mohammed Musa lectures on the Communication and Media Studies Programme at the University of Zimbabwe. He was head of the Mass Communication department at the University of Maiduguri, Nigeria. He was also Chairman of the Board of Directors, Bauchi Radion Corporation in Nigeria. He graduated with MA and PhD degrees from the Centre for Mass Communication Research, University of Leicester. His publications have covered news agencies, news production, media professionalism and New International Information Order issues, and he has carried out a major research project on international and Nigerian media reporting of the Gulf War.

Colleen Roach is a writer and researcher specialising in communications and cultural issues. She worked at UNESCO during the years of 'battle' over the 'new world information and communication order' and has been a professor of communications for the past 11 years.

Annabelle Sreberny-Mohammadi is Professor and Director of the Centre for Mass Communication Research at the University of Leicester. Her recent publications include *Small Media, Big Revolution: Communication, Culture and the Iranian Revolution* (with A. Mohammadi, 1994), *Questioning the Media* (with J. Downing and A. Mohammadi, 2nd ed. 1995), *Women, Media and Development in a Global Context* (1995) and *Globalization, Communication and Transnational Civil Society* (with S. Braman, 1996).

Pradip N. Thomas was formerly Asia Regional Co-ordinator at the World Association for Christian Communication (WACC). He is now WACC's Director of Studies and joint-editor of the international journal *Media Development*. A graduate of the Centre for Mass Communication Research, University of Leicester, he has contributed articles to various journals on the political economy of communications in India, alternative communications, ethno-religious conflict and the media, and public service broadcasting.

Richard C. Vincent is Associate Professor of Communication at the University of Hawaii, Manoa, and has a PhD in communication from the University of Massachusetts, Amherst. He specializes in mass communication theory and research, with emphasis on international media. He has published widely in both scholarly journals and books, and is author (with Johan Galtung) of *Global Glasnost: Toward a New International Communication Order?* (1992) and *Glasnost' – USA: Missing Political Themes in US Media Discourse* (forthcoming).

Foreword

This book has its origins in conversations between the editors about the way world communications research was changing in the 1990s. Although this may have seemed on the surface to revolve around such issues as the declining state of English pub culture, the inability of Scottish football to travel, and the relative merits of takeaway pizzas in Rome and Leicester, underlying these conversations was a deep unease about the analysis of global cultural change.

The editors were fortunate in having some discipline imposed on their thoughts by the active intervention of one or two key thinkers in this area working at the admirably open-minded and energetic base of the World Association for Christian Communication. Neville Jayaweera, who was then working at WACC, started out as a partner in this enterprise; however, his subsequent duties in Scandinavia, on diplomatic call for Sri Lanka, absorbed his time and efforts. Michael Traber, recently retired from WACC, has been a friend and support throughout the development of this project, and the book would have been impossible without his quiet, but effective, encouragement. To other staff at WACC, especially Philip Lee, and Pradip Thomas, we also owe a great debt. More formally, we gladly acknowledge to WACC out gratitude for the grant which enabled much of the editorial work for this project to take place across a growing diversity of locations. Bob White, of the Gregorian University in Rome, has been supportive throughout, alongside Mike Traber as co-editor of the series to which this book contributes.

Editing a book with contributors scattered across four continents, and with its editors never in the same country for more than a few days at a time, poses problems of international communication which make the concerns of this volume only too tangible. We are grateful to our contributors for their patience and forbearance, when many might have assumed their efforts would never see the light of day. We are especially grateful to Wendy Monk at Loughborough, for her invaluable editorial assistance, carried out with characteristic efficiency and good humour, at a stage when editorial energy was flagging. International communications are of the essence in a project such as this, but as ever the support that really matters is that closest to hand. We both want to thank our families for their now expected patience and tolerance of long, expensive phone calls, and occasional disappearance into editorial purdah for days on end.

Our saddest duty is to record our desire to dedicate this book to the memory of our good friend, Barry Troyna. Barry was, throughout his life, a tireless fighter against racism wherever it was to be found, and someone who keenly understood the international forces which lie behind the indignities and cruelties of racial conflict and oppression. However global culture and communications change, the key issues remain the same.

Peter Golding
Phil Harris
June 1996

Introduction

Peter Golding and Phil Harris

Wandering round an upmarket shopping centre in swelteringly sunny Penang, days before Christmas, it was a trifle disconcerting to riffle through the Christmas tree baubles and admire the artificial snow décor on the mock Tudor shop windows. In a fearsomely expensive Tokyo hotel the restaurants compete to offer the most elegant of chic European cuisine. Mooching round the acrid and sticky dust trails behind a Lagos street market it was impossible to miss kicking endless lines of lager cans. At the back of the awesome baroque structures of the former royal palace, high above the Danube in Budapest, stands one of the largest, reddest Coca-Cola machines you could ever wish to see. 'You can see who won, can't you?', our guide queried ruefully.

In frantic response the Vietnamese government was not the first in launching a campaign against 'cultural poisons', as retailers were forced to hide British breakfast cereals and French wines under blankets while police tore down advertising billboards displaying foreign goods. Even more desperate measures in the digital age are required, as the Chinese government announced in 1996 rules intended to increase its control over cyberspace by forcing computer networks to use approved links and forbidding the spread of information that would 'hinder public order'.

Something, it is clear, is happening to the diversity and reach of world cultures. For the archetypal travelling academic or journalist, doing their best to ape the smart familiarity and high-tech purposefulness of the jet-set executive, one airport lounge can seem confusingly much like another, one English-dominated international seminar indistinguishable from a dozen more. This troubling semblance of the superficial trappings of a global culture has lurked behind much discussion of international media culture for many years. Cultural oppression or global village? Threat or promise?

What can one more book add to this substantial literature? News editors have a distinct advantage over book editors. They don't have to worry that history is rapidly going to overtake their product and render it obsolete. Disposable and ephemeral as their work is, they need only be concerned about the opposition scooping an item by a few hours, or the apparent advantages of broadcast media exploiting the immediacy of telecommunications over the less instant technologies of print. The book editor takes an altogether more leisurely and lofty view of time's tread. Yet so often this can become a trap.

These cautionary thoughts have been prominent in our minds in the preparation and production of this collection. When first mooted many years ago, the collapse of the Soviet empire, the redundancy of Cold War practice and rhetoric, the formal disappearance of apartheid, the rapid dwindling of US hegemony, and the resurgence of nationalisms, ethnic, local and regional, were either wholly invisible or only just beginning to surface. The pace and significance of the change in the international order in the dying years of the millennium have caught us all unawares.

Yet it was nagging doubts about our capacity to understand and analyse even such changes as we had recognized, that prompted the book in the first place. Our focus on communications and media issues led us to the surprising observation that this most international and interdisciplinary of fields of study had become curiously insular in its approach. While exciting and vital debates about the nature of the changes in international politics and social dynamics were attracting the attention of other intellectual and political fields, communication scholars were increasingly, and unproductively, becoming self-enclosed in their own ever more introspective dialogues.

Of course the sense of change can be much exaggerated. Social scientists of all persuasions enjoy the sense of living on the cusp of social reconstruction. As futurologists wrestle with the implications of new information technologies it is easy to get caught up in a seductive rhetoric which sees us as just about to turn the corner into a new, post-modern, or information age. Most of the world's population would be somewhat intrigued and bewildered by the visions conjured in seminars and think-tanks from Berkeley to Paris, while enduring privations resulting from the eternal verities of global inequality and exploitation.

It is worth pausing to remind ourselves how deeply rooted such simple structural features remain. The 1980s were indeed the 'lost decade' for much of the poorer two-thirds of the world. At the start of the decade roughly 60 per cent of the world's population lived in countries whose per capita income was less than 10 per cent of the world average. As the 1990s arrived some were emerging from the morass of destitution. But this was a small minority, mainly in the East Asian bloc of 'newly industrializing countries'. While aid was hastily diverted to the struggling economies of Eastern Europe (prompted by commercial opportunism and American alarm at the political instability generated by collapsing economies and a power vacuum), the poorer countries, of Asia and Africa especially, listened to uncomfortable advice about 'structural adjustment' while watching over soaring debt and falling primary commodity prices.

The combination of growing northern protectionism, declining aid, higher real interest rates, and growing debt has further consolidated the endemic crisis of Third World economies. By the year 2000, as the rest of us gaze in wonder at millennium celebrations and ponder the luxuries of the digital future, about a billion people will be living in absolute poverty. The statistics of these diverging experiences are always staggering, and rarely illuminating, but as Paquet-Sévigny has reminded us, their scale is mammoth. 'Some 70 per cent of world income is produced and consumed by 15 per cent of the world's population. In the 41 least developed countries, average per capita income is well under $300, in sharp contrast to the $14,500 average of developed market economies ... Each year in the developing world, 14 million people die before their fifth birthday' (quoted in Ihonvbere, 1992: 990). Massively mounting debt engendered a new form of economic bondage, exacerbated by declining incoming private capital flows.

The advice from the North has been stern. As an OECD report puts it, the problem is 'fundamental institutional and human resource weaknesses'. It wags its finger disapprovingly and offers firm guidance: 'It is clear that a critical factor in enabling developing countries to participate dynamically in world trade, and thus to adjust to the fundamental long-term forces now in play, is a flexible robust, business sector. The individual business unit is the key institution for intermediating between national capacities and the world economy.' The need is for 'market and efficiency-oriented growth policies and their effective implementation by strong and competent governments' (OECD, 1990: 58). It does not take much imagination to translate these epithets. As the report goes on 'constructive labour relations are an important aspect of private sector development', and there is a 'need to rationalise the parastatal sector' (ibid.: 80–1). The reward for the obedient, of course, will be, in that wonderful euphemism, structural adjustment loans.

What emerges then is a pattern that goes full circle. Moving forward from Bretton Woods in 1944, through the rise of the Non-Aligned Movement at Bandung in 1955, or more completely in 1961, and the arrival of the Third World on the international agenda of economic decision-making at UNCTAD in 1964, brings us to the brave new world of the 1990s with the Western economies on the edge of recession, and the Third World riddled with dual economies, massive debts, and over a billion people living in stark and absolute poverty. On the demand side we find a rising appetite for imports fuelled by a pattern of demand nurtured by cosmopolitan elites, and consequently a growing dependence on the North for research and development, technology, and education.

Communication scholars have never ignored the global dimension to their subject. The myopia and insularity to which we allude is not that of parochialism, but of intellectual provincialism. The interest of communications research in international dynamics has gone through three phases. The first involved a happy optimism, in which the media would be 'magic multipliers', bringing development advice instantly, effectively and extensively to the information-hungry multitudes. Pioneers like Wilbur Schramm evolved elaborate and inventive conceptual frameworks and research programmes whose practical application was energetic and well meant, if the political programme underlying them was only too evident (Golding, 1974, 1977). A second, and more critical phase construed the spread of Western imagery and culture as a new form of imperialism, cultural imperialism, which was more insidious and more effective in cementing the dependency of the post-colonial periphery than the fiscal crudities of earlier decades. Finally the concept of globalization appeared, '*the* concept of the 1990s' (Waters, 1995:1). An all-embracing capture of the distinctive features of late modernity, cultural flows and information technology were prominent and defining facets of this characterization of the modern world.

This certainly took us beyond the all too narrow debates increasingly common within communication and media scholarship. Those debates have found themselves truncated in two ways. First, they have too frequently been confined within an *administrative* frame of reference, generating ritual recitals of the meetings, declarations and conferences which are the wayside landmarks of the post-war trek towards cultural sovereignty. The emergence of the Non-Aligned Movement to provide a political accompaniment to pressure for a New International Economic Order led inexorably to the cardinal involvement of UNESCO as a forum for what became the insistent demand for a New World Information and Communication Order. Culminating in the establishment of the MacBride Commission and, later, the International Programme for the Development of Communications, the oft told story of the political campaign which took the USA and UK out of UNESCO is critically reviewed in the chapters that follow, especially those by Hamelink and by Roach. But the literature which swelled alongside these debates was so often a litany of gatherings and manifestos, from Nairobi to Algiers, to

Lima, to New Delhi, to Colombo. It became harder and harder to stand back from such academic tourist guides to see the economic and social dynamics underneath. The reduction of history to a documentary paper chase was quite inadequate to the complex social, political and economic dynamics in play.

Secondly, the frame of reference was excessively focused on the mass media. After all, the charter document from UNESCO was a *Mass Media Declaration* (1978), and the public debate from both sides was very often about the presumed attempt to foster control and licensing of journalists in Third World authoritarian regimes, while clinging to the tenets of liberal freedom of the press in the West. This seemed fundamentally inadequate to the questions of culture, identity, and globalization with which writers outside communication research were becoming increasingly exercised.

Crucial to the limited vision developed in these debates was the sense of a David and Goliath model inherent in the term 'cultural imperialism'. Centre dominated periphery, imperialists held dominion over dependencies, and all was increasingly held in place by the power of the media above all else. The term cultural imperialism began to limit rather than illuminate discussion. Garofalo (1993: 18) has usefully summarized the weaknesses of the concept under four heads. Firstly it overstates external determinants and undervalues the internal dynamics, not least those of resistance, within dependent societies. Secondly, it conflates economic power and cultural effects. Thirdly, there is an assumption that audiences are passive, and that local and oppositional creativity is of little significance. Finally, there is an often patronizing assumption that what is at risk is the 'authentic' and organic culture of the developing world under the onslaught of something synthetic and inauthentic coming from the West. Now we would only go so far with this impatient rewriting. Garofalo calls for an important riposte to the more deterministic models of cultural flow, and rightly draws attention to the undue simplicity of much that flowed from 'cultural imperialism' models. However, as in the parallel debates within 'Cultural Studies' in Western scholarship, the rediscovery of the resistant and creative, even subversive, power of audiences can too easily slip, even within self-consciously radical discourses, into a romantic celebration of the cultural insubordination of consumers. Welcome music to the indignant ears of MTV, Coca-Cola, McDonald's and the rest, but perhaps just a trifle optimistic in its rejection of even the more simplistic accounts of cultural oppression.

Nonetheless, it became clear that 'cultural imperialism' needed unpacking in both its component terms. The lingering Leninist tones of imperialism lent it too deliberate and calculated a meaning. For many this was necessary and appropriate. Objectives were planned, campaigns constructed, objectives clearly set in the boardrooms of the military-industrial complex. Petras has argued, for example, that 'United States cultural imperialism has two major goals, one economic and the other political: to capture markets for its cultural commodities and to establish hegemony by shaping popular consciousness', though '[T]he principal target of cultural imperialism is the political and economic exploitation of youth' (Petras, 1993: 139). He goes on to define cultural imperialism as 'the systematic penetration and domination of the cultural life of the popular classes by the ruling classes of the West in order to reorder the values, behaviour, institutions, and identity of the oppressed peoples to conform with the interests of the imperial classes' (ibid.: 140). Within this scheme the 'mass media have become an integral part of the US system of global political and social control' (ibid.: 142). We would not wish to part too far from the accusations and analysis inherent in that account. But its presumption of clear and pre-meditated goals, seamless collusion between class and social segments, unproblematic adoption of a categorization of 'imperial' and 'popular' classes, and elision of any contradictions between economic and cultural processes, leaves such analysis only too open to the criticisms adduced by such writers as Garofalo. As Amin and Barnett show in their chapters in this book, the dynamics of 'imperialism' have become complex and inconsistent in the latter years of the century, however, much of the old forms of inequality and mendacity that lay behind them still remain.

If 'imperialism' needs unpacking so too does the term 'culture'. Before we reach, Goering-like, for our revolver every time we hear the term, it is only necessary to look beyond the mass media to recognize the scope of the symbolic and normative impact of one society on another. As Kieh notes in reviewing the roots of Western influence in Africa, education in that continent 'is a social institution which expresses capitalist cum Western socio-political intentions, aspirations, and interests' (Kieh, 1992: 9). So too, he notes, in dress, consumption, entertainment, fine arts, and politics. Annabelle Sreberny-Mohammadi takes us further down that route in Chapter 3, reminding us not least of the power of tourism among the flows within what Appadurai terms the 'ethnoscape' – 'the landscape of persons who constitute the shifting world within which we live' (Appadurai, 1990: 297). International tourism has resisted the inroads of recession in the 1990s, receipts rising by 6.8 per cent in 1992 alone. In that year Africa received some 17 million tourists. Good news (a large and growing increase year on year) or bad (with 12 per cent of the world's population Africa gets just 1.6 per cent of the world's tourism receipts)? Behind the statistics lie other processes. The growing attraction of exotic locales, of 'travel' rather than 'holidays', takes us to the allure of 'eco-tourism', in which the sustenance of local culture is an important requirement for the inducement of the Western visitor. 'Culture-based' travel and 'eco-tourism' are expected to grow by up to 30 per cent a year through the 1990s (Cleverdon, 1993).

But unravelling the shorthand of 'cultural imperialism', necessary though it is, only gets us so far. We still need to get 'beyond cultural imperialism' to capture this complex and crucial stage in our social evolution. Whatever the form and character of the new international order, it remains deeply and starkly inegalitarian, in ways which mark the lives of the privileged minority as much as the impoverished majority. Corporate giants continue to dictate the flows and substance of the goods and material which form and reform this order. Yet only so much has changed. As Garofalo (1993: 30) insists, 'the new diversity of global culture must not be allowed to paper over hierarchizations of race and ethnicity, let alone the age-old inequalities associated with gender and class'. What has changed is the form, and just perhaps the mechanisms, by which these persistent schisms are reinvented.

In attempting to capture what is new about 'the ensemble of institutions through which the new imperialism functions' (Steven, 1994: 294), the pace and dazzling prominence of technological advance are bound to impress. Yet the jury is still out on what these innovations may mean. Just as the impact of the 'transistor revolution' in the 1960s was far from as predicted, so too for more recent gadgetry. The cassette recorder facilitated cheap and easy production, duplication and dissemination of local music and styles in many regions, yet also became the dominant form for global distribution of the ever more ubiquitous transnational music industry. Video recording gave new political energy and resource to the Kayapo and other Indian groups in the Amazon basin, yet also secured the full integration of the television and film industries in the further domestication of Western leisure patterns. The Internet is being heralded by aficionados as the means for horizontal communication and global networking which will revolutionize relationships both local and global, yet its commercialization in the mid-1990s looks all too familiar to observers of past technological promise.

To interrogate these developments will require the reconnection of debates about communications and media with wider questions in the social and human sciences. Thus far the notion of globalization has failed to meet that need. Firstly, its focus on the cultural always detaches the epiphenomena of change from their structural imperatives. To argue, as Waters (1995: 124) does, that 'material and power exchanges in the economic and political arenas are progressively becoming displaced by symbolic ones, that is by relationships based on values, preferences and tastes rather than by material inequality and constraint', is a breathtaking commentary on a world patently characterized by unprecedented extremes of material experience and opportunity. We are a long way, surely, from believing that parallel style wars among the urban youth of Tokyo, Dar es Salaam, Lima and New York are a greater reality than the desperate efforts to eke out some form of subsistence among the billion or so of the world's inhabitants living on less than a dollar a day.

Secondly, the concept of globalization underestimates the persistence of the nation state as political form and economic entity. It is tempting to observe – as many have done who believe they are observing the final triumph of a singular form of economic system, Western capitalism – that the end of diversity has finally come at modernity's zenith. Fukuyama advances this particular cosmopolitan proclamation thus: 'there has emerged in the last few centuries something like a true global culture, centering around technologically driven economic growth and the capitalist social relations necessary to produce and sustain it' (Fukuyama, 1992: 126). But the confusion between political project and the stubborn verities of economic and cultural existence is substantial. While the new international division of labour has certainly relocated production and the circuits of goods, people and capital, the extent of variations between the levels of success of national economies suggests something other than globalization. The USA in particular remains immune to such dissolution of national boundaries: 'The ratio of imports and exports to GDP stands at 21 per cent, unchanged since 1980. Foreign investment in US stocks and bonds has risen, but in 1993 it remained only 6 per cent of US stocks' (Fox Piven, 1995: 111). As Fox Piven summarizes her account, 'in other words productive capital has in fact remained within national borders.'

Thirdly, as for capital so too for consciousness. As Billig has recently reminded us, what he terms the daily 'flagging' of nation and nationality forms an inescapable and formative backdrop to everyday experience and rhetoric. The boundaries between 'us' and 'foreigners' are not just the lines around which the racism of ethnic antagonisms are drawn, though they serve that purpose only too well. 'These habits of thinking persist, not as vestiges of a past age, having outlived their function; they are rooted to forms of life, in an era in which the state may be changing, but has not yet withered away' (Billig, 1995: 139). The global culture we may presume to observe is itself the transnationalization of a very national voice, the universal triumph of a supremely local and parochial set of images and values. 'Hum a Gershwin tune anywhere from Boston to Bangkok and probably someone can finish the chorus' (Schwartz, 1973: 1).

We have invited our contributors to explore these dilemmas. Most importantly they attempt to reconnect the fundamental themes of social science with the complex flows and forces which form the world of media and communications. Getting 'beyond' the media is our primary task, to recognize that much of what is being thought and addressed outside the realm of communication scholarship is of utility, and indeed essential, to the task that analysts of international communications have set themselves. 'Only connect' was the aphorism borrowed from E.M. Forster in a thousand discourses on communications. Our aim is simply to 'only reconnect' the unduly limited dialogues of media research with the wider conversation of international analysis. To this task we commend both our contributors and our readers.

January 1996

1

Reflections on the International System

Samir Amin

Never more than today has humanity shared the feeling that the Earth is one and indivisible and that all peoples of the planet belong to a sole system, notwithstanding the extremely divergent positions they occupy within it: an integrated natural system, as illustrated by ecological interdependence; an integrated economic system to the extent that the Eastern bloc countries have abandoned their tradition of relative autarky; even an integrated cultural system following the extraordinary intensification of communications which has resulted in the most advanced forms of Western technology being transferred to the most remote villages on the planet.

Interdependence is certainly not a completely new phenomenon. Capitalism has been a worldwide reality since its very origins when, five centuries ago, it set off to conquer the Americas. Upon deeper reflection, one might even pose the question of whether this interdependence is not even older, as the importance of the 'silk routes' from the fifth century BC would tend to illustrate. Nevertheless, the structures of this integrated system have undergone continuous developments and this calls for clear identification of the qualitative changes at each stage of history.

From the industrial revolution to the First World War, throughout the nineteenth century, the world was united in its specific forms (colonization, British hegemony, etc.). These were considered unacceptable by both worker and socialist movements as well as by movements striving for national liberation of colonies. From 1917 to Gorbachev and Deng Xiaopeng, the twentieth century was characterized by the collapse of this unity and by the conflicting coexistence of a declining capitalism and a 'new expanding socialist system'. We have now entered a third phase which will lead, in the twenty-first century, to a more general development (of capitalism?) based on a universal form of world unity which will perhaps (or undoubtedly) be more beneficial to all concerned than was the case in the nineteenth century.

This is the argument I will discuss here, knowing full well that the exercise of predicting the future is particularly hazardous given the current situation of major change, the contours of which are still not clear. This discussion raises a whole number of very different questions:

- What is the nature of the system undergoing change? Is it necessary and indeed sufficient to qualify it as 'capitalist'?
- What is the potential role of a unified world in the 'market'?
- How does the crisis of socialism fit into this change?
- Is the development of awareness of solidarity among peoples in the process of reaching a new qualitative plateau based on common universal aspirations such as democracy and the desire to avoid nuclear and ecological catastrophes?
- What is peculiar about the range of different 'potential' (and 'desirable') futures, taking into account objective constraints which are common to all?

Changes in the modern economic system

The modern economic systems of advanced capitalist nations have been formed gradually over a period of several centuries, on an essentially national basis: the formation of these systems was the product of a configuration combining social alliances and conflicts in a way that was specific to each nation. The bourgeoisie was therefore able to install its own stable hegemony, thus forming a bourgeois national state with its unique political culture. Take, for example, the distinction between the alliances created within the financial and industrial bourgeoisie and the aristocracy of the *ancien régime* (England, Germany and Japan), between the new class of rich peasants originating from the rural peasant revolution (France), and later the alliances forged with the middle class. The development of the workers' movement, operating under stable political conditions, in conjunction with the advantageous positions occupied by the bourgeois national states which were crucial to the world system (imperialism), later on also favoured an historical compromise between workers' social democracy and capital. Since then Western style democracy has operated efficiently on the largely accepted basis of multi-party politics, made possible by a further consensus: that of the capitalist enterprise as a means of economic regulation with the 'market' above and beyond question. The fact remains that the 'market' is in no way extraneous to social formation, which operates on a purely 'economic' basis, as expressed in widely accepted Western bourgeois ideology (is not this very blunder merely the expression of the economic alienation that defines this ideology?). The market itself is governed by social relationships which create bourgeois hegemony. In other words, price and income structures are specific and therefore national, and these national economic systems are self-centred in the meaning that I have given to this concept. However, these structures are in no way autarkical. On the contrary, the double opening up towards the peripheral capitalist world that they dominate and exploit (whether that be in colonial forms or not, depending on the circumstances) and towards competition between centres affects the reproduction of these systems and determines the features specific to each of them.

The same was true of economic systems created through so-called socialist revolutions. These systems were even more 'self-centred' and nationally based, if only because of blockades which forced them into a marked autarky. Moreover, since they were the direct result of people revolting in the countries in question (which had been condemned to peripheral or semi-peripheral status by the worldwide expansion of a capitalism that really existed), these revolutions could not even have been considered 'bourgeois', that is to say controlled by this class. Rather these revolutions were pitched against this very same class which, by nature, was incorporated into the world expansion of capitalism and ultimately accepted the status the world system had in store for it. Consequently they were not as socialist as they imagined themselves to be. The developments triggered by such revolutions were founded on a new kind of 'national popular' hegemony. Here the originality of price and income systems reflected social reality in economic terms. That this took place thanks to a non-democratic political system and bureaucratic planning was certainly important. It was a reality which called for complex explanations, not only from historical, social and cultural viewpoints, but also in terms of the effects of the ideology of the socialist movement which produced the revolutionary intelligentsia in the countries in question (Leninism, Maoism). It is therefore not surprising that such popular national hegemony should be replaced by political democracy and the 'market' mechanism. Indeed, such popular national hegemony demanded that the system move in this direction.

On the other hand, the ways in which peripheral capitalism was created were, by their very nature, non-national (not self-centred). The price-income system that operated here was not the result of a social hegemony constructed on a national basis, but rather the fruit of an asymmetrical alliance whose international dimension was the principal vector, an alliance between dominant capital on a world-wide basis and subordinate/dominant local classes, whether these classes had preceded capitalism or had been a product (as the bourgeoisie has been) of the worldwide expansion of capitalism.

The national character of social formations thus created has itself modelled an economy that can be characterized as international since those who truly use the system (nation states, enclosed within customs and monetary frontiers) are businesses that are essentially nationally based in terms of property and the location of activities, operating according to a logic which is a product of the national social hegemonic structures of their central partners.

A new stage of development

This structure is entering a new stage of capitalist development and the extent to which the worldwide application of this has entered a new phase of development marked by qualitatively new features should not be underestimated.

A new form of capitalist enterprise had already appeared in the post-Second World War boom (1947–70) – the multinational (or better still 'transnational'). The transnational, originally associated with US hegemony for which it promoted the 'free enterprise worldwide' argument (socialist countries excepted), operated in a world side by side with the robust elements of national policies; specific fiscal policies, tolerated protectionist policies, sectoral subsidies (especially in the agricultural sector), autonomous monetary controls regulated within the framework of fixed exchange rates and the gold standard, etc.

Nevertheless, the gradual relaxation of such elements has led to a weakening of national productive systems by de-localizing segments of the production process and by reducing barriers to foreign investment. However, the decisive qualitative step was made only when the gold convertibility of the dollar was done away with in 1971. Since then a system of flexible exchange has created a climate in which financial transfers have taken place at an unprecedented rate. This transformation was boosted by the ideological offensive of the 1980s, which accelerated privatization and systematic deregulation: in a word, the incredible rise of so-called 'neo-liberalism' boosted by the Thatcher–Reagan style which apparently convinced even Social Democrats to abandon many of their traditional fundamental humanistic values in the name of so-called 'economic efficiency'.

One of the best analyses of the diverse dimensions of this development towards the creation of a 'world productive system' and the substitution of an 'international economy' by a 'world economy' is that of Michel Beaud (1989). G. Arrighi (Amin et al., 1990) has placed emphasis on the worldwide changes in the structure of the workforce that accompanied this development. He argues that the distribution of this force between the 'active army' and various segments of the 'reserve army' has undergone a cyclical-style transformation: in the phases of rebuilding the world economy these two armies have re-established contact via the reconstitution of a reserve army in the centres affected by unemployment, the development of the 'informal economy' recreated in the centres and by the growth of the active army in semi-peripheral 'newly industrialized' areas. Thus the rupturing of the world economy has further isolated the different segments of the workforce throughout the world.

In any case, the new trends have called into question the efficiency of national policies based on local hegemonies, alliances and national social contrasts. New local systems have had to adapt rapidly to the logic of worldwide social alliances and contradictions. The optimistic conclusion from Arrighi is that this integrated worldwide expansion does create in the long run an international atmosphere which, from an objective point of view, is conducive to internationalist workers' solidarity. Unfortunately, this evolution is still a long way off and current developments tend to suggest the contrary.

A second, symmetrical, conclusion would be that what has been created is, on the one hand, an international atmosphere for capital, relegating to a secondary role intra-imperialist struggles which would subsequently be restricted at best to 'mercantile' competition and, on the other, the wiping out of any peripheral national bourgeois aspirations tailored to consumers' needs and accepting their inferior status.

Socialism was based on the idea of universalism and its derivation was 'proletarian internationalism', i.e. the idea that working people everywhere on the planet have fundamentally common interests, while competition and aggressive attitudes are those of the ruling classes. This ideal is not utopian, but corresponds to an objective need if we want to avoid 'barbarism'. Yet I strongly feel that internationalism has to be rebuilt on the basis of the real common interests of the working peoples and classes (not exclusively 'proletarian', since capitalist world expansion did not 'homogenize' societies on the basis of an exclusive bourgeois/proletarian contrast as socialists thought), and that this reconstruction requires recognition of a phase of national-popular autonomous developments in the peripheries. Simultaneously, the growing interdependence of capital (the globalization of finance, etc.) has created more solidarity among the bourgeois ruling classes than in the past, when competition overshadowed solidarity, thus creating some sort of capitalist 'internationalism' (or 'cosmopolitanism').

Nonetheless, the worldwide expansion of capital takes place in a world still controlled by a system of inter-state relationships, where even political consciousness has not resulted in a 'world government' in any embryonic form. The effectiveness of national policies has been cancelled (and this is reflected in the everyday language of those in power who believe there is no way of escaping 'world constraints'), but nothing has replaced them from the moment in which US hegemony, called into question, no longer enabled the American state to play the role of 'world policeman'. Behind the long-term disorder created by this situation lies a deeper evolution in the operation of the worldwide law of value: the world price system has gradually imposed itself as the system of reference, which in turn has been internalized by all countries, and where this geometrical equation has proved impossible, as in many peripheral nations, 'dollarization' (Salama, 1989) has replaced local currency as a means of economic calculation. However, as will be seen further on, this deeper insight into the world law of price value has not led to harmonization of social conditions but, by virtue of operating within a restricted general market, has further accentuated differences.

In spite of the triumphant tone of liberal ideology with the wind in its sails, the future form of the worldwide expansion of capital under way is uncertain because of its interaction with three new types of economic problems (technological revolution, the worldwide expansion of finance, and the development of comparative competitiveness between the United States, Japan and Europe). There has been growing uncertainty due to the dramatic entrance on the scene of new problems (environment, arms, communications). Moreover, the collapse of 'real socialism' has further increased that uncertainty.

The new technological revolution has only just begun. In the most likely shape that it will take in the foreseeable mid-term future – based on computerization – this is an area which can lead to massive capital savings, contrasting with the call for large-scale physical investments that was implied by preceding revolutions (railways in the nineteenth century, the car and urbanization in the twentieth century). There have been major savings in numerous raw materials and energy. Productive infrastructures are being lightened (this may be interpreted in the figurative, i.e. less important, or literal sense). Such savings have taken place within a general structure of income distribution (both at a worldwide level and within industrialized nations) resulting in savings which have not found outlets in productive investment. Competition has furthered this disequilibrium – by virtue of business looking to modernize rather than expand – doubtless explaining the forward flight of capital in speculation over the choice of productive investment. In a longer-term perspective, new elements might be called upon to play a more prominent role in the technological revolution, requiring massive investments: systematic environmental action, biotechnical development, exploitation of space and the seabed, new forms of energy, including nuclear. However, in addition to the political and even ethical problems raised by the options available in these areas (we do not yet know how they will be resolved), knowledge in these fields is still too much in its formative stage for us to do anything more than speculate (meaning, even more speculation than in the past). Besides forward flight of capital in speculation for want of anything better, which itself has been encouraged by deregulation and flexible changes, this worldwide expansion is also the result of a US counter-offensive to face up to its relative decline. As Parboni (1985) has shown, the withdrawal of the gold standard and the flexibility of changes have prolonged the hegemony of the dollar standard, whereas Japanese and European economic progress would normally have forced the world system to create another new international standard. The dollar standard survives in the absence of anything better due to the general interdependence of banks and of financial construction in 'reinforced concrete' on which basis they operate and which technically makes a classic (1929-type) financial clash avoidable. Yet how long can the growth of internal and external debt continue at rates which are disproportionate to the material bases of economies? Debate on this question is far from over. Beyond these trials and tribulations, however, would not the worldwide expansion of finance be the long-lasting consequence of a qualitative transformation in the level of centrally located capital, leading to the setting up of a new worldwide financial capital (different from that of the past, which remains nationally based and which inspired Hobson, Hilferding and Lenin) subordinating productive activities? If profit redistribution (and/or tendency to harmonize its levels) has basically operated until now on product market competition (however oligopolistic it may have been), are we not then seeing the beginnings of a new redistribution mechanism determined by fluctuations in the appreciation of capital on financial markets? A transformation of this nature might, then, be envisaged as having long-term duration. Yet this also indicates the extent to which liberal ideological discourse has the virtue of evading rather than answering questions.

It is quite obvious that under these conditions future worldwide structures are not hardened facts defining the framework in which competition between the United States, Japan and Europe unfolds. In fact, it is this competition (its development) which determines the structures of the worldwide expansion, the shares of each of the major three poles, as well as those of eventual new regional powers which could be controlled by the major centres through monetary and other institutions.

The awareness of environmental interdependence has certainly made an irreversible entrance onto the world stage and we should be thankful for it. Nevertheless the very principles of capital are powerless to control these constraints. This is because the 'market' is a set of mechanisms operating on a short-term basis (maximum 15 years), whereas the environmental effects of the development of productive forces are situated on a much longer-term time-scale. As a result, it is absolutely impossible to avoid a catastrophe without first accepting the principle of rational planning (a particularly unfashionable term!) which goes against the 'market'. It is absurd to think that one can face up to the problem by interiorizing external costs (this would be nothing more than a makeshift solution). One might even question whether the democratic principle we are familiar with (the electoral system) is capable of enabling the planet to be controlled environmentally. By too often neglecting to highlight impending contradictions in the system, many environmentalists are simply sustaining a fatal double hypocrisy. On the one hand the working classes – even in the democratic West – do not have the last word in economic decision-making, and on the other, countries of the Third World equally have no real responsibility for the deteriorating condition of the planet.

Parallel to this destructive dimension of development, there has been a qualitative increase in arms power, capable of destroying the entire planet. Needless to say, this development calls into question the traditional channels of diplomacy, normally forced to avoid recourse to war when there is an unexpected threat which might escalate into a major conflict. Ultimately, the prodigious intensification of communications has already had its effect upon our 'village planet': there has been a qualitative progression in universal aspirations and consumer and living patterns. But even there one might question whether this worldwide dimension has not actually accentuated the contrasts by giving them the dimension of deep frustrations.

Moreover, the intensification of communications operating within the bona fide world capitalist system has not been a liberating or democratizing factor; quite the opposite in fact. The observer who does not see Western life on a daily basis is always struck by the incredible brain-washing of the dominant media. From Liberal and Conservative to Socialist opinion, consensus has meant adopting identical attitudes towards all the major problems. Pluralism, which has been praised as synonymous with democracy, has become devoid of all content, with differences artificially accentuated by competitors in political spheres on minor and parochial questions. At a time when we are proclaiming the end of ideologies, the West has never been so intrinsically tied to such a singular ideological discourse.

This book deals basically with this particular dimension of the contemporary world system, i.e. the intensification of communications. It is a very important dimension, certainly recognized as such by professional politicians; yet overlooked too often by social scientists (except those who specialize in this field) and almost ignored by economists. This intensification of communications has, in my opinion, an unavoidable – and positive – aspect: the building of an integrated (even if differentiated) universal mankind; and I am not one of those constantly regretting the 'past' and thinking that 'cultures' should be maintained as they are and forbidden to evolve. National specificities and cultures are bound to continue their endless evolution and generate more universalism. Yet simultaneously I believe that the type of culture which is conveyed by the mass media, operating in the framework of the global capitalist system, is bound to be poor, sometimes even degrading, frustrating and 'Eurocentric' (cf. Amin, 1989). The responsibility of those working in this field is therefore of particular importance. The struggle for a real democratic alternative requires an enlightened consciousness of those problems. Democracy cannot be reduced to a blueprint of 'free elections', it requires constant in-depth real debates over issues and forbids the 'manipulation' of opinion through media.

Alternative futures

The parameters of a potential new integrated worldwide expansion remain uncertain. The shape it will take is dependent on conflicts that will inevitably continue, in spite of liberalist ideological discourse. For all that, even in the most unlikely outcome that conflicting national and social forces will agree to put aside their vehemently conflicting interests and subject themselves to the strict logic of 'worldwide integration through the market', the newly recreated world would be a dreadful one to live in. Thus the future remains open to potential alternative evolution and there is nothing to justify not thinking about and not fighting for the promotion of a better global project. I do not feel here that I am victim of some voluntary subjectivism, because the potential choices which underpin future projects are integral features of historical objectivity.

The exploration of potentially different forms of evolution calls for examination of alternatives with regard to three types of development:

- contrast between the centre and the periphery governed by the logic of the system;
- East–West relations;
- competition between Western nations, briefly departing from the logic of unilateral integration through the market which is the essence of the Western project.

At the heart of this analysis lie proposals regarding the world law of value, based on world commodity markets (and of a corresponding world price system) and a world market for capital, but excluding an international integrated market for the workforce. This truncated form of liberalism – and there is no other kind in the true existing form of capitalism – leads, by the combination of forms of its worldwide application analysed previously, to an acceleration in the creation of a passive reserve work army in the peripheral areas of the system. This is particularly the case in the newly industrialized areas which are incorrectly termed 'semi-peripheries', when in fact they are the real peripheries of the future, the 'Fourth World', bearing testimony – and a permanent one at that – to the devastating effects of capitalist expansion (Amin, 1990a, 1992). Developments under way within the economy and within the sphere of cultural and political organization in the world cannot diminish the imminent polarizing nature of 'really existing capitalism', but can only accentuate the contrasts within which it expresses itself. The policies of submission to unifying the world via the market – which for the peripheral areas is called 'adjustment' (but which I would qualify as unilateral, whereas in fact we are talking about restructuring when concerned with centres!) – cannot 'neutralize' the new polarization and thus cannot form a new acceptable alternative to a popular national alternative which is needed even more than ever.

Undoubtedly, the centre–periphery contrast is in the process of transformation, the former contrast of industrialized nations versus non-industrialized areas giving way to new polarization mechanisms which are based upon financial, technological, cultural and military domination; consequently the 'comprador' peripheral bourgeoisies are incapable of adjusting to worldwide expansion to their own nations' benefit. The popular classes, who have been the victims of these developments, are unquestionably still in a state of confusion following the exhaustion of the former movements for national liberation. It is difficult to predict the next concrete step in uninterrupted popular revolution that always threatens to break up the worldwide system in the peripheral areas which, in the long run, remain 'tempestuous zones' (Amin contribution in Amin et al., 1990).

Will the genuine crisis of socialism end in the total integration of Eastern bloc countries into the world system (being subjected to the universal rules of the market)? Here I can point to three questions which are linked and whose developments I have analysed elsewhere (Amin, 1990b).

- the democratic question: are we heading towards the straight restoration of forms of bourgeois democracy, or are we heading in the direction of a democracy that contains social elements enabling social (non-capitalist) control of the economy?
- the question of the market: are we heading towards a total submission to the constraints of a market which is necessarily cut-throat? Will it be a pedestal on which private enterprise might be restored? Or will we intelligently associate a renovated non-bureaucratic planning system with a market that it encompasses?
- the question of the international opening: are we heading towards an external openness that is untenable, or can we intelligently combine a greater degree of openness with the principle of delinking (i.e. national popular control of this openness)?

Without going into the detail of these developments, which are marginal here, attention should be drawn to four conclusions that are relevant for an analysis of worldwide expansion.

First, in general, even if in different degrees, the levels of development and international competitiveness obtained by the former Eastern bloc countries and China would not be sufficient to enable those countries to aspire to high positions within the world capitalist system.

Secondly, the answer to the three questions above will be determined by an intense class struggle which is already under way (albeit in a non-vociferous form). Within the ex-Eastern bloc countries there is a large minority (perhaps 20 per cent) which might benefit from the restoration of capitalism. However, this minority will be able to gain access to Western living standards, on which they base their aspirations, only by suppressing the popular classes due to the insufficient levels of development and international competitiveness attained by the socialist nations.

Thirdly, in this struggle, which is similar to that in the Third World, the peoples of the various Eastern nations are unequally armed. In some of the former Socialist bloc countries, a certain level of ideological weaponry could theoretically enable them to impose a progressive solution to their struggle. But in others, the risk is that of being swept away by the attraction of annexation to Western Europe, without being able to understand why their position/place in the world system would be closer to that of the newly industrialized countries (NICs) than to the Western societies where advanced forms of social democracy dominate. In this case, the drift from a transitional democracy to a strong form of government imposing capitalist discipline is not out of the question.

Fourthly, the bi-polarization that has characterized the post-Second World War period is without doubt destined to undergo a number of deep-reaching changes, but is not likely to disappear in all its respects. Unquestionably, the ideological bi-polarization which has resulted from so-called socialist revolutions from 1917 onwards will be erased if capitalism is restored to the countries in question. In the case of a more progressive development, everything would depend on the knock-on effect that it had upon people in the West. This is because such a profound change might simply leave things in a state of chilled relations if Western workers continue to believe their consumption levels are still superior and that there is nothing the East can teach them. Yet it might also set off a renewed socialist consciousness in the West. This would still mean, however, that military bi-polarization would remain real. Whatever the state of equilibrium between 'superpowers' may become, they will continue to hold the supreme trump card of being the only ones with the capacity to 'blow up the planet'.

To date, the contradictions that may have existed between Western nations have not gone beyond commercial competition, and neither the Japanese nor the Europeans have ever dared take up a position which the United States would look upon most unfavourably. Will this necessarily be the case in the future? This remains open to question. Some believe that these conflicts must become worse and in the final analysis lead to a relative break-up in the unity of the world market and to the setting up of zones of influence around the dominant poles (United States, Japan, Germany and Europe). The consolidation of détente in East–West relations should make this an even more likely possibility, with the US military shield being rendered obsolete. Nevertheless, there are some doubts as to the potential solidity of a common European neo-imperialist policy; with Europe caught between the competition of industrialized peripheral areas better placed as regards traditional industries, than Japan and the United States, which are better equipped in technological fields, will it be able to stamp its own authority on this framework?

Global capitalism and democracy

From the point of view of the different interests of the peoples of the planet, unifying the world system by the unilateral basis of the market is not desirable. Nor is it the most likely outcome of developments under way, so acute are the conflicts which fatally entail submission to the so-called unilateral criteria of the 'market' operating in a 'Darwinian' world space. Western ideological discourse, which has made this a strategic option, aims at concealing the acuteness of these conflicts. From this perspective I have analysed 'the discourse on democratization'.

My thesis in this respect is that the polarization produced by 'really existing capitalism' creates in the peripheries such dramatic conditions at all levels (economic: growing poverty; social: massive marginalization; cultural: frustrations, etc.) that it makes democratic rule almost impossible. Therefore I do not accept this fashionable idea of today that 'market' (read, capitalism) generates (or needs) democracy. No, 'really existing capitalism needs' autocratic powers in the peripheries. That is after all the lesson of history. Democracy appears here, in a truncated and weak version, from time to time (as is the case now) as an expression of the crisis of autocracy, its failure to deliver, rather than an objective need of the system. In that sense, autocracy in the peripheries is not a 'vestige of the past' but a consequence of the modernization operating in the frame of global polarization of wealth and power.

More than ever before, the onus is on the forces of the Left to promote a credible alternative to this catastrophic option.

Conclusion

The only strategy which makes any sense for progressive forces worldwide must be incorporated into the building of a 'polycentric' world, on the basis of which an internationalism of peoples from the three areas (West, East, South) might find a new lease of life. Any such construction would link up the different areas that form it in a flexible manner, enabling specific policies which are required to be put into effect. These would be dependent upon different levels of development and upon objective grounds.

One must immediately recognize that problems people face throughout the world differ from one region to another. There therefore needs to be: a sufficient degree of autonomous space to enable people to promote their own interests; and reconciliation between general interdependence and the legitimate concern of becoming autonomous. The logic of unilateral adjustment by the weakest which benefits the strongest exclusively needs to be replaced by the logic of mutual and reciprocal adjustment.

For the nations of the South and Eastern Europe, polycentrism means the pursuit of delinked development policies in the sense of external relations being submitted to the needs for internal progress and not the opposite, which is the gist of unilateral adjustment by the market. This strategy fits into the perspective of potential advances towards socialism (by the democratizing and reinforcing of its popular national content), but not into that of 'restoring capitalism' to the Eastern bloc nations and in accepting the 'compradorization' of the countries in the South. It must equally enable progressive advances to take place in Western nations by the opening up of non-commercial outlets and by other reforms based on socializing economic control. As far as Europe is concerned, this is incorporated into East–West rapprochement, itself based on respecting the diversity of situations, which is the complete opposite of the 'rollback vision'.

With particular regard to the Third World, this strategy places greater importance upon the concept of progress (in the organization of productive forces), however detrimental it may be to immediate 'international competitiveness'. It prioritizes on the agenda the aims of an agricultural revolution which should take place with maximal possible equality, as well as the transformation of 'informal' activities to become the basis for transitional popular economy. It calls for an effective combination of planning and the market, upon which any democratization concerned with incorporating a popular social content must be founded. The polycentrist vision that it inspires provides the countries and regions of the Third World with a degree of autonomy which is not open to them by either the model of world unification or by a policy of regionalization determined by the main competing industrial poles.

As far as action to be taken at the level of international organization of general interdependence is concerned, this strategy aims at encouraging the development, in an embryonic form, of a 'democratic world government' (as opposed to domination by the Group of 7) as illustrated by the introduction of a world tax earmarked for ecological operations, for instance. In addition, it proposes to reduce the tensions that have arisen due to the massive stocking of weapons, notably by the superpowers. Finally, its ambition is to give a new lease of life to the democratic institutionalizing of world control by reviving interest in the United Nations.

To conclude, I would say that the international system is not 'bound' to move in the directions it seems to be moving in if we extrapolate the current trends. There are always alternatives – this reflects a real range of the choices societies have. The current trend would necessarily lead to 'barbarism', i.e. uncontrolled contradictions and ugly violent conflicts leading to nowhere but growing frustrations. The alternative to this bleak future has a name: the struggle for a socialist alternative at all levels, national and international.

2

States of the State and Third Worlds*

Tony Barnett

This chapter has four goals: briefly to review some issues raised in recent discussion of the nature and role of the state in the 'Third World'; to show how these debates relate to a much older tradition of thought about the state; to suggest that it is difficult to make general statements about the nature and role of the state in the 'Third World' because that concept is itself problematic.

The fourth task is to suggest that while much has been achieved from the application of essentially Marxist analysis, this has too often resulted in mechanistic and deterministic interpretations of that body of theory. The result has been premature generalization, an inevitable focus on class relations and a neglect of issues of culture. In particular, the relation between local cultural idioms and the conduct of politics in a world where the nation state has become the dominant political cultural form has not received the attention it deserves.

The state and the Third World: two inventions from Europe

When we speak of 'the state', we usually mean the nation state. Whereas it could be argued that both nations and states had existed prior to the expansion of European power, the nation state is a European invention. This should always be remembered. Likewise, the 'Third World' is also an invention.

The state

The nation state originates in the development of capitalism in Europe. It provided a mechanism whereby a 'national' culture, language and identity, together with law, could be linked to the development of a system of production and exchange based on money and markets within a defined territory.

It was always important that the state controlled civil society. Early questions about the state (posed at the time of its development in Europe) concerned the balance of this control between the state authority and the citizen, the nature and extent of that authority, the rights and duties of the citizen: thus the efflorescence and continuation of a steady stream of debates such as those to be found in the writing of Hobbes, Locke, Rousseau, Bentham and Mill in an earlier time, and continuing into the present century from von Hayek, Keynes, Friedmann to contemporary political-economic policy debates across the world.

The invention of the state also required the construction of a social space for the individual. This construction and definition of 'individuals' is a major preoccupation of those who concerned themselves with the state and its power throughout the eighteenth and nineteenth centuries. The invention of the state, the introduction of a distinction between the state (as the regulator of 'civil society') and 'civil society', required at the same time the invention of the individual as 'citizen' – a category which abstracts from the particular social and economic features of specific individuals, characteristics such as class, status, gender and ethnicity. This process of abstraction resulted in a system of thought and definition of the relationships between people (in part through law) which could often be used by those holding political and social power to blame the 'victims' of structurally determined inequalities which either pre-existed the coming of the market system (as with gender – depending on how one concludes the capitalism-patriarchy debate) or other social categories (such as those of status and class) which to a greater or lesser extent were developments of the system itself.

The Third World

The 'Third World' was, if not a European invention, an invention in relation to European culture and economy. Its purpose was to explain certain historical and personal experiences among the colonized, to define their place within a world system of economic and political relations, and furthermore to define this place in terms of supposed common political and economic interests shared by the colonized in relation to their colonizers.

The idea of the 'Third World' arose from independence struggles. It was often monopoly of force which enabled colonial regimes to come into being and to continue to exist. Independence struggles required a reinterpretation of the state form by the educated colonials in order that they could take power in and through those independence struggles. 'Third World' was a convenient piece of jargon to unify masses of people (rather than intellectuals) whose main basis of communality, beyond local and regional ethnic and religious identifications, was their experience of colonialism. Hence the Bandung Conference of 1955 which held out hopes of new paths to economic and social 'development' for those parts of the world which were not part of the capitalist 'First World' or of the socialist 'Second World' – the 'Non-Aligned states'.

At the same time, 'Third World' also provided a focus for metropolitan radicals to find common cause with the colonized. However, like 'dependency' a decade or so later, it was a political concept which, when imported into social theory, disguised more than it explained.

It must now be recognized that the 'Third World' has dissolved into many different forms of state, economy and society. As a concept, it played an important role in the period of decolonization and the early years of independence. It was, though, more a slogan than an analytical category. Today, there are greater differences than resemblances between the societies and states of, say, Malaysia and Uganda or Peru and Sudan. They have little in common. It may be argued that they are all more or less 'dependent' economies, but to say this is not enough. Whatever 'dependency' means, it is too broad a concept to describe relations as diverse as those between the USA and El Salvador, the USA and Korea or, to extend the concept, between Russia and Kazakhstan.

Thus, if there were to be a general theory of the post-colonial state, it would have to be able to illuminate economic and political forms as different as military dictatorships, authoritarian one-party rule and Leninist democratic centralism, as well as various approximations to liberal and social democracy.

Theories of the state

The myth of the state

The idea of 'the state' is complex. It has been used to describe a series of entities, variously combined, depending on the political, moral and theoretical interests (in both senses of that word) of the writer.

At one level, it refers to the existence of a system of permanent administration and finance, demarcated territory, control of military and civil power through a social and cultural apparatus. At another level, it is a cultural concept describing a political idea, a myth within which people live their lives (Cassirer, 1946). This idea, this myth, appears in our lives as though it were 'natural' – we recognize its existence each time we complete an official form, change our civil status, produce our driving licence for the police, apply for or use a passport, cross a 'national' boundary, or pay our taxes. The idea assumes some minimal degree of commitment to (and benefit from) 'national identity'. Today, this myth is assumed to provide the main base of identity for most of the world's people in the last decade of the twentieth century. It is apparent that in many of the states of Africa, Asia, the Middle East, and to a lesser extent Latin America, it does not constitute the main base of identity. With the passing of the Soviet Union and its satellite states and of Yugoslavia it is also apparent that European nation states as constituted in the post-Second World War (and in remnant form in the post-First World War) settlement in Europe no longer always form firm bases for identity. Emergence of sub-national aspirations in the Caucasus, the Balkans and in Canada indicate that a world made up of nation states can no longer be seen as an immutable order composed of stable entities.

This should not surprise us. States are not, of course, 'natural'. We live in a world of social invention. A social invention has two parts – a material part, the administration and daily relations which maintain its existence and play some role in the production or reproduction of continuing social existence; and the ideal, the myths, ideologies, discourses and philosophies which legitimize and facilitate the reproduction of those social relations (Bourdieu, 1977; Bourdieu and Passeron, 1977).

In a sense then, the state is a 'real myth'. There is a unity to these two parts of the state as we experience it, as it shapes and defines our lives. Myths are an important part of the way we organize our social and economic lives. There appears to be a 'national' economy and we act in relation to this belief even though, in many circumstances, it becomes increasingly difficult in practice to identify where the 'national', 'regional' and 'world' economies are distinct. But we must remember that many decision-makers, policy-makers and economic actors also act in the belief that there is a national economy. This belief is an important factor in their actions.

The origins of the state

> In the course of the 16th century, the Absolutist state emerged in the West. The centralised monarchies of France, England and Spain represented a decisive rupture with the pyramidal, parcellised sovereignty of the mediaeval social formations, with their estates and liege-systems. (Anderson, 1974: 16)

National states came into existence at particular times. In most of Africa, the Middle East, Asia and Latin America, the European-style state (as opposed to the indigenous states which had existed in some parts of the world and differed in many respects from those invented in Europe) made its appearance as a result of the establishment of colonial administrations. Administration and the state were imposed on societies and economies which had often existed without any form of state, or in some cases with no cultural or linguistic identity beyond the local.[1]

Colonial governments did not attempt to construct nation states, merely administrative states. For a variety of reasons, these states were often divided along ethnic and/or religious lines. Sometimes these divisions were for the 'protection' of minorities defined by colonial governments as being at risk of domination by a majority, for example the protection of the 'pagan/Christian' southern Sudanese from the 'Arab/Muslim' northerners; in other cases, it was a clearer case of divide and rule, as with the policy of indirect rule in Nigeria and other parts of Africa (Lugard, 1965). And in yet other cases, there was a clear identification of ethnicity with economic function in the colonial economy – the Chinese in Malaysia, the Indians in East Africa and the Pacific are obvious examples of ethnic populations imported as labourers who later became traders. The social-evolutionist ideologies and nineteenth-century theories of race which were central to the discourse of the imperial governing class provided categories of thought which did not and could not envisage the possibility of the creation of nation states within the colonial empires.[2] The discourse of colonial rule often emphasized racial and cultural differences rather than the homogeneity which is assumed by the nation state. And, indeed, it must always be recalled that colonial populations were more usually ethnically, linguistically and religiously heterogeneous than homogeneous. The degree to which particular sub-populations within a colony were privileged or disadvantaged varied, partly through design, partly through accident – and we should never forget the role of accident in history![3]

The varieties of colonial state influenced the specific organizational form and administrative tradition inherited by the successor post-colonial state. Other factors which affected state formation included the particular circumstances arising from economic developments in each area, as well as forms of resistance to colonialism and, related to these, the forms of political, social and economic organization which had pre-existed colonial rule or developed in relation to its encroachment.

> When the European states extended their military power in support of their commercial activities, other rulers were obliged to copy the form of power of the Europeans in order to defend themselves and also formed states. States . . . come to constitute a system of competitive agencies, each alone or in a group of allies, striving to expand in political, military and economic terms at the expense of its rivals, or at least to ward off the threats of other states. The competition forces, to a greater or lesser

degree, measures of uniformity upon the competitors; if one government acquires a new and more powerful weapon, its nearest rivals are obliged to follow suit in order to defend themselves. (Harris, 1977: 149)

The development of the English state (perhaps the first European state, although others might argue that medieval Spain is also a contender for this title) was based on processes of bureaucratization, monopolization of force, creation of legitimacy, and cultural and linguistic homogenization of population.[4] In particular, the land-holding nobility lost much of its power, the sovereign was able to accumulate funds and thus 'buy' the services of a bureaucracy. Much of this purchase of bureaucratic and administrative services was based on the ability to borrow – which in the end weakened the power of the sovereign. Indebtedness meant the creation of a 'national' debt. At the same time, pre-existing religious ideas provided the basis for a theory of 'divine right' and thus legitimized the special privileges of power. Wars against competing European powers (particularly the Spanish) contributed to the development of a national identity, a factor in the development of a broadly homogenized population (or at least a myth of homogeneity) which, in its mature form in later centuries, permitted the development of an ideology of 'nationalism'.

In Western Europe, the idea of 'nation' developed from the fourteenth century and more rapidly from the sixteenth century. The notion of 'nation' implied an identity of culture, language and geography and thus the basis for a politics based on the assumption of 'the nation' with its attendant potential for expression in an ideology of nationalism, the possibility of competition between nationalisms and nation states. During this period, the distinction between 'the state' and 'civil society' was made and became all-important in the transition whereby the state had rights over those who lived within its geographical boundaries. The process reached its peak in the mid-nineteenth century with the establishment of Germany and Italy as nation states.[5] In many respects, the principle and discourse of 'nation' and 'national self-determination' was enshrined as the 'natural' political order in Europe and for the world as recently as the settlement of the Treaty of Versailles in 1918.

Thinking about the state

These developments were not unproblematic. The debates about the relationship between states and individuals were often phrased in the idiom of religion, philosophy and natural rights. Thus, in his *Leviathan* (1962), Hobbes (1588–1679) explored the unpleasant necessity (as he saw it) for strong central government. He was a monarchist, but not out of any firm attachment to the king.[6] Rather, his acceptance of the authority of the Great Leviathan over the individual arose from a strong sense of the advantages of civil order in those troubled times. Once the dominance of the theological authorities had been weakened he saw that, in the resulting world of 'individuals', competition could lead to civil disorder. Hence his argument that human beings created the state by contracting together to protect their own best interest, which is to survive. For Hobbes, the state was seen as an unfortunate necessity, an outcome of the enlightened self-interest of freely contracting individuals.

John Locke (1632–1704), whose lifetime overlapped with that of Hobbes, took up the other side of the issue, emphasizing the consent of the governed. He looked at the rights of the individuals against the state rather than examining the reasons for the unfortunate necessity of the state's existence. In his *Two Treatises of Civil Government* (1988), Locke presented a picture of the state as resulting from a free contract made between presumably equal individuals – a state founded on consent and on majority opinion. Parallel debates were, of course, going on in other parts of Europe. The writings of Rousseau (1712–78) are a later example (see *The Social Contract*, 1969), as are those of that great metaphysician of the state, Hegel (1770–1831).

Hegel took discussion of the state in a somewhat different direction. He emphasized that the ideal nature of the state reflected the spirit of a people and its culture – the expression of an ethical idea. In his work we see the state as not only other than civil society, but also as its tutor, regulator, moral guardian and an active cultural and spiritual reliquary of all that a 'nation' (prior to and without the state) had learned during its centuries of existence. It followed that for Hegel the Prussian state could be seen as an expression of national genius and the high point of the development of the 'German' nation's historical journey towards a nation state.

Much more pragmatic, and more legalistic in its expression, was the British liberal tradition as expressed in the work of Burke, Bentham and Adam Smith. Although Burke flirted with romantic ideas in some respects akin to those of Hegel, being concerned with the way in which the English state and state form preserved 'the wisdom of our ancestors',[7] the overriding view is one of the state as referee in the game (mainly economic) of civil society.

By the mid-nineteenth century, the liberal state as reality (found in the organization of actual societies such as France and Britain) and as political charter (for nationalities as different as those of Bismarck and Garibaldi) was well established and spreads to most parts of Western Europe, bringing with it the unresolved and (irresolvable) problem of the correct relation between the state and its citizens.

However, while the nineteenth century was a time when many Europeans came to see themselves as members of 'nations', and thus having rights to become established as 'nation states', some historical nations were bound to lose out in the process. The growth of nationalism during this era also brought into existence the problem of 'peoples' and 'nations' without states. This problem was not to go away, and it forms a constant theme in the history of the twentieth century, appearing as a set of 'national problems' – these include the 'Balkan problem' (re-emerging as this is written), the Jews, the Palestinians, the Kurds, the Armenians (and the many other nationalities of the USSR), the Sikhs, the Eritreans and – for a British writer – not least of all the Irish, the Scots and the Welsh. The importance of the state as the legitimate expression of ethnic consciousness/culture in the twentieth century lies at the root of many current problems – problems which could be and have been exploited for superpower purposes, and which now reappear in a new form as the Soviet empire, that 'graveyard of nations', is swept by the hurricane of its 'wind of change'.

States and 'development'

States and state forms in the non-European world grew directly out of the colonial experience. With a few exceptions, such as Thailand, contemporary states are the successors to colonial governments. Even the exceptions are responses to the encroachment of colonial powers in adjacent areas. The clearest example of this is Ethiopia, where one powerful regional ethnic group, the Amharas, established its hegemony and the nationhood of 'Ethiopia' at the same time as Britain and Italy were themselves struggling for control of areas in the Horn of Africa.

Most contemporary nation states in Asia, Africa, the Middle East and Latin America are either part of the response to colonialism or the direct creation of colonialism. As is well known, the 'national' boundaries of African and Asian states often cut across pre-colonial cultural and ethnic entities, those of Latin America reflect the aspirations of local settler interest groups within the Spanish and Portuguese empires expressed in the idiom of nineteenth-century nationalism, while in the Middle East and North Africa, colonial boundaries (derived from the French and British division of the administrative units of the Turkish empire) cut across a fundamental 'Arab' identity, itself questioned by the existence of other local identities based on ethnicity (the Berbers in Algeria, the Kurds in

Iraq) and of communion (the division between Shi'i and Sunni Islam and between Marronite Christians and Muslims in Lebanon).

The result is often a complex mixture of diverse identities, languages and cultures bundled within territorial boundaries representing the hegemony of one dominant group or an uneasy hegemony of several groups. In varying degrees, all nation states are always uneasy balances of ethnic and class identities and interests. The precise degree of unease, and the issues which may serve to produce a legitimation crisis – religion, tribe, class, language – will depend on the specific history of a state as well as its economic viability. In most of the states of Asia, Latin America, the Middle East and Africa, state legitimacy depends explicitly and to a considerable degree on the politics of 'development', which term often forms a part of the political discourse.

In contrast, 'development' was never part of the political discourse of Western Europe. When economic growth occurred in Europe, it was as part of the personal enrichment of the members of a class, and it often took place under the auspices of a *laissez-faire* liberal state. However, the supposed non-involvement of the state in economic life was belied by reality. In various degrees and in different guises, in nineteenth-century Britain, Bismarckian Germany and later in Japan, the state itself was a very important focus of economic growth and 'development' (see Moore, 1991: Chapter 5).

In the case of non-European state formation in Africa and Asia in the present century,[8] there were two important influences on the process of development through the state. The state first appeared here dressed in the garb of a civilizing mission in the colonial period. It appeared in a different guise in the post-independence period when 'development' became a conscious goal of independence and decolonization. This was the period of 'third worldism' after the Second World War, when 'state' and 'development' constituted the stuff of nationalist struggle and of the attempt to establish national identities and nation states. And the two main influences which formed these developmentally oriented states were the centralized colonial state on the one hand and the Soviet experience, which in its turn also emphasized national planning and centralization and the suppression of difference within its own borders, while paradoxically appealing for anti-colonial struggle abroad – thus influencing many of those fighting against colonialism.[9]

There are many reasons why these two sources should have been so influential. One, the pragmatic, was that the colonial state structures of administration, the organization of the administrative world, were what independence leaders inherited in those heady days immediately after the midnight lowering and raising of flags. The second, also pragmatic in its way, but ideal as well, offered a way forward which was an alternative to the capitalist model, a way forward which had been integrated into many nationalist struggles often heavily influenced by Soviet support for independence movements. In addition, this form permitted the easy integration of the independence party into government and the administration of the state. Nowhere was this more pronounced than in Africa where transition to the so-called one-party state (with its populist appeal) was thus made possible and legitimized. In Ghana, we see this in an early and pronounced form, where, after independence in 1957, the structure of Nkrumah's Convention People's Party and the structures of the state soon became inseparable.[10]

Marxism, critique and the criticism of the liberal state – the basis for understanding states in the Third World

By the late 1960s, Western academics were becoming increasingly radicalized. The Vietnam War, difficulties of welfare capitalism and the advent of a new generation of post-war intellectuals, themselves often beneficiaries of post-war welfare capitalism and sometimes from a social milieu different from that of traditional Western elites, all contributed to criticism of what was happening in many of the new states. In addition, non-European intellectuals, who were themselves critical of the way in which things were turning out in their countries, began to look for a way of understanding the corruption, waste, political compromises and lack of progress which were apparent in the newly independent states. In the intellectual climate of the times, one source of critical understanding of what was happening was Marxism and, in particular, its theory of the state.

Marxist theories of the state have deep roots in Western philosophy. The idea of critique is central to both. At its base is the idea that beneath appearances lies a deeper reality. Thus, beneath the appearance of the capitalist state lies another reality, the reality of relations of production and their attendant class structures. Marx claimed to be a materialist. In the context of social analysis, this means looking behind ideas, legitimizing theories and social and political 'myths', to tease out the underlying socio-economic processes which logically (Sayer, 1983) produce the ideas people have about the 'natural' order of society. An essential part of the Marxist method is to look beneath appearances to some assumed 'deeper' reality, to look behind the dominant legitimizing beliefs (such as those of the liberal state) and ask how they relate to the productive organization of society.

Engels said that the core of Marx's contribution at the philosophical level was that he 'stood Hegel on his head'. Put simply, and applied to the problem of the state, what this means is that the state must not be approached as an ethical ideal – tutoring and forming civil society. Critical analysis must look beneath that ideological appearance to the material reality which produces the structure of ideas, the taken-for-grantedness within which people exist:

> the state – the political order – is the subordinate and civil society – the realm of economic relations – the decisive element. The traditional conception, to which Hegel too pays homage, saw in the state the determining element and in civil society the element determined by it. Appearances correspond to this. As all the driving forces of the action of any individual person must pass through his brain and transform themselves into motives of his will in order to set him into action, so also the needs of civil society – no matter which class happens to be the ruling one – must pass through the will of the state in order to secure general validity in the form of laws. That is the formal aspect of the matter – the one which is self-evident. The question arises, however: What is the content of this merely formal will – of the individual as well as of the state – and whence is this content derived? Why is just this willed and not something else? If we enquire into this we discover that in modern history the will of the state is, on the whole, determined by the changing needs of civil society, by the supremacy of this or that class, in the last resort by the development of the productive forces and relations of exchange. (Engels, 1973: 83)

> out of [the] contradictions between the interest of the individual and that of the community, the latter takes an independent form as the state, divorced from the real interests of the individual and the community, and at the same time as an illusory communal life, always based, however, on the real ties existing in every family and tribal conglomeration . . . and especially . . . on the classes, already determined by the division of labour, which in every such mass of men separate out, and of which one dominates all the others. (Marx and Engels, 1965: 107)

In these two extracts, the state is seen (a) as an illusion of communal life: thus patriotism and nationalism are illusions; and (b) as having its origins in the way that production is organized. But, above all, the state is seen as a charter, a creation myth, a legitimation of the status quo and, in particular, of the class relations of the status quo.

Clearly, the Marxist analysis of the state stands as a counterpoint and challenge to the liberal theory. It asks a number of very important questions. These include: why do people believe the liberal theory of the state? And, arising from this, in whose interests is it that such a belief should be widely held in a society?

In fact, there is much more than one 'Marxist theory of the state'. In the work of Marx and Engels at least two may be discerned and, in this century, Marxist scholars have developed a number of others, some of which may actually be at variance with the original Marxian formulation – depending upon how people choose to interpret the work of Marx and Engels. One apparently straight-forward Marxist theory of the state is summed up in the familiar quotation: 'The state is but a committee for managing the affairs of the whole bourgeoisie' (Marx and Engels, 1975: 35). This might be called the executive committee model. It is a view which suggests that the state plays an enabling role, administering and coordinating the various spheres of economic activity in order that the interests of the bourgeoisie are maintained. It is a view which assumes a direct relation between the economic interests of the ruling class, the administrative and legal apparatus and the general ideas expressed in national religion and culture.

Except to the most simple-minded, the history of the last century does not suggest that life falls into such easy patterns. Such an approach is overly determinist. Not to put too fine a point on the matter, the state cannot be seen as a kind of sausage machine – the economic interests of the bourgeoisie being fed in at one end, and action which is in their interests coming out the other. The problems with this view are manifold. Among them one might note that:

(a) 'the bourgeoisie' is not a unified social category; it is internally divided and these 'fractions' have different and competing interests;

(b) state policies have often benefited classes other than the bourgeoisie;

(c) there is an unwillingness to engage with questions of ethnicity, religious affiliation and historical experience, all of which are actually taken very seriously by people, but which are here assigned to the category of 'ideology' and 'superstructure'. It may be argued that welfare and industrial legislation are ways of keeping the working class quiet, but at the same time they reflect a state which is responding to the demands of labour as well as to the bourgeoisie. Thus the state is also an arena of class struggle, struggle which is not always won by the bour-geoisie. Questions of ethnicity and religious affiliation are taken very seriously by many people and do not only represent or disguise class interests. They are real forces in human affairs and their power must not be underestimated.

There is, though, another model which can be derived from Marx's writing. This is of particular concern because it forms the basis for many attempts to theorize the 'Third World' state which, when addressed from this perspective, becomes characterized as 'the post-colonial state'. This may be called 'the Bonapartist model', deriving its name from Charles Louis Napoleon Bonaparte (1808–73), better known as Napoleon III, who took power in France by means of a *coup d'état* in 1851, changing his position from President of the Second Republic to King.

The general lesson which Marx drew from these events was that in the France of that time there was such a high level of division among the ruling classes – the bourgeoisie and the landowners – that a power vacuum existed. This enabled the *coup d'etat* to occur. He comments acerbically that:

> France seems . . . to have escaped the despotism of a class only to fall back beneath the despotism of an individual without authority. The struggle seems to be settled in such a way that all classes, equally impotent and equally mute, fall on their knees before the rifle butt . . . Only under the second Bonaparte does the state seem to have made itself completely independent. As against civil society, the state machine has consolidated its position so thoroughly that the Chief of the Society of December 10 suffices for its head, an adventurer blown from abroad, raised on the shield by a drunken soldiery, which he has bought with liquor and sausages, and which he must continually ply with sausage anew. (Marx, 1985: 72–5)

The importance of this model is that it has been extended to explain some of the manifestations of the state in Africa, Latin America, the Middle East and Asia. Consider for example the regular military coups in Thailand over the last 50 years (most recently in 1985), the hundreds in Africa since 1956, and the dozens in Latin America in the last 150 years.

There is also a Leninist variant of the Bonapartist model. This was embodied in the 1917 Revolution in Russia. In *The State and Revolution* (Lenin and Service, 1992), and by his actions, Lenin presents another view of the state which, under the leadership of the vanguard party as the vehicle and means for revolution, stands for 'development' – for communist revolution was never concerned with economic progress if not explicitly with something more obscure, 'development'. In this variant, the revolutionary party, on taking power – in the name of peasants and workers – must completely dismantle the old state and replace it with one which revolutionizes society in a way that benefits those in whose name power has been taken. State terror is an important component of this model, which has been used to legitimize most coups and counter-coups around the world in recent decades. It is also, of course, a rationale for the establishment of one-party states and for the organizational form of 'the party/state' as embodied in 'democratic centralism'.

Of these two broad theories of the capitalist state to be found in the writings of Marx and Engels, the more familiar is the 'executive committee model'. However, it is the secondary theory, the Bonapartist model, which forms the basis for much writing on Third World states. It was first applied by Hamza Alavi in a celebrated article (1972) analysing the post-colonial state in Pakistan and in Bangladesh. In this article, Alavi argues that the power of three social classes or categories – the indigenous bourgeoisie, the metropolitan bourgeoisie and the indigenous landowners – was evenly balanced and so the state personnel could act with some degree of independence, although in the overall interests of these three classes. This arrangement of forces Alavi describes as an 'overdeveloped' state, beyond the control of the indigenous class forces, thus accounting for the frequency of authoritarian government in Third World states. An important and problematic innovation in theory was the role of the 'metropolitan bourgeoisie', prompted no doubt by the recognition that mere political independence did not mean economic independence and that a world system of economic and political relationships still constrained the choices of governments of nominally independent states in a world of states.

The state in Africa

It is this approach which has occupied the theoretical centre-stage in discussions of the state in Africa. Given the intellectual roots of these debates, it has not been fashionable to attempt to include cultural factors in discussions of the recent history of the state in that continent. Instead, the debates have largely revolved around the applicability or otherwise of class analysis to the African state.[11]

This perspective has been subjected to much criticism, especially when applied to Africa. In particular, taken as a *general* theory of the post-colonial state (which may not have been Alavi's intention), it is difficult to see how to identify the existence of the assumed class groups sociologically and then how to show with clarity that there is a power vacuum arising directly from the nice balance of their interests. In addition, the whole approach is very instrumentalist, adopting a variant of the sausage machine approach referred to above. There is also an element of teleology: the argument that because state personnel appear to have things their own way, this must be because there is a power vacuum.

By and large the issues as they have been discussed in relation to sub-Saharan Africa have been concerned with assessing the possibilities for 'real' development to occur in societies where the capitalist mode of production has not developed in a pure form, but exists in relation to other 'backward' modes of production (such as subsistence agriculture with few links to the market and based on household labour and communal land tenure), the relation between capitalist and other modes being held together by the state. Thus, if 'development' involves mobilization of economic resources and the pursuit of economic growth (as well as changes in social ethos and social relations), it is vital for the non-market, non-maximizing economic systems of traditional Africa to be integrated into the large 'national' economy and, by implication, into the international economy. Hence, African states can be said to face problems similar to those confronted by the colonial governments – integrating different modes of production (which might include, among others, subsistence production, petty commodity production, export-oriented plantations, as well as fully-fledged capitalism) into the nation through any means available – education, language policy, manipulation of markets, political mobilization, naked coercion.

In some cases, 'real development' has been taken to mean development which benefits the mass of the population by changing the organization of relations of production so as to increase overall production and enable more egalitarian distribution of that product. In other cases, 'development' has meant only the revolutionization of productive forces, with less emphasis placed upon distribution.

Viewed from this perspective, the state becomes the focus of the struggle for power. However, the question then arises as to what forces are participating in the struggle. Given the supposed simultaneous existence of different modes of production, the class nature of the society is by no means clear. It is not really appropriate to talk only of a bourgeoisie (local or metropolitan) and a proletariat or even lumpenproletariat (a term which some observers have used). Further, it should be noted, these terms do not invite consideration of the entire issue of 'gendered' relations of production, particularly important when considering peasant production where the internal organization of the household economy is based on gender and age differentiation of the workforce. Class terminology, which describes important aspects of capitalist societies, faces difficulties when applied to societies in which capitalism is neither fully developed nor the sole mode of production. This point is taken up below in relation to Hyden's discussion of the nature of the state in Africa.

In the early 1970s, in the aftermath of the immediate post-independence euphoria, observers began to raise serious questions about the way that state personnel seemed to be using their position to enrich themselves and do very little if anything either for 'the masses' or for the transformation of productive forces. In Africa, this revolved around the following question: when African politicians and party officials spoke in the name of 'socialism', was this merely manipulative rhetoric, or was it a benign stance frustrated in practice by 'external' interference? Was responsibility for the evident failures of the post-colonial state, particularly in Africa, to be placed at the door of national leaders and national governments, or was it to be pinned on something called 'the capitalist world system'? Debates also turned on the question of whether or not state personnel could be considered a 'class' (a group with a specific relation to the means of production, in Marxist terminology), whether they were representatives of indigenous classes, or whether the concept of class was in fact inappropriate in such societies, and discussion should really concern itself with understanding the actions of groups of people who had some common interests, similar occupations, but were not really 'fully formed' classes.

John Saul, who worked in Tanzania during the 1960s, when that country was seen by some European and North American radicals as the great hope for a socialist development trajectory in Africa, argued in his article 'The State in Post-colonial Societies: Tanzania' (1974) that these clerks, schoolteachers, public employees, etc., who became the first officials of the new state, could move in either direction. They could act in their own interests or in the interests of 'the masses'. It was an 'uncertain moment'. Saul considered that it was too early to say which way they would jump:

> The contradictory situation and experience of these typically transnational and partial ruling groups is mediated through the transformations, incoherences, oscillations, 'false' and illusory representations and reconciliations at the level of ideology. (1974: 75)

In contrast, the Tanzanian writer Issa Shivji (1975), whose work was the object of Saul's critical response, argued that in Tanzania the state itself had very early taken on a strong class character and that state personnel were often identifiable as the real exploiting group. He argued that despite the socialist rhetoric: 'The state . . . asserted its class character regardless of ideology. But in so doing it laid bare the fundamental contradictions between the exploited and the exploiter' (1979: 155).

A fundamental point was at issue here. This concerned whether or not state personnel in the modernizing state were to be seen as benevolent technocrats (the term 'izers', from 'modernizers', was coined to describe them in this role) or as self-interested exploiters (perhaps best described, as they are in East Africa, as the *waBenzi* – KiSwahili for 'the Mercedes-owning people'). An additional point is the use of 'socialism' as part of the manipulative ideology. In

Tanzania, the questions certainly remained unresolved, and may never be resolved as that country, along with many others, now turns away from 'socialism' – African or otherwise – under the impact of decades of independence and World Bank structural adjustment programmes.

In the context of Cameroon, but relevant to the wider debates, the place of the state as the creator and facilitator of the process of accumulation, and of the relation between state functionaries, state structure and civil society, is nicely described by Bayart:

> Whether it embraces socialism or not, the state has become a principal economic initiator. Everywhere, it has amplified its incorporation into the world capitalist system. And it is inclined to pursue a sort of accumulation based on the over-exploitation of the peasantry. At the same time, a maximisation of the economic role of the state cannot be dissociated from the process of individual accumulation which it facilitates at all levels, irrespective of the ideological stance. Every position of [political] power relation is indisputably one of private enrichment because of the personal advantages that it procures. Even the business category of the population who do not belong to the public sector heavily depend on the state apparatus for capital accumulation. This is mainly based on their ability to manipulate laws [about customs control, fiscal fraud, etc.] and the administrative procedures [export/import licences]. It is therefore meaningless to make a distinction between the informal and formal sectors of the economy. This is because both are contributing to the hegemonic quest and the creation and consolidation of the dominant classes in society.[12]

What then has happened in Africa since those heady days of the 1960s? In some countries, such as Sudan, where there was for many years a stand-off between commercial and industrial capitalists (as well as interference by the USA and others (see Barnett and Abdelkarim, 1988)), the Alavi model tells us something of use. But in other regions of the continent, for example in Kenya or Côte d'Ivoire, it is fairly clear that some form of capitalism is developing, and within a state in which a local capitalist class, in alliance with state personnel, has a high degree of control. Here, the Alavi model is of less use. Yet we still need to explain why it is that while capitalism does appear to develop in some cases, it does not provide the economic growth (however maldistributed) to be seen in other states in the Third World, notably those of South-East and East Asia. It is this disjunction of experience between different states in Africa, and between them and states in other parts of the world, which places in doubt the generality of any one theory of the state in Africa, Asia and Latin America. Can there really be one theory which explains the form and actions of the state in Brazil and

Argentina as well as in Paraguay and Uruguay, or in Korea as well as Vietnam?

A refreshing break from the schematic and unempirical approach which characterizes much of the writing which has been derived from Alavi's original and important analysis of Pakistan and Bangladesh is to be found in the work of Goren Hyden.

Hyden begins dolorously (but I fear realistically) by saying that: 'As most of Africa's new states are reaching the age of a human generation, very few can look back on a period of real progress' (Hyden, 1983: xi). Hyden's approach, based on his years teaching at the University of Dar es Salaam and as Ford Foundation Representative in Nairobi, recognizes that there is a major methodological problem in writing about the state insofar as the detail of policy processes and decision-making is often hidden. Thus, the observer is usually in the position of making statements of the order of 'this happened, therefore "the state" must have done that for the following reasons'. Sometimes such observations may well be correct, but usually we have no way of knowing.

Hyden argues that the writings of both Saul and Shivji, despite their differences, present the problem as one of a struggle between progressive and reactionary forces. He argues that this a wrong agenda because in Africa there is a 'peasant mode of production' functioning side by side with either capitalism or socialism. This mode is based on petty land ownership or common tenure. It has been unable to sustain large political structures (with some exceptions) because its productivity is not such as to allow a surplus to accumulate which would support the state superstructure. It is a society which gets on very well without the state, indeed has no need for the state:

> Because the state is structurally superfluous from the point of view of the individual producer, it is not difficult to see that the peasants experience any policy aimed at improving his [*sic*] agriculture as a 'foreign' intervention. Because he owns the land, or at least has the undisputed right to till it, his ability to escape such policy demands is much greater than that of a tenant under feudal rule or a worker under capitalism. (Hyden, 1983: 7–8)

That African states are erected on such a 'base' means that an 'economy of affection' exists at the same time as a capitalist organization of society – of which the state itself is a major element. This 'economy of affection'

> denotes a network of support, communications and interaction among structurally defined groups connected by blood, kin, community and other affinities, for example religion . . . to be sure, the economy of

affection is most prevalent in the rural community but it is an integral part of society at large. Its influence stretches right from the grass-roots to the apex of society. (Hyden, 1983: 8–9)

It is important to note that this peculiarly peasant form of social organization, based on overlapping affiliations and obligations, is an important part of the survival strategy for rural peoples and also for the urban poor. It may also be important for the wealthier, who can use it as the basis for gaining political power and authority through a web of patronage and reciprocal obligation.

Perceived from within the African rural community, the first experience of the state was of the colonial state – it was an interference, made demands (tax, labour, crops). In short, it was experienced as exploitative. With the departure of the colonialists, the state was thrown open to the economy of affection – independence leaders had argued that the state was exploitative, it must be overthrown. This overthrow occurred, Hyden argues, but the post-colonial state was then 'swamped' by the demands of the economy of affection:

In this respect the post-colonial state, in spite of a superficial structural resemblance with its colonial predecessor, is very different. It has created one of the most problematic paradoxes in contemporary Africa: the existence of a state with no structural roots in society which, as a balloon suspended in mid-air, is being punctured by demands and unable to function without indiscriminate and wasteful consumption of scarce societal resources. (Hyden, 1983: 19)

Hyden's conclusion is that the way forward lies in increased capitalist development, because only that will destroy the economy of affection and implant a more rational organization of society. This will involve the allocation of resources through the market (thus giving peasants an incentive to join the wider society) and will at the same time be the basis for the development of a class strong enough to compete with international capital represented by the multinationals. A point of view, it will be noted, which is close to that of the World Bank and its policies for structural adjustment, and also, paradoxically, to some of Marx's writings on colonialism and capitalism – particularly when he writes of capitalism 'battering down the walls of China' (Avinieri, 1969), as well as to those of B. Warren (1980).

Thus, Hyden concludes, for Africa, socialist, centrally planned economies (and the state forms which accompany them) are not the way forward – the economy of affection is too strong. Instead it must be destroyed by the forces of the market – a conclusion which is now fashionable in many parts of the world.

The state in South Asia

Discussion of the state in India contrasts somewhat with the debates about the African state. In the part of the world where Alavi's now classic analysis has its roots, we find a discussion of the state which increasingly moves away from the simple Marxian formulation. One observer has argued for a 'realist' view of the state in India, a view in which

> the actual institutions of the state – the executive, the judiciary, the bureaucracy, the police and the military, commercial and cultural institutions, etc. – may be wielded against the interests of the supposedly dominant class . . . without resort to the formula which treats as axiomatic the proposition that while the state apparatus may work against the apparent interests of the dominant class it does so ('structurally') in order to secure those interests over a longer term. (Harriss and Mishra, 1983: 22)

Such a 'realist' approach implies a need for careful empirical study of the government administration, policy development and institutional interrelationships in India.

In contrast to this, Mitra (1977) and Patnaik (1979) have argued a more conventional Communist Party of India (Marxist) line that the Indian economy as a whole can be understood as the outcome of a coalition between the bourgeoisie and the large landowners, what they characterize as a 'duapolistic' arrangement between the rural oligarchy and the industrial bourgeoisie (Harriss and Mishra, 1983: 23) – a view closely based on the 'executive committee' model.

Thus, we appear to find two sharply differing views of the nature of the Indian state and, perhaps more importantly in the present context, of the way in which it is to be analysed. There is almost a sharp opposition between those adopting an inductive approach – arguing for more and better information – and those arguing from a deductive position – from the model to the evidence.

K.N. Raj's idea of an 'intermediate regime' (1973), later elaborated by P.S. Jha (1980), seems to provide another perspective. An 'intermediate regime' is one where the government is dominated by a lower middle class in alliance with a rich peasantry. This alliance ensures the failure of policies which might have benefited the industrial bourgeoisie, and thus accounts for the failure of Indian industrialization during the 1970s and early 1980s, while at the same time explaining the simultaneous 'success' of Indian agriculture in adopting the 'Green Revolution'. Such an argument has the appearance of an ex-post analysis – asking the question 'who benefits?' and from an answer to that question assuming some kind of class intentionality (whether 'structural' or conscious) as being the origin of the situation. Such a mode of argument has not, of course, been restricted to the Indian debates.

Contemporary states

Much of what has been said so far derives from discussions of states in Africa. But states in Africa and elsewhere are not to be analysed as though they share common features. We cannot assume *a priori* that they do. Each state reflects its own history, the cultural and linguistic traditions of its populations, as well as its own unique relation with a 'world system'. The differences in the terms of the debates, the differences in economy, culture and society within Africa and between Africa and India (as well as between these and other parts of the world) should indicate that there is a certain futility in talking of 'the state' in the 'Third World'.

As there is no longer any 'Third World', so the theoretical category of 'the state in the Third World' or 'the post-colonial state' has begun to dissolve. Simplistic instrumental theories (such as the executive committee model) exist side by side with abstract formulations, such as those of Poulantzas (1968), in which the state ceases to exist except as something which seems remarkably similar to the Hegelian 'idea'. At the material level, nation states in Western Europe are at an uncertain moment, on the edge of greater centralization under the guise of 'decentralization', or transition to federal structures. In Eastern Europe, the dissolution of the Soviet empire constitutes another uncertain moment where nationalism could all too easily tip over into nationally based repression and centralization with the attendant danger that nationalism as a special form of ethnic identification may become institutionalized, privileging one particular ethnic identity by attaching it to the state in the complex ethnic mix once more revealed by the crumbling of Soviet hegemony. To this explosive mixture, in addition, the influence of multinational corporations and the ambitions of Western nations are providing various forms of tinder.

By contrast, in Africa the state may continue as an interfering irritant, a source of corruptly obtained advantage or a massive irrelevance for many people. In East Asia, South Korea, Singapore and Malaysia, states grow strong and create national identities in relation to a developing capitalism. Technically and socially, they are able to control populations. In Africa, the more subtle means of control are by and large absent, and politics often seems little more than a succession of military coups sometimes accompanied by random state terror, attempts by state personnel to control the limited wealth accumulated through a deformed and peripheral capitalism. Thus, Worsley says of Africa:

> The nationalist mystique . . . is grounded in an institutional praxis, that of mobilisation for development: part . . . of the contemporary drive to catch up . . . The states which emerged during the epoch of a world system dominated by multinational corporations and Superpower rivalries had acquired experience of mobilising the masses during the Independence struggles. After Independence, they try to continue that mobilisation, for the possibility of developing capitalism along classic laissez-faire lines is a pipe-dream since its major pre-requisite – capital – is missing. Not much capital gets generated in the first place, and much of what there is gets exported. What does exist, in abundance, is labour. For these latecomers, then, the only possible development strategy is a labour-intensive one. The outcome is the emergence of highly-centralised state systems, either one-party states or military ones. (Worsley, 1984: 292)

Hyden argues that in Africa the state floats above civil society like a tenuously tethered balloon. In Singapore and Malaysia, the state is so strong as to be able to suppress most opposition, sack high court judges, but at the same time can provide sufficient material welfare to a majority of its population to meet their rising expectations while issues of liberal democracy remain unexperienced and unexpected by most citizens.

In some respects, we see an odd evolutionary/unequal development laid out across the world. The nation state, while a European invention, received its greatest thrust in the latter part of the nineteenth century. Together with the colonial state, it reflects the machine metaphor of nineteenth-century capitalism. It is no accident that Weber was a major (if often unrecognized) theorist of the state's operation through his detailed dissections of bureaucracy and other forms of authority. In Europe, we see perhaps the beginning of the end to that machine metaphor, as communications technology and social experiences and aspirations allow (but not without a struggle from those wedded to the machine metaphor and wishing perhaps to transfer it to supra-nation state federations) for the emergence of greater regionalism and localism, together with all the attendant dangers of ethnic conflict. In Africa, the essentially military colonial state, now inherited by Africans, remains as a part of an extractive capitalism which tries to capture a meagre surplus from the population on the excuse of developmental accumulation. In parts of East and South-East Asia, the development of capitalist production organization, locally as well as multinationally based, ensures that control can be exercised, assuredly not in the interests of all, but sufficiently so as to defuse opposition for the moment.

The conclusion of the survey is that in the same way that there is no such thing as the 'Third World' any longer, in the sense that since the concept was a political and polemical one, deriving from the history and experience of anti-colonial struggle, it can no longer be argued with integrity that there is 'a theory of the state in the Third World'. We now need studies of specific states in Africa, the Middle East, Latin America and Asia which show us how real states operate,[13] rather than analyses which take as their point of departure theories which were constructed for other purposes in another time. In particular, we need to be aware that insofar as 'states state' (Corrigan and Sayer, 1985) – with all that this implies for the role of culture in politics – so they affect cultural construction and the actions of government in relation to the people who live within the boundaries of any particular state.

Only when this work has been done should we attempt the reconstruction of a unified theory of the state.

Notes

* This chapter covers developments up to the final draft completed in 1992.

1. The term 'tribe' is sometimes used to describe such local identities. I do not wish to use this term, first because of its association with notions of 'the primitive', and secondly because it is really quite inappropriate as a description of local identities based on such diverse identifications as craft, religion, caste, status and nation.

2. The taken-for-granted world of colonial administrators was constructed from many sources. Among those were mainstream Church of England beliefs. Additional components would have been drawn from origins as diverse as the racial theories of Gobineau (1933), Spencer's ideas about social evolution (1967) and the popular literature of the time, such as the works of Rudyard Kipling (Pinney, 1986).

3. Or, put another way, this points to the importance of chaos theory for social theory. Much socio-historical explanation has been too deterministic, failing to recognize that minute variations in the initial state of a system can result in major changes in a future state of that system.

4. The origins of the English state cannot, of course, be defined precisely. Some authors would begin with the Norman Conquest, others later, some earlier. For an excellent discussion of the issues and source, see Corrigan and Sayer (1985).

5. An important contribution to the establishment of the principle of the nation state in Europe is to be found in Johann Gottlieb Fichte's (1762–1814) 'Addresses to the German Nation', delivered in Berlin during 1807–8. These were responses to the victories of Napoleon I at Jena and Aurestadt in 1808 which effectively established French imperial hegemony in much of West and Central Europe, threatening to suppress many ethnic and 'national' identities. Fichte's writing affected thinking not only in Germany but also in Italy and other parts of Europe.

6. Indeed he was not partisan and he attempted to think the issues through very thoroughly. Elements of his thought were appropriated by both sides in the English Civil War, and both sides were offended by it. *Leviathan* was publicly burned in Oxford in 1685.

7. Edmund Burke, Speech on the Middlesex Elections, 7 February 1771: 'The circumstances are in great measure new. We have hardly any landmarks from the wisdom of our ancestors to guide us' (Ayling, 1988).

8. Of course the whole process starts much earlier in the case of India.

9. It must not be forgotten that the Soviet Union had played a part in anti-colonial struggles for many decades, starting very soon after the October Revolution. See Carr (1966: 232–71).

10. This type of regime could of course be found in many other African states at different times in the past three decades. It has been described as a 'party-mobilizing regime'; see Chazan et al. (1988).

11. The exclusion of 'culture' from the analysis is not surprising in view of the way in which it was used as a catch-all variable in modernization theory and reduced to an economically determined false consciousness by some Marxists.

12. Bayart (1985: 329). I am grateful to John Mope Simo for drawing this work to my attention and for providing this translation.

13. Such as may be found in an embryonic form in E. Clay and B. Schaffer's book, *Room for Manoeuvre* (1984).

3

The Many Cultural Faces of Imperialism

Annabelle Sreberny-Mohammadi

It would have been far better for these poor people never to have known us. (Captain Cook's journal entry on 'Tahiti')

The notion of 'cultural imperialism' became one of the staple catch-phrases of the field of international communication. Yet, from the beginning, the concept was broad and ill-defined, operating as evocative metaphor rather than precise construct, and has gradually lost much of its critical bite and historic validity.

Schiller's early definition of cultural imperialism was highly inclusive: the 'sum of the processes by which a society is brought into the modern world system and how its dominating stratum is attracted, pressured, forced and sometimes even bribed into shaping social institutions to correspond to, or even promote, the values and structures of the dominating center of the system' (Schiller, 1976: 9). Yet, while acknowledging the powerful cultural impact of colonialism, Schiller's interest lay in documenting the rise of American corporate power and its ideological expansion worldwide via the media, so that the earlier processes and carriers of Western culture were essentially ignored.

Similarly, while Hamelink acknowledged that 'throughout history, cultures have always influenced one another', he actually tends to dismiss the cultural impact of colonialism by saying that 'in European colonial history ... the distance between the exclusively Western culture and the indigenous culture is kept as wide as possible' (Hamelink, 1983: 4).

The process of cultural imperialism, or 'cultural synchronization' as Hamelink preferred to call it, 'implies that a particular type of cultural development in the metropolitan country is persuasively communicated to the receiving countries. Cultural synchronization implies that the traffic of cultural products goes massively in one direction and has basically a synchronic mode' (Hamelink, 1983: 5).

Essentially such an argument rewrote the Frankfurt School analysis of the power of the 'culture industries' (Adorno and Horkheimer, 1972) on a global scale. The post-war expansion and power of the Western culture industries is indeed unparalleled and well documented, not only in television but in 'films, records, cassettes, women's magazines, and children's comics' (Hamelink, 1983: 9), and is an arena of continuing theoretical and practical concern. Yet to label this dynamic process 'cultural imperialism' is to invite two unacceptable reductions in analytical focus.

The first is to reduce 'culture' solely to the products of the culture industries, while the second – which follows from the first – is a tendency to assume the limited cultural impact of the earlier 'political and military' dynamics of imperialism. Thus cultural imperialism was often elided too much into 'media imperialism' (Boyd-Barrett, 1977), a more narrowly-focused construct, and Western cultural impact was perceived as a post-Second World War phenomenon carried out mainly through the activities of multinational corporations.

More recently, Tomlinson (1991) effectively unpacked the various discourses – about media, about nationality, about the culture of capitalism and about modernity – which congealed within the one term of 'cultural imperialism'. Hall (1992) also focuses on the discourses that emanate from the impact of 'the West on the Rest' and the spread of modernity.

Yet by focusing on the realm of the discursive, the dynamics of cultural contact become invisible. Tomlinson situates the general problematic of cultural domination within the global process of 'the imposition of the social institutions of modernity . . . capitalism, bureaucracy, urban-industrialism . . . a Western praxis' (Tomlinson, 1991: 162), yet is not particularly concerned to explore precisely how those very broad institutional forces operate.

Hall too, while concerned to analyse the global spread of modernity, pays little attention to any particular social carriers of Western influence. Said writes that 'imperialism consolidated the mixtures of cultures and identities on a global scale' (1993: 407), but his focus is also on the textual, specifically the novel, as it carried the cultural discourses of imperialism. Even Mattelart's work on the 'ideological apparatuses of imperialism' concentrates on the multi-nationals' 'control of culture' (Mattelart, 1979).

Thus, between the political economic analyses of the post-1945 globalizing media industries and the more historically grounded discourse analyses of the globalizing myths of modernity remains a space, an historical examination of the practices imperialism institutionalized that carried the social and cultural infrastructure of modernity. If Raymond Williams (1961) oriented us to the essential ordinariness, everydayness, of culture, then part of the function of a global cultural analysis is to identify the many ordinary, everyday ways that life in the South has been affected by the social structures of imperialism. In our epoch of high modernity, it has become easier to see imperialism as perhaps the core mover in shaping the world we now inhabit, as the global carrier of the social practices of 'modernity' in all its manifestations.

Imperialism did not maintain its rule merely through suppression, but through the export and institutionalization of European ways of life, organizational structures, values and interpersonal relations, language and cultural products that often remained and continued to have impact even once the imperialists themselves had gone home. In short, imperialism was in itself a multi-faceted cultural process which laid the ground for the ready acceptance and adoption of mediated cultural products which came much, much later.

As Hobsbawm argues, 'the colonial conquests of European forces had been achieved not by miraculous weaponry, but by greater aggressiveness, ruthlessness and, above all, disciplined organization' (Hobsbawm, 1989: 16). Gann and Duignan likewise claim, rather too benignly, that 'European immigration to Africa . . . represented . . . a much-needed transfer of modern skills. We accordingly interpret European imperialism in Africa as an engine of cultural transfusion as well as of political domination . . . Imperialism . . . acted as a means of cultural transformation. Among other things, the whites brought to Africa modern forms of education, medical facilities and a host of economic techniques' (Gann and Duignan, 1969: 23).

If we use a more inclusive, anthropological definition of 'culture', there were and are many more carriers of Western culture to the Third World than the corporate channels of the culture industries, and the cultural milieux of many developing countries were already 'contaminated', deeply and perhaps irreversibly altered by Western cultural penetration, long before any modern media arrived. Without acknowledging the deep structure of cultural affiliations and orientations that imperialism brought with it, many of the practices of modernity, the more obvious inequalities of economic and technological development cannot be successfully engaged. As Laitin (1983: 317) has noted, in the post-colonial world 'many aspects of the imperial relationship remain and even prosper . . . the economic, military and technological', but also 'the more elusive but no less significant cultural ties'.

Imperialism as cultural contact

Some caveats to begin with. This is not an analysis of the root causes of imperialism nor a recapitulation of the contentious theoretical debates about its cause(s). Nor is it an analysis of the popular rhetoric of imperialism (MacKensie, 1984, 1986) nor the cross-cultural encounters which ensued (Kiernan, 1969). Nor do I assume necessary and equal impacts of modern culture on the host cultures of these various carriers. The point here is only to map these out. Also, while I acknowledge that there were many different, usually nationally based, forms of political and economic imperialism, I do not make much of the Anglicized, Gallicized, Germanized, Lusitanized or, later, Americanized, flavours of the process. What I hope to show are the multi-faceted ways in which imperialism fundamentally altered the material, psychological and social environments of the Third World, broadly conceived as their 'cultures'.

Despite the burgeoning of work in post-colonial studies, little has been taken on board by media scholars. This chapter attempts to disaggregate some older dynamics of cultural contact which have not been much examined by communications scholars, yet which may serve as points of critique of contemporary models of international communication and intercultural contact.

Map-making and nation-building

With the current rise of ethnic conflicts centering on territorial divisions, it makes sense to start by pointing out that many of the actual political boundaries between nation states, as well as the manner of representing these cartographically, bear the imprint of colonialism. All maps bear certain distortions of the collapse of three dimensions into two, but they also carry cultural distortions, creating preferred imaginings of the lie of the world.

Mercator's projection, in common use since the 1500s, distorts the comparative size of continental landmasses, as well as evoking a Eurocentric vision of the Mediterranean as the centre of the world. Peters's projection, by equalling the distances between lines of latitude, provides a representation more in line with actual size, and has been adopted by UNESCO and other international bodies.

Many existing national boundaries are more the result of inter-colonial rivalries and pay-offs than any demarcation of cultural and ethnic groupings. This was true of the late nineteenth-century 'scramble for Africa'. As Ajayi argues,

> the most fundamental aspect of the European impact was the loss of sovereignty which it entailed for practically every African people. Europeans exploited their technological superiority to establish their political dominance throughout the continent . . . Perhaps the most significant exercise of this sovereignty was the extent to which the act of

partition was effected. The territories into which Africa was divided marked entirely new departures in African history . . . the new boundaries, once the Europeans themselves were agreed on them, were intended to be permanent and no longer to expand or recede at the will of Africans. (Ajayi, 1969: 504)

The colonial powers – Britain, France, Germany and Italy – with Russian agreement, also drew many lines in the sand which created the map of the modern Middle East, bestowing on future generations numerous struggles about territory and identity – Kurds, Armenians, Palestinians – that are still being played out (Fromkin, 1989). But more significant even than the actual boundaries is the thinking that lay behind these, and other divisions: the notion of national political determination which grounds some claims but disallows others. It is here that the expanding field of political geography makes its contribution in showing how the Eurocentric understanding of nationalism became the ideology which defines the current world economy, that 'no less than states, nations are created and reflect the politics in which they are made' (Taylor, 1989: 188). It is not only, as Appadurai has said, that 'the nation and the state have become one another's projects' (1990: 303) but also that the criteria for legitimate claims about nationhood shift, from linguistic to religious and other 'ethnic' bases, or are simply ignored in great power *realpolitik*.

The contradictions of anti-colonial nationalism in the Third World are very real, reflecting progressive popular movements against European hegemony, yet running the rapid risk of becoming new nationalist hegemonies, often as ruthless and undemocratic as those they replace. The (re-)construction of a nation and the encouragement of an inward-looking singular cultural identity within the boundaries of a political state are part of the unanticipated cultural consequences of imperialism.

Missionaries and the export of religion

One of the earliest and most pervasive forms of Western cultural exportation was Christian missionary activity. There is a great deal of research in missionary history, both linking missionaries to the prevailing political and economic forces within Western societies and examining the impact of such activity on the non-Western cultural milieux they encountered.

Missionaries were often the advance guard of colonialism, with an explicitly cultural mission, carrying the white man's burden of civilizing the 'noble savage' in preparation for the economic and administrative roles that the colonizers would require of them. Academic research on this topic includes analyses of Christian encounters in many different cultural settings including China, the Philippines, Iran and Latin America (Fairbanks, 1974; Poikal, 1970; Mansoori, 1986; Zirinsky, 1993; Lewis, 1988) and many different time frames. Some brief examples provide the flavour and findings of such work.

In 1797, two years after its founding, the London Missionary Society sent out missionaries to Tahiti, concerned to convert if not through persuasion then by terror. By setting island chiefs against one another, and declaring illegal the wearing of flowers, singing other than hymns, tattooing, surfing or dancing, slowly the peaceful, happy native culture was extinguished. And so too were many Tahitians, from the syphilis, tuberculosis, smallpox and influenza brought by the outsiders: they declined from a population of 200,000 to 6,000 at the end of 30 years of missionary rule (Lewis, 1988: 4). By 1850, the British and French between them had carved up the Pacific.

Clymer (1986) discusses the manner in which the Spanish brought Roman Catholicism to the Philippines by 1521 and maintained control until 1898 when the American Bible Society and the British and Foreign Bible Societies became active. Of the Americans, Clymer writes:

> The missionaries constituted an important and articulate segment of the American colonial population. They helped shape attitudes in the Philippines and in the US about Filipino culture and about the American presence in the islands; on occasion they helped shape policy too. They helped reconcile Filipinos to their new fate and were allies of the government in what both perceived as a 'civilising' mission. (Clymer, 1986: 8)

The Americans set up YMCAs, gave courses and lectures, published magazines, and organized wholesome recreation like volleyball. Mission schools provided an industrial education, aiming to 'save souls' but also to promote societal transformation and humanitarian reform. Missionaries were the 'advanced agents of civilisation', trying to end slavery, polygamy and cannibalism, and cope with – what they saw as – the generally dirty, lazy and immoral Filipinos. Such was the 'white man's burden'.

China experienced different waves of missionary activity, including Franciscans in the thirteenth and fourteenth centuries, then Jesuits, and much later Protestants. Barnet and Fairbank (1985: 5) argue that 'the full story of Christian proselytism in China still needs to be appraised as a whole'. They do suggest (1985: 18) that Protestant missions were more than 'simply a religious movement' as they played a central role 'in the meeting of cultures' and thus a contradictory role in the expansion of the West and the regeneration of China.

American missionary activity at the turn of the century was considerable, growing from 934 foreign missionaries in 1890 to almost 5,000 a decade later, and to over 9,000 by 1915 (Hill, 1985). Some missionaries were critical of their own impact. Already in 1906 Helen Barrette Montgomery wrote that Western interest in the Pacific was a result of commercial exploitation that was less than a blessing to the island natives for, though the islanders were 'rude, uncivilized, bewildered by superstition, decimated by wars, and brutalized by customs', they possessed their own primitive laws and customs, and were free, strong and occupied beautiful territory (1906: 135).

One of the most evocative areas of cultural contact, and one which points out all the dilemmas and ironies of Western Christian contact with the 'other', is black American missionary activity in Africa. Williams's study (1982) shows not only the central importance of the Church as the core of community organization in rural black America but how the growth of independent black churches was a mechanism by which black Americans adapted to their low status in post-Reconstruction America (Williams, 1982: xiv). Yet at the same time, black Americans had assimilated much of the dominant Western attitude to 'the dark continent' of Africa, and their missionary evangelism carried these values abroad. As Williams argues, 'by the late nineteenth century, Africans and Afro-Americans were two peoples, separated in culture but united by color and struggles to control their own lives' (Williams, 1982: 124), and black missionary projects were a crucial part of the renewed intercultural encounter. He suggests that although there were individual exceptions, like William Shephard in the Congo, most nineteenth-century black American missionaries 'had a low opinion of indigenous African culture. They saw themselves as civilized people who were trying to bring civilization to Africans, and they did not identify with non-Western lifestyles.' Williams explains this sense of cultural superiority in terms of Afro-American inferiority at home: 'The chance to see themselves as a black Elect coming to save a continent was, not surprisingly given their backgrounds, irresistible to the missionaries. Unfortunately, this elevated self-image was at the expense of understanding and appreciating African cultures' and thus blocked the growth of any genuine Pan-Africanist sentiment (Williams, 1982: 124). Many black Americans, such as Alexander Crummell, John J. Coles and Floyd Snelson, were strong supporters of imperialism, believing it to be part of God's plan to open the continent to Westernization and enlightenment (Williams, 1982: 134).

Although there were emigrationist and anti-imperialist sentiments, most mission supporters looked forward to the 'redemption' of the black man.

Jacobs (1982: 23) argues similarly that different forms of Christianity were brought to Africa by European colonialism, and that American missionaries played a comparatively minor role before 1945 in the development of the African Church while post-war activity was dramatic. In 1900 there were a little over half a million Christians in Africa, 35 million by 1960, and almost 130 million by the early 1980s (Jacobs, 1982: 24). The ambiguities of missionary work in undermining indigenous African culture were multiplied when the missionaries were themselves black Americans, sent to Africa because whites felt them to have a natural resistance to the climate and fevers of Africa. Yet when missionary emphasis shifted from conversion to trusteeship – developing self-governing, self-supporting and self-propagating churches in Africa – the domination of the African Church by Europeans included the black missionaries, and European hostility towards black American missionaries began to develop. Black American missionaries stressed education for Africans and the Protestant churches developed schooling in Africa. The Europeans also feared black American missionaries' support for Marcus Garvey's 'Africa for the Africans' notion from 1916, and their support for anti-colonialist, political movements in black Africa (Jacobs, 1982: 21). Roth argues that many black Americans themselves suffered from racism within the mission movement, but the cultural issue ran far deeper.

> By 1900, only the most naive observer of what some called 'aggressive Christianity' could deny that the coming of Christianity and civilisation usually spelled the going of African society . . . more long-lasting was that more subtle destruction of African mores and customs. The nature of mission work inevitably accelerated this destruction, since concepts of the non-material world were at the core of African civilisation. When the black missionary in Africa assisted in the erosion of African society, he was simultaneously destroying his own past. Thus, missions to Africa involved carrying forth American civilisation, towards which the Afro-American felt ambivalent, in order to modify African civilisations, about which the American black also had mixed feelings. (Roth, 1982: 36)

Of course, missionaries made many notable contributions to the continent of Africa, as elsewhere. They recorded an enormous amount of information about traditional African society in auto-biographies, diaries and letters, and in the artefacts brought back to the United States. They helped project a more positive image of the continent and to dispel some of the Western myths and negative stereotypes about Africa and its peoples; they also aided in social and political reform, especially in the development of education in Africa and in the United States. Jacobs's summation is that 'although missionaries have been accused of only disrupting African traditional society, some positive impacts are now being realized' and the long-term impact of missionary movement in Africa is not yet fully assessed (Jacobs, 1982: 236).

The period after 1945 was another major era of American missionary expansion. For example, the Summer Institute for Linguistics and the New Tribes Mission set out across Latin America to 'settle and civilize' Indian tribes, often supported financially and administratively by Latin dictators (Lewis, 1988). Lewis gives some vivid examples of the subtle – and not so subtle – cultural and economic effects that missionaries could have. One, a Mr Fernley who ran the mission in Chichicastenango, Guatemala, also ran in the late 1940s the first tourist shop outside Guatemala City, where he had amassed an outstanding collection of *huipils*, the traditional, hand-embroidered blouses worn by Indian women. These he obtained from the women either by exchanging the blouse for metal bowls, which replaced the decorated gourds they used, or for manufactured blouses sporting Disney characters. In Venezuela in 1987 it was discovered that half of 2,300 Panare Indians had been converted and then forced to pay monthly dues to their missions or sell their land, or even prostitute their daughters (Lewis, 1988: 180). Survival International now monitors such activity and has asked missions to respect tribal religion and culture.

While the full impact of missionary activity in different areas still remains to be assessed, and while more 'positive' readings seem to be coming forward, there is little doubt that beyond the specifics of Christian teaching – a profound alteration in and of itself – missionaries can be considered amongst the first active carriers of broader Western culture to 'enlighten' the Third World.

Education

> On the Black continent, it began to be understood that their true power lay not in the cannons of the first morning but in what followed the cannons. Thus, behind the gunboats, . . . the new school. The new school had the nature of both the cannon and the magnet. From the cannon it took the efficiency of a fighting weapon. But better than the cannon it made the conquest permanent. The cannon forces the body and the school fascinates the soul. (Kane, 1986: 49)

Another profound carrier of Western values and a major outcome of colonial contact was the development and spread of European formal education with its disciplinary divisions and hierarchical organization, providing the social as well as professional skills for the would-be post-colonial elites. Education is also the arena where ambivalent sentiments about cultural alteration are most acute. Quite opposing views are represented, for example, by Szcylowitcz's positive (1973) and by Carnoy's negative assessments (1974).

Altbach argues that probably no single 'export' is more crucial in the export of the structures, values and outlook of imperialism than education, specifically university structures which are a direct product of the Western tradition and have little to do with the intellectual or educational traditions of the Third World. The imposition of metropolitan models of politics, administration and education reinforced economic dependency through cultural reliance on Western models of education and learning. 'The institutional models, the curriculum, the pedagogical techniques and basic ideas concerning the role of education in society were all Western' (Altbach, 1987: 51).

Yet, in the main, education was provided only so far as to satisfy the colonial need for local low-level functionaries or to satisfy missionaries' consciences about their 'civilizing mission'. Britain was more supportive of higher educational provision than was France, although Britain favoured such development more in India than in its African colonies; the Belgians actually banned the development of post-secondary education in their colonies (Altbach, 1987: 49). According to Gilbert (1972: 384), loyal Indian universities were expected to produce small numbers of middle-class civil servants, leaving little room for intellectual autonomy, and in fact developing a culture of subservience. Educational policy also had linguistic implications (see the section on language, p. 61–3 ff.). It was felt that vernaculars could be effectively used to promote religious values and would in the long-run be more valuable to African development; much of British literature, including Bunyan's *Pilgrim's Progress*, Aesop's *Fables* and Lamb's *Tales from Shakespeare* were translated into African vernaculars to be taught by local teachers. At the same time, ironically but probably inevitably, English-language instruction came to be highly valued by those Africans who wanted their children to receive education, and missionaries offered English instruction as an incentive to get children to come to school (Wardhaugh, 1987: 159). Thus, while English was extensively used, 91 vernacular languages were being used in the primary schools of black Africa by 1950. The post-colonial legacy was that English was seen as a pragmatically useful language but local languages were valued; the other side of the coin was that comparatively few people had been educated at all.

French practice was rather different. As part of their *mission civilatrice*, the imperial power required the use of French in all schools except Koranic and other religious schools, although they actually educated very few locals, who became the small but powerful post-colonial elites.

Ali Mazrui (1975) has gone so far as to argue that the university is the single 'most sophisticated instrument of cultural dependency', cultivating a taste for Western lifestyles, and thus imports, and Western academic values that devalue African culture – such an argument reinforcing the notion of the 'thickness' of cultural imperialism.

The institutionalization of Western-style education helped, if not to create *ab initio*, to widen the gap between local elites and the masses as a whole, and between urban dwellers and rural masses. Educational qualifications became a passport into government bureaucracy and a life of comparative luxury; even after independence, the lack of trust between elites and masses makes it very hard for many Third World development programmes to be effective. Often, higher education institutions proliferated while the lack of primary educational facilities for all school-age children endured. In some countries, steps to extrication from this form of cultural dependency have been taken. In Tanzania, for example, there is increasing use of Swahili over English, the replacement of expatriate teachers with Tanzanians and the Africanization of the curriculum.

As in most other spheres, the colonial legacy in education remains a mixed blessing in the current educational environments of the Third World. For example, the limited development of colonial schooling for the most part meant little attention was paid to the development of textbooks and teaching materials, which have remained scarce (Altbach et al., 1988). Often, texts imported from the metropole were the only books available, while sometimes catechism and the Bible were felt to be sufficient for colonized populations. Only in rare instances – as in French West Africa – were new books written and curricula developed, although these inevitably emphasized Western views of Third World societies concerning singing, dancing, farming and so forth (Altbach et al., 1988: 4). Thus, at independence, both scarcity and dependence characterized most Third World educational structures, and the basic infrastructure to produce texts – printing presses, publishing houses and supplies of paper – did not exist (Altbach et al., 1985). The politics and economics of paper, in and of itself, is a fascinating microcosm of the structural inequalities produced by imperialism.

Educational provision, curricula content and teaching materials are thus important sites of inherited economic dependency, complicated policy-making and deep-rooted cultural conflicts, which may centre upon the language of instruction, or the nature of the 'knowledge' imparted, or the very purpose of an educational system within its national socio-economic and political frameworks. One outcome of the limited development of higher education in much of the Third World, along with difficulties in generating sufficient employment for graduates, is the brain drain, the quasi-permanent export of intellectual talent to the West and a major retardant to development.

Education in the Third World reflects the deep-rooted cultural impact of imperialism and, as a result, the continuing dilemmas of development.

Administration

No imperial power could rely on its own nationals alone. A small but cooperative native elite was vital, and education in the broadest sense, as just discussed, was vital. But beyond training in literacy, in the specific disciplines of Western knowledge, values relevant to bureaucratic structures had to be imbued, including those of professionalism and administrative propriety.

Coquery-Vidrovitch (1969) describes how by 1907 there were 489 officials in French black Africa but many of them were not trained, so the French set up *écoles coloniales* to train their administrators. Delavignette argues that independence ended the regional governments-general but retained the local administrative units. 'The new African republics were built in place of the colonial territories, without modifying the shape or content of each territory . . . French Africa and British Africa remained under independence what they had been during the colonial period' (Delavignette, 1970: 276).

Administration is closely allied to a whole complex of orientations referred to as 'professionalism'. Referring to media professionalism in particular, but with implications for other fields of practice, Golding (1977: 292) has argued that professionalism is 'an ideology that has been transferred in parallel to the transfer of technology and as part of the general stream of cultural dependence'. This transfer of an ideology, without necessarily the transfer of the practice, has been achieved through three mechanisms: institutional transfer, training and education, and the diffusion of occupational ideologies (Golding, 1977: 293) and was a crucial non-material underpinning of the entire infrastructure of imperialism. Midgely (1981) coined the term 'professional imperialism' in his analysis of dynamics of social work in the Third World, and Arnold (1988) critically examined the penetration of Western values and practices in medicine.

The increasing globalization of training, the development of international MBAs and distance learning programmes, are all part and parcel of this dynamic, the export of Western bureaucratic ideology, sometimes its process, to the South.

Language

> You taught me language; and my profit on't
> Is, I know how to curse: the red plague rid you
> For learning me your language!
>
> (Caliban to Prospero, *The Tempest* I.ii.363–5)

Some claim that the most profound and long-lasting cultural impact of imperialism was and is language practice. So Laitin (1983: 317) argues: 'Of all the cultural ties that still bind Africa to Europe, it is the continued use of European languages as the official languages of African states that remains most significant.' Yet, as he brilliantly develops, language policy reflects the basic dilemmas of Third World modernization so that, for some, linguistic nationalism goes against the progressive thrust of internationalism (Luxembourgeois), while others see indigenous language as the necessary assertion of popular national cultures struggling against colonial powers (Leninist) (Laitin, 1983: 323–5).

Different colonial powers had somewhat different attitudes to the use of vernacular languages or those of the colonizers. The British, Germans and Belgians tended to learn one or more vernacular language and conducted much of their business in vernacular tongues. At the end of some centuries of British colonial rule in India, only 1 per cent of the population could speak English (Altbach, 1987: 51). The French, however, felt their language was the apotheosis of high culture and advanced civilization, and conducted their education, administration and all manner of communication in French (Wardhaugh, 1987). Mazrui (1977, quoted in Ngugi, 1986: 30) has argued that 'European languages became so important to the Africans that they defined their own identities partly by reference to those languages. Africans began to describe each other in terms of being Francophone or English-speaking Africans. The continent itself was thought of in terms of French-speaking states, English-speaking states and Arabic-speaking states.' Ngugi has criticized this argument, saying that 'Arabic does not quite fall into that category. Instead of Arabic-speaking states as an example, Mazrui should have put Portuguese-speaking states.

Arabic is now an African language unless we want to write off all the indigenous populations of North Africa, Egypt, Sudan as not being Africans' (Ngugi, 1986: 31).

Here Ngugi raises the term which lurks implicitly behind much of the debate in international and inter-cultural communication, the notion of the 'indigenous'. He resolves the question of what is indeed indigenous to a particular part of the world through some kind of historical sleight-of-hand, never defining the 'now' or how long its history. Thus the key word in the quotation above is 'Arabic is *now* an African language', in place and in use prior to European expansion, yet also highlighted as not having always been used in these African nations. Ngugi's own work is a passionate exploration of the dynamics of language politics in Africa, and culminates in his personal declaration that 'this book is my farewell to English as a vehicle for any of my writings. From now on it is Gikuyu and Kiswahili all the way' (Ngugi, 1986: xiv; see also Ngugi, 1991). Language politics is a central part of African cultural resistance against neo-imperialism. Ngugi takes up the argument, often espoused in regard to Third World nations, that the colonial language has not been rejected since it serves as a politically neutral language standing above the conflicts of tribe and region; he goes so far as to reject the label 'African literature' as applied to works written in colonial languages by Africans, wishing to call them 'Afro-European . . . [or] Euro-African' (Ngugi, 1986: 33).

This radical position was opposed by Senghor and other 'negritude' poets who write in French, claiming it to be the lingua franca of the multitude of diverse African states that were created out of French colonialism.

The establishment of national language policy after independence has been extremely complicated. Often education, administration and law are conducted in the European language, whose continuation is both expedient and efficient. In many ex-colonies the European language has been adopted as the 'official' language while vernacular languages are sometimes adopted as 'national' languages. The continued use of colonial languages within higher educational systems cuts university students off from their humbler fellow-countrymen, orients them continually towards metropolitan centres, and reaffirms an already existing elitism.

Laitin suggests that a policy of linguistic dissociation is needed for a number of reasons: that such a strategy might help African people overcome the debilitating psychological effects of colonialism; that it might be the basis for innovation in the technical and political fields, a different linguistic vision helping creatively to solve problems; that it might help to foster a receptive audience for progressive social policies, greater regime sensitivity to the needs of its own peripheral areas and help to stem the brain drain (Laitin, 1983: 368; see also Laitin, 1991).

In the future, however, it seems likely that far more people of the South will be fluent in more languages, including European ones, than Northeners, another odd cultural twist of the imperial legacy and its 'linguistic imperialism' (Phillipson, 1992). In the twenty-first century, it is southerners who are the likely cosmopolitans.

Travel and tourism

> Tourism is the largest scale movement of goods, services and peoples that humanity has perhaps ever seen. (Greenwood, 1977: 129)

Of the various kinds of cultural contact before mediated contact, tourism was still in its infancy, but has since become one of the major forces of cultural contact, having grown into a multi-billion-dollar industry projected to become the world's largest industry by the turn of the twenty-first century (Nicholson-Lord, 1990). Early travel was the privilege of a moneyed elite carrying bourgeois table manners and vocalizations. The democratization of travel and leisure – more money, more time, more monotony at home – has also meant its massive increase, with later popular hordes carrying blue jeans and chewing gum, syphilis and swear words.

Tourism flows North–South, from industrial to Third World.

> It is perfectly legitimate to compare tourists with barbarian tribes. Both involve mass migrations of peoples who collide with cultures far removed from their own. There is, however, one major difference. The old Golden Horde (a Tartar Empire led by Genghis Khan's successors) was a nomadic, non-monetary people which threatened the settled urban civilizations of Europe. Today, the pattern is reversed. Tourists come from the industrial centres but, this time, it is they who are fanning out through the world, swamping apparently less dynamic societies, including the few pre-industrial ones which still remain. In the past, it was the great commercial centres of the world like Constantinople and Vienna which were threatened. Today, it is the Nomads of Affluence, coming from the new Constantinoples – cities like New York, London, Hamburg or Tokyo – who are creating a newly dependent, social and geographic realm: the pleasure periphery. (Turner and Ash, 1976: 11)

The impacts of tourism are multiple and profound. Even the economic analysis of tourism is complex. It may generate entrepreneurial activity and stimulate a growth in employment, but such economic benefits are unequally spread, and often have environmental impacts, particularly in building and development projects like airport construction, road expansion, hotel development and establishment of sewage plants. Larger ecological problems can also be a consequence of tourist development, such as deforestation, water pollution, threatened eco-systems, trade in wildlife and the threat to certain species, erosion of beaches and depletion of local resources. Lea (1988) examined the pleasure periphery in Southern Africa (Botswana, Lesotho and Swaziland), where a tourist boom was experienced in the late 1960s to the mid-1970s based on the 'forbidden fruits' of gambling and inter-racial sex enjoyed by visiting South Africans. But economically, about 60 per cent of tourist revenue leaked back to South Africa to the two parent transnational corporations and other businesses based there, while slot machines and porno houses took their toll of the local population whose low incomes could not support such habits.

Impacts on social relations and sexual mores may be even more profound. Western tourism has been motivated by the three s's: sun, sea and sex. One major impact has been the commodification and commercialization of sexuality, the most extreme instances of which are to be found in the sex tourism industry in the Philippines and Thailand. This is merely one area where the gender bias of cultural imperialism is at its most evident – in male Western and Japanese exploitation and degradation of Eastern women (Enloe, 1990).

Clearly, the demands and desires of tourism are external to the developing country. As Nash (1977: 46) argues, 'exogenous forces, which emanate from one or more metropolitan centers, involves the generation of touristic needs and tourists, the selection or creation of tourist areas, and the establishment of direct and indirect tourist–host transactions'.

One effect is that often 'traditional' culture is 'commodified' and packaged for touristic consumption, and its original meaning for its people changed in the process. Greenwood (1977) shows how the performance ritual of the Alarde of Funeterrabi, which recreates their victory over the French in a seventeenth-century siege, has become a tourist attraction, so that instead of an annual event it is now held twice in one day to accommodate tourists, and it has become harder to find volunteers to participate. The indigenous culture becomes a commodity over which tourists have rights, no longer the expression of a people's history and identity. By making it an explicit and paid performance for tourists, it can no longer be believed in the way it was before; thus, 'the commoditization of culture in effect robs people of the very meanings by which they organize their lives' (Greenwood, 1977: 137).

Ascher (1985: 81) notes that the economic, social and cultural effects of tourism are just beginning to be better known. 'Far from being a panacea, it requires considerable precautions if it is to be economically advantageous. Its socio-cultural effects may be fraught with consequences for local societies. When it goes beyond certain limits, it is likely to plunge developing countries even more deeply into an international system of dependency.' Ascher's assessment is that 'it is not tourism which permits development but development which permits tourism' (1985: 83) and that developing countries need a national policy *vis-à-vis* tourism, including shared investments (infrastructure, hotels, air transport); securing transfer of strategic 'technologies' (management systems, marketing technologies) and devising appropriate forms which are geared to each country's resources and heritage.

MacCannell argues that 'tourists are purveyors of modern values the world over – and so are social scientists' (MacCannell, 1976: 5)

> The characteristics of modernity . . . are advanced urbanization, expanded literacy, generalized health care, rationalized work arrangements, geographical and economic mobility and the emergence of the nation-state as the most important socio-political unit. These are merely the surface features of modernity. The deep structure of modernity is a totalizing idea, a modern mentality that sets modern society in opposition to both its own past and to those societies of the present that are premodern or un[der]developed. (MacCannell, 1976: 7–8)

Its critics complain that 'tourism has "cocacolonised" the world. It has homogenized places, "trinketed" cultures, degraded traditions and rituals and made proud people slaves' (Nicholson-Lord, 1990: 6).

Technology

At the heart of many of the dilemmas of development lies the issue of the transfer of technology. Export of highly developed and sophisticated technologies to the Third World, often controlled by transnational corporations (TNCs), brings environmental problems, and economic and other 'ties' without the basic scientific knowledge to build on and expand such technologies. But many Third Worlders are wary of arguments that they should receive 'only' limited and appropriate technologies and be forever left behind in the technological race.

Some talk about 'human needs technology' to face the massive problems of ill-health, malnutrition and poverty in the Third World (Clarke, 1985; Goulet, 1975). Yet TNCs have bigger research and development (R&D) budgets than most Third World nations (Clarke, 1985: 176); scientists are trained in an industrial, profit-oriented mode but not in the solving of basic human problems. There is a significant cultural component to all technological issues, particularly the component of 'self-colonization' or an acceptance of the superiority of Western values and practices. 'Self-colonization' reinforces an extroverted look to the industrialized world for help rather than the support and development of internal R&D and appropriate technologies from within. Thus technology transfer often reflects a deep loss of confidence in one's own culture and raises the question of how far techno-economic dissociation can proceed without corresponding measures in the cultural realm (Hveem, 1983).

Other cultural impacts

If the above documents some of the major institutional carriers of 'modernity', there are many other areas of impact that are worthy of exploration. Appadurai's (1990) model of the five 'scapes' of global interaction includes the 'ethnoscape', by which he means the movements of people across the globe. All cultures have deeply imprinted patterns of behaviour, for example in their use of space, patterns of eye contact and other non-verbal mannerisms (Hall, 1969) which feel 'natural' to those that inhabit them, but appear radically 'different' to those that do not. Westerners brought a different dress code, often used by Third World states as a crucial signifier of modernity and as a frequent site of struggle against Westernization. The Islamic Republic has lambasted cosmopolitan intellectuals as 'tie-wearers', for example. They brought Western patterns of child-rearing and family life; of cuisine – from dried baby milk to packaged Western foods – and of leisure pursuits, such as cricket, now quite indigenized in the way it is played in Bombay or Barbados, and many other cultural habits and tastes. Given my bracketing of much contemporary cultural production and its export, I have said nothing about the spread and impact of advertising, or about popular music, or about the transfer and adoption of Western tastes in general. But all those current phenomena are already better known and documented by media scholars than the historical aspects I have described.

Conclusion

Imperialism has been a double-edged sword, impacting, albeit unequally, both on the colonized and the colonizer (although the dynamics of the latter are not analysed here). Imperialism must be seen as the major global diffuser of modernity, its 'cross-cultural carrier'.

The cultural impact of modernity has brought about what Clignet (1971) has called a 'double alienation' in much of the South, an alienation from one's own tradition and cultural heritage, but also an alienation from the metropolitan culture to which there is only selective exposure. As Fanon (1973) has evocatively written, the cultural encounter with the colonized created a long-lasting Caliban complex, an internalized sense of inferiority that lingered long after the colonialists had returned home:

> Every colonized people – in other words, every people in whose soul an inferiority complex has been created by the death and burial of its local cultural originality – finds itself face to face with the language of the civilizing nation; that is, with the culture of the mother country. The colonized is elevated above his jungle status in proportion to his adoption of the mother country's cultural standards. He becomes whiter as he renounces his blackness, his jungle.

Hence also Memmi's socio-psychological investigation of the nature of dependence, into which both provider and dependant are locked and which does indeed satisfy certain needs (Memmi, 1984).

Contemporary theorizing about the structures of modernity needs to be supported by detailed historical investigation of the sequences, relative importance and enduring impacts of the institutions, structures and 'culture' of modernity, and its interface with older non-Western cultural environments.

In suggesting these areas of cultural impact, I do not mean that their impacts were the same everywhere, or similar across race, class and gender divisions. I do suggest, however, that such phenomena appropriately fit within the analysis of the 'cultural impact of imperialism'. It is relatively easy to discuss the 'cocacolization' of the world, even the 'seikoization' of global time; this chapter aims to serve as a reminder of the many, varied and deeply integrated structures of modernity that were in place long before these other, more superficial cultural changes. Many Southern cultures had already been irrevocably changed long before any electronic media arrived.

At the same time, I do not want to be thought of as suggesting that the institutional dynamics and social practices outlined here, supportive of various hegemonic discourses of imperialism, had direct, unmediated effects – but to examine effects, we need detailed case-by-case analyses showing the mixed and contradictory dynamics of adoption, adaption, resistance, reconstruction. Indeed, at some level, even my attempt here to delineate some central carriers of Western cultural practices suggests a too singular and total model – the realities were and are far more complex and varied (see Thomas,

1994 for such an argument as well as an extensive bibliography). The contradictory legacies of imperialism are beginning to be picked up in the literature of post-colonial studies, including the hybridity of much of contemporary Southern cultures, but have made remarkably little impact as yet on debates in international communication. If this chapter serves to help open out the terms of debate on cross-cultural contact and impact, in which the media are merely one strand, I will be pleased.

The poles of broader argument might be represented by B. Warren (1980) who has long argued that imperialism is part and parcel of the global spread of capitalism and brings concrete benefits in its wake, and by Amin who continues to argue for 'delinking', a 'disengaging . . . from the world system as it is in reality' (1992: 141) as the only viable strategy for the Third World which can never catch up with the level of development of the centres. But between, on the one hand, a too sanguine acceptance of the necessary costs of 'progress' and, on the other, a too pessimistic vision in which autarky becomes the only (im)possible solution, lies a lot of middle ground. Modernity has created a paradoxical global unity (Berman, 1988: 15) which remains deeply problematic in its patterns of inequality and domination. Yet it may also hold some opportunity. A recognition of the many inextricable linkages that bind us is part of an emergent global consciousness that might just do some good.

4

MacBride with Hindsight

Cees Hamelink

The MacBride Report in historical context

The final report by the International Commission for the Study of Communication Problems represents one of the concrete outcomes of an eventful debate that lasted almost a decade (UNESCO, 1980a). The two other legacies of this international information debate of the 1970s are the Mass Media Declaration of UNESCO[1] and the UNESCO International Programme for the Development of Communication.[2]

The debate and its outcome have to be seen in the light of crucial developments in the general context of international relations and in the more specific context of the United Nations system.

The confrontation in the 1970s around the issue of a new international information order obviously evolves from a series of interrelated features of world history between 1945 and the late 1960s. In this period, a large number of new, post-colonial states emerged in Asia and Africa. In their struggle to become sovereign entities, they had to confront, in addition to political and economic dependencies, the cultural legacy of former colonial relations.

The first generation of post-colonial nationalist leaders was intent on creating national integration in state structures that were internally threatened by the existence of multiple nationalities (often artificially thrown together) and externally beleaguered by a forceful cultural diplomacy enacted through Western foreign policy and business interests.

In the early 1950s, the first collective performance by the post-colonial states began. In those years, the political cooperation between African and Asian countries, in particular, was at stake, as the 1955 Bandung Conference demonstrated. In the 1960s, this coalition was extended to include the Latin American countries, which brought economic problems in particular on to the agenda. Actually, since the mid-1960s, the non-aligned movement has given increasing attention to strategies for the development of economic links among the countries of the South. Alongside the non-aligned movement, the so-called Group of 77 came into existence at the first UNCTAD conference in 1964.

These two overlapping groups showed the ambivalent position of the South: it found itself caught between strengthening horizontal linkages and coping with remaining links with the former colonial powers. That these latter links had an important cultural component became clear in the early 1970s. In particular, the non-aligned summit in Algiers (1973) began to extend South–South cooperation to the area of cultural development.

An important component of the background history leading to the information debate was also the expectation (particularly during the First United Nations Development Decade, 1961–70) that the technological achievements of the developed countries would contribute decisively to the resolution of global disparities between the rich and the poor. It was assumed in the 1960s that technology, which had lifted the advanced industrial nations to unprecedented levels of material wealth, could do the same for the poorer nations. The transfer of the latest and the best from the developed countries to the developing countries seemed the most adequate instrument for development. Towards the 1970s, the tone of the development debate became notably less optimistic.

Technology had been transferred, albeit mainly in the shape of end-products and often with disadvantageous conditions for the recipients, but sharp disparities in access to and distribution of technology remained and the basic problems of structural poverty and exploitation had not been resolved.

In the field of information/communication technology, the results of processes of transfer suggested, by the late 1960s, that the primary beneficiaries (of telephony, educational television and satellite communications) had been foreign manufacturers, foreign bankers and national administrative and military elites. In fact, in most countries the introduction of modern information/communication technology had not resolved any of the basic problems, but had rather added to the obstacles in the way of independent and self-reliant development. In most developing countries the pattern was that advanced technology was not primarily introduced to meet the basic needs of the people, but as the support system for the expansion of transnational business.

The needs of this business system added yet another vital component to the environment in which the information debate originated. Since the early 1950s there had been a rapid growth of transnational industrial and financial companies. These spread their affiliates across the globe and began marketing, advertising and trading in many of the developing countries. As part of the growing world business system, information/communication conglomerates developed into one of the leading sectors. The world's flows of news and entertainment began to be controlled by ever fewer companies, often closely interlocked among themselves and with other industrial and financial interests.

Throughout the 1970s the debate on the information issue (which took place primarily in UNESCO) developed in the context of an economic dialogue between the North and the South which was largely inspired by the threat of a North–South confrontation over oil prices. In 1974, the United Nations General Assembly adopted the Declaration and Programme of Action on the Establishment of a New International Economic Order. In the same year the Charter of Economic Rights and Duties of States was adopted. In 1976 the UNCTAD–IV at Nairobi accepted the Integrated Programme for Commodities and a new financial institution was created to support the effort to stabilize the world's commodity markets, the Common Fund.

In terms of political practice all this meant very little. As a matter of fact, by the end of the 1970s the North withdrew from this dialogue as the oil-threat had subsided. The UNCTAD–V in 1979 at Manila marked the point at which the North–South round of negotiations on a fundamental restructuring of the world economy effectively ended. A few efforts to renew the dialogue in the early 1980s (such as the Cancun Summit, 1981, or UNCTAD–VI in 1983) met with no success.

To this 'real world environment' should be added the specific history of the United Nations which goes back to the late 1940s. The origins of a persistent controversy about the solution of global information inequality are to be found in the immediate post-war years at the time of the incipient United Nations. This controversy is rooted in an early 'division of labour' within the United Nations system that embodied a distinction between political and technical tasks in dealing with international information questions.

Early in the history of the United Nations system it was already a rather common claim among the Western member states that the specialized agencies of the United Nations should be technical rather than political. Political issues were to be dealt with by the UN General Assembly, whereas the other agencies, among them UNESCO, were supposed to provide technical assistance to the implementation of the normative principles elaborated by the political body. In the field of information this meant that the UN General Assembly would be responsible for news and freedom of information, and UNESCO would deal with the improvement of the technical conditions for news production and exchange and promote the free circulation of educational and cultural materials.

As a result of this division of labour, UNESCO began to implement a programme of technical assistance. In 1957, a UNESCO report on the global 'information famine' motivated the United Nations General Assembly to request the Economic and Social Council (ECOSOC) in 1958 to formulate a programme for the development of communication and information media in the developing countries. ECOSOC invited the specialized UN agencies to contribute to this programme.

In 1962, ECOSOC recommended to the General Assembly that the UNESCO contribution to the programme should be integrated with the efforts of the First United Nations Development Decade. The technical assistance programme thus established and implemented lasted throughout the 1960s and turned UNESCO into a forum of consensus on information matters. In the 1970s, however, the non-aligned countries recognized that this technical assistance did not alter their dependency status, that the 'information famine' persisted and that in fact their cultural sovereignty was increasingly threatened. They therefore opened the debate on the need for normative standard-setting regarding the mass media. The key agenda issue for this debate was the demand for a New International Information Order.

This 'politicization' of the media debate did in fact revitalize the spirit of the 1948 UN Conference on Freedom of Information (held in Geneva from 23 March to 21 April 1948). This conference had in various resolutions articulated normative prescriptions for the conduct of the mass media.[3] Despite its 'technical' mandate, the UNESCO General Conference had referred to these norms in a series of resolutions that it adopted since 1964.[4]

Moving away from the imposed 'technical' mandate was perceived by the Western member-states as undue 'politicization'. In the ensuing confrontation, the Western delegations formulated as their essential policy objectives:

- to avoid the adoption of a legally binding instrument on the demanded New International Information Order;
- to adopt a regulatory instrument only if it would reflect Western preferences;
- to maintain a consensus on the primacy of technical assistance in information matters.

During the UNESCO general conferences of 1976, 1978 and 1980 the Western minority managed to achieve these policy objectives against the expressed preference of the majority of member states. In the end, the debate did not yield the results demanded by the developing countries. Their criticism of the past failures of technical assistance programmes was answered by the creation of yet another such programme: the IPDC (see Glossary). Apart from the inherent difficulty that IPDC represented a definition of global information problems that in the past had not worked to the benefit of Third World nations, the programme would also from the outset suffer a chronic lack of resources.

Regarding the core of the debate (the political-regulatory demands of the developing countries), a compromise solution emerged in the form of the Mass Media Declaration. The most crucial observation about the declaration is that it has little legal significance. Although by themselves declarations have no stronger legal force than recommendations, they are important in international law since they can be forerunners of binding treaties,[5] or can evolve into international customary law.[6] Declarations can also be generally considered as having legal force.[7] There is however also the possibility that a declaration is too controversial to contribute to international law.[8]

The legal significance of a declaration largely depends upon whether it is adopted unanimously, is worded in strong obligatory fashion, is referred to in later debates as important and binding and intends to interpret or clarify existing legal principles or rules. On these criteria the record of the Mass Media Declaration is very poor indeed.

There was unanimous adoption, but in the explanation of their votes several delegations undermined the legal significance of this acceptance. Switzerland, Denmark and Austria voiced strong reservations and the Dutch delegation, while congratulating UNESCO, stated that 'if it had narrowed its scope to its own interests, it would never have felt the need for an international instrument of this kind' (see Hamelink, 1989a).

Third World delegates (for example Benin, Indonesia, Jamaica, Nepal, Guinea, Algeria) also stated reservations by expressing that they had wished for a more normative instrument.

The declaration is not worded in strong obligatory language. It is less prescriptive than other instruments adopted by the international community.[9] The declaration's language is more liberal than the UNESCO constitution (with its reference to 'employing the means of mass communication for the ends of peace') or the *Universal Declaration of Human Rights* (with its reference to social duties). The declaration does not seriously interpret or clarify existing legal principles. Consequently, it is not likely to evolve into either a binding treaty or customary law or to be considered legally relevant.

In this historical context the MacBride Report emerged. The commission was appointed in 1976 following a recommendation of the 19th General Conference of UNESCO held in Nairobi. This conference confronted a deep controversy over the draft declaration on the mass media, and the establishment of a 'reflexive group of wise men' was proposed as a compromise formula to resolve the conflict. As the Director-General stated in his closing address in Nairobi, the conference had found a way out of the controversy by asking the Secretariat

> to inquire more deeply into the role, aims and conditions of communication. As I had occasion to state earlier during the discussion on this item, I intend, within the framework you have laid upon me, to undertake wide-ranging consultations in support of the work we have been asked to do, making use, if necessary, of a discussion group, so that at its twentieth session the General Conference may be presented with a comprehensive study on the problems of communication in the modern world.[10]

The discussion group became the commission chaired by Sean MacBride and it reported at the twentieth session of the General Conference in 1980 at Belgrade.

The work of the commission inevitably reflected the climate of compromise in which opposing parties within UNESCO sought to accommodate their conflicting interests. The final report was accepted by consensus – with one abstention, Switzerland – and some of the Western delegations (among them the Dutch) praised its 'moderate tone' and 'balanced approach'. As this unanimous acceptance suggests, the report is 'more a negotiated document than an academic presentation'. This was the comment by two of the commission's members, Gabriel García Márquez and Juan Somavia who also observed: 'the work of the commission has been a worthwhile effort to reach a certain level of consensus among participants with divergent viewpoints in the context of the United Nations' (UNESCO, 1980a: 281).

Márquez and Somavia came to the conclusion that the element of compromise might enhance the practical and political value of the report. Several members of the academic community who had been deeply involved in the debate on the New International Information Order were less convinced of the value of the report and pointed to a series of shortcomings (Hamelink, 1980).

In an assessment of the report, Alfred Opubor pointed to its atheoretical nature, Kaarle Nordenstreng commented on its ahistorical nature, Tamas Szecsko referred to the inadequate coverage of the socialist experience, Nabil Dajani criticized the emphasis on materialistic values at the expense of moral issues, and Herbert

Schiller exposed the insufficiency of the report in dealing with the systematic patterns in the control of communication technology.

The recommendations

At the end of its report, the MacBride Commission produced a series of 82 recommendations. In order to assess their effectiveness I have selected crucial recommendations in five core areas of concern. These are communication policies, technology, culture, human rights and international cooperation.

The purpose of the exercise is to establish to which extent these recommendations have been implemented in the past decade and to understand why implementation or lack of implementation occurred.

Communication policies
The pertinent recommendation states:

> Communication be no longer merely regarded as an incidental service and its development left to chance. Recognition of its potential warrants the formulation by all nations, and particularly developing countries, of comprehensive communication policies linked to overall social, cultural, economic and political goals. Such policies should be based on inter-ministerial and inter-disciplinary consultations with broad public partici-pation. The object must be to utilise the unique capacities of each form of communication, from interpersonal and traditional to the most modern, to make men and societies aware of their rights, harmonise unity in diversity, and foster the growth of individuals and communities within the wider frame of national development in an interdependent world.[11]

In short, the commission recommends the formulation of national, comprehensive communication policies.

Some 15 years later, one has to conclude that the proposed policies have not become realities. Only in a few countries has a beginning been made with national communication policy formulation in the comprehensive way the report recommends. (Obviously, in many countries there are various forms of partial policy-making with relevance to communication. One may find such implicit communication policies in industrial policies, technology policies, or even cultural policies.) Several factors can help to explain this assessment.

First a factor of a rather general nature can be identified. If communication policy is understood as public policy the problem is that not all problems that emerge in a society will be matters for public policy-making. Most problems remain in the private realm. Some become public concerns and may reach the systemic agenda, i.e. a society's agenda for public discussion. Few issues end up on the institutional agenda, i.e. the agenda for political action. This is the agenda of problems public policy-makers will act upon.

The communication issue is at present hardly anywhere on the institutional agenda. Therefore the first prerequisite for communication policy-making is very seldom met. It is not very likely that this will change soon. Reasons for this are related to the mechanisms through which an issue gets on the institutional agenda. Firstly it is necessary to observe that the political system will usually try to keep problems off the agenda. Many politicians perceive the management of potential conflict as their primary task and this makes them wary of making decisions. This can be facilitated by denying problems a status on the institutional agenda.

If problems nevertheless achieve this status a number of mechanisms or their combined operation is usually at work. Politicians may expect important political mileage from dealing with certain problems. In other words, such problems may have image potential.

Problems can also achieve agenda status through a crisis, protest activity, lobbying by powerful interest groups, or media coverage. None of these mechanisms is likely to be operative for the problem of communication. Not many politicians expect this issue to have electoral quality, and it is difficult to imagine crises or demonstrations over communication problems. Few, if any, interest groups will stage communication lobbies and, in general, the mass media pay little attention to themselves. Whereas there is of course news and commentary about media mergers, for example, these are usually treated almost exclusively as financial events, while nothing is said about the potential socio-cultural impact.

Secondly, if it is problematic to get the communication issue on the institutional agenda, it is certainly unrealistic to expect the formulation of comprehensive policies. The theoretical argument in favour of this position may have some appeal, but this does not hold out against the strength of the suspicions against the possible implications of comprehensive policy-making. These suspicions (that prevail among both governmental and non-governmental actors and are equally strong in different political circuits) are a major obstacle against even minimal improvements of existing partial policies and provide a convenient excuse for doing nothing at all.

In most national situations the notion of integrated policy-making runs against the preference of powerful local lobbies (media entrepreneurs, state bureaucracies) to maintain the existing institutional and regulatory arrangements. Among governmental actors the concept of 'comprehensive' raises the prospect of breaking down imperial niches (in separate fields such as telecommunications, broadcasting, press, film) and losing power to new overarching structures. Among commercial actors the same concept adds to the fears that communication policy-making is really state interference in disguise.

Thirdly, the policy recommendations assume that actual policy processes are relatively well-organized processes of discrete rational steps. In reality, however, the policy process is 'messy', badly structured, and largely determined by personal preferences and ad hoc motives. In the political reality, decision-making usually does not follow a rational-comprehensive approach, but is characterized as a 'muddling through' strategy.

Fourthly, the recommendations were to be implemented in an international climate that had become increasingly dominated by the 'new realism' of the 1980s that demanded deregulation rather than public policy-making. For many social domains, the emerging policy principle became 'more market, less state'. The drive to retreat from public ownership in important sectors of the economy did not remain restricted to the industrialized market economies. Increasingly the developing countries also became affected by the retreat of the state. Powerful donor countries such as the USA, the UK and France, and donor agencies such as the IMF, USAID and the World Bank recommended this strategy to these countries as an effective way towards economic development.

Privatization in the communication sector meant by implication a shift away from public policy-making.

Technology

The pertinent recommendations included:

> Devising policy instruments at the national level in order to evaluate the positive and negative social implications of the introduction of powerful new communication technologies. The preparation of technological impact surveys can be a useful tool to assess the consequences for life styles, relevance for under-privileged sectors of society, cultural influence, effects on employment patterns and similar factors. This is particularly important when making choices with respect to the development of communication infrastructures.

> Setting up national mechanisms to promote participation and discussion of social priorities in the acquisition or extension of new communication technologies. Decisions with respect to the orientation given to research and development should come under closer public scrutiny.

> The concentration of communications technology in a relatively few developed countries and transnational corporations has led to virtual monopoly situations in this field. To counteract these tendencies, national

and international measures are required, among them reform of existing patent laws and conventions, appropriate legislation and international agreements.[12]

In short: the commission proposes responsible technology decision-making with extended public involvement and regulatory measures in favour of developing countries.

With regard to technology decision-making a current assessment would have to conclude that by and large the reality of technology choice is not characterized by careful premeditation and/or public consultation.

Among the factors that explain the non-implementation of the recommendations are the modalities of technology choice that prevail in most countries. Since 1980 the leading motive in many developing countries has been the enormous anxiety about missing the alleged benefits of the imminent information age. At a very rapid rate advanced information/communication technology (IT/CT) was imported into many countries and in recent years the political leaders in Africa, Asia and Latin America have made statements reflecting the urgent need to catch up with the electronic world and their concern about lagging behind.

Throughout the past ten years the introduction of much IT/CT into the Third World has happened in a totally uncontrolled way or was made by ad hoc decisions. In the main, the emphasis is on equipment procurement and very little interest is given to the control of imports, the creation of independent assessment capacity, adequate legislation (in the areas of fiscal law, trade policy and the protection of intellectual property) and the assessment of social impact. The reality of technology choice seems primarily to be steered by mindless determinism and technological opportunity.

The lack of coherent policy-making here may be related to such factors as the relatively recent explosive development of the field, the unclarity as to where in public administration the responsibility for IT/CT resides, and the degree of technical complexity that demands specialized expertise. Moreover, the 'new realism' climate in this area strongly mitigates against public policy-making.

The general anxiety about missing the revolution implies that the majority of policy decisions relate to the spending of public funds on the acquisition of the latest technology. In such resource allocation, the opportunity syndrome is often at work: since the technology is available it should be purchased. Thus policy-making is driven by technological development and fails to adapt technology to defined social priorities. This is corroborated by the fact that in most cases the actual technology choice is open to very few actors. The process of IT/CT choice most commonly lacks any proper assessment of impact or elaborate public consultation, or even comparative shopping.

Among many illustrative cases about the lack of choice in socially responsible technology, the introduction of a national satellite system in Mexico could be cited. After three years of negotiations among a restricted number of agencies (such as the government executive, the Secretariat for Communication and Transport, and the commercial television company Televisa), a public announcement was made on 24 March 1983 that as from 1985 Mexico would have a national satellite called 'Morelos'. On 1 June 1983 the Secretariat for Communication and Transport announced that the 'Morelos' system – initiated and operated by the federal government – was contracted to Hughes Communication International for the manufacturing of the satellite, to McDonnell Douglas for the rocket and to NASA for launching. The approximate costs for placing and operating the satellite would be US\$ 140 million. The 'Morelos' system would be used for television, radio, telephone, telegraphy, telex and private data networks.

Characteristic of the whole process were the following elements:

- There never was a comprehensive analysis of needs and possible applications.
- There was no full consultation with all the potentially involved parties (such as future users and those affected by uses).
- There was no precise calculation of the additional costs of operating the Earth segment of the system.
- The Mexican technicians would have to be trained abroad and would remain low-level operators.
- There was no process of tendering as formally prescribed by the federal law on acquisitions.
- Other offers (by RCA or France) were not made public and the choice of Hughes was not publicly justified.
- The option of upgrading the existing microwave system was not seriously contemplated.
- The potential vulnerability of the 'Morelos' system (allowing the US Department of State, the Hughes company and 'Televisa' to control Mexican telecommunications) was not seriously debated.
- The price was too high; a comparable system could have been procured on a competitive market for less than US\$ 100 million (see Hamelink, 1988).

The proposed regulatory arrangements have not been enacted. The controversies around the proposed UNCTAD Code on the Transfer of Technology have remained irresolvable since the early 1970s. The international patent system has not been revised to accommodate the interests of developing countries. Continued debate around intellectual property rights has pointed more to benefits for developed market traders than to improvements for small intellectual property producers in developing countries. In most of the developing countries, the development of local research and development capacity is hindered by inadequate patent protection. The existing patent systems (legacies of the colonial past) do not protect traditional technologies and inventions in the informal sector.

A partial explanation of this discrepancy between recommendation and reality can be found in the increasingly crucial role that the international business community plays in the regulatory process. Particularly in the 1980s, this community became a very active lobby in the various rule-making fora (such as ITU, GATT, since replaced by the World Trade Organization, or WIPO – see Glossary) and has been successful in influencing the direction of international communication politics towards the accommodation of its concerns. The hesitation on the national level radically to alter intellectual property arrangements is to a considerable extent caused by the fact that the decolonization process is still more rhetoric than reality.

Culture
The pertinent recommendations state:

> We recommend establishment of national cultural policies, which should foster cultural identity and creativity, and involve the media in these tasks. Such policies should also contain guide-lines for safeguarding national cultural development while promoting knowledge of other cultures. It is in relation to others that each culture enhances its own identity.

> Communication and cultural policies should ensure that creative artists and various grass-roots groups can make their voices heard through the media. The innovative use of film, television or radio by people of different cultures should be studied. Such experiments constitute a basis for continuing cultural dialogue, which could be furthered by agreements between countries and through international support.[13]

In short: the commission recommends policies that foster cultural identity and cultural dialogue.

Assessing the success of these recommendations, one has to conclude that such national cultural policies have not emerged, that the media have become rather more involved in the creation of global than local culture, and that there are few indications of a more intensive cultural dialogue in the world.

This situation can probably be explained by pointing to the following factors. The recommendation was highly unrealistic, given the enormous confusion and tension in many countries about the issue of national cultural integration against the background of the existing variety of ethnic cultural expressions. Nor did the recommendation take into account the realities of the international media market in which the dominance of one type of programming is hard to avoid (Hoskins and Mirus, 1988). During the 1980s, the proliferation of commercial TV continued, more countries became dependent upon imports and only the largest producers were able to supply. In 1983, the leading US companies exported half a billion dollars' worth of TV products, often in co-production or in the disguise of national production firms. The promotion of a universal homogeneous visual code has probably fostered global cultural integration rather than cultural dialogue.

Nearly 20 years after the MacBride Commission was set up, one has to observe that probably the most successful single company, almost spanning the globe, is McDonald's. As a McDonald's executive remarked when the company began selling its 'fast food' in Moscow (January 1990), 'We're going to McDonaldise them.'[14]

Some countries even generously prepare the vehicles for such invasions. For example, Kenya embarked in 1989 upon a plan to launch a second TV channel, financed by advertising and drawing upon Ted Turner's CNN. On 15 November 1989, the chairman of the Kenya Times Media Trust (publisher of the newspaper of the ruling Kenya African National Union) stated: 'This will be a global commercial television channel that will be run for 24 hours throughout the country. We have already negotiated contracts with leading television companies to ensure satisfaction to our subscribers. These companies include Cable News Network and Sky TV. We have also negotiated contracts with various motion picture companies' (Winsbury, 1990: 36). The recommended cultural dialogue is also hampered by existing copyright laws that continue to favour the strong producer countries and provide little protection for the musical heritage of small people. (This is well documented in Wallis and Malm, 1984.)

The recommendation would also seem to have suffered from an overestimation of the mutual interest people have in each other's culture. Western news, for example, continues to be predominantly about a few core countries and much of the Third World remains invisible. If, however, we take by way of illustration the large newspapers of a country like India, one finds equally little coverage of other Third World countries. There is among Indian journalists little professional interest in getting the latest news from other Third World countries. The real interest is in domestic political events.[15] This may reflect the reality that for a majority of world citizens the world does not really extend beyond the borderlines of their own cultural community.

One might have assumed that the further expansion of international tourism in the 1980s would have contributed to an increase in the dialogue between cultures. Although there has undoubtedly been some growth in Western tourism to the Third World, some 80 per cent of the international tourist flow remains in the industrialized nations. For those tourists who adventure the 'cultural dialogue', the cultural experience usually does not extend beyond sunbathing on tropical shores.

Human rights
The pertinent recommendation states:

> We recommend all those working in the mass media should contribute to the fulfilment of human rights, both individual and collective, in the spirit of the UNESCO Declaration on the Mass Media and the Helsinki Final Act, and the International Bill of Human Rights. The contribution of the media in this regard is not only to foster these principles, but also to expose all infringements, wherever they occur, and to support those whose rights have been neglected or violated. Professional associations and public opinion should support journalists subject to pressure or who suffer adverse consequences from their dedication to the defence of human rights.

> The media should contribute to promoting the just causes of peoples struggling for freedom and independence and their right to live in peace and equality without foreign interference. This is especially important for all oppressed peoples who, while struggling against colonialism, religious and racial discrimination, are deprived of opportunity to make their voices heard within their own countries.

> Communications needs in a democratic society should be met by the extension of specific rights such as the right to be informed, the right to inform, the right to privacy, the right to participate in public communication – all elements of a new concept, the right to communicate. In developing what might be called a new era of social rights, we suggest all the implications of the right to communicate be further explored.[16]

In short: the commission recommends that the media expose human rights violations and support the defence of human rights. It also suggests the development of the right to communicate.

Throughout the last two decades, the media have continued a pattern of distorted international reporting of human rights violations. There is still very uneven coverage of violators and victims, as has been extensively argued and documented by Chomsky and

Herman.[17] It also needs to be acknowledged that the proliferation of advanced information/communication technology in many countries has posed new and serious threats to the realization of human rights. The 'information age' arrives in many countries with a monumental invasion of citizens' privacies. Rapidly increasing volumes of personal information are collected, stored and sold through vast electronic systems. Profitable markets are emerging for personal information.

As economic activities converge, as in the banking and insurance sectors, there is a strong incentive to share the personal information that such companies have been collecting. These entities have also realized that their information resources may not only be used for internal purposes, but can also be offered at a price to a general market.

In many countries the public sector has an overwhelming urge to monitor the citizenry. This has gained new momentum with the installation of advanced information/communication technology. This is bad enough in itself, but now the public sector has also become market oriented and has begun to commercialize many of its functions. This means, for instance, that public information collections are sold to private purchasers.

The 'information age' has also brought a proliferation of electronic employee monitoring: secret video and audiotaping even in bathrooms, the opening of electronic mail, the use of video display terminals to check employee performance, and the omnipresent telephone bugging. Whatever the excuses or arguments for such surveillance activities, they amount to a fundamental violation of human rights and are conveniently facilitated by the new technologies.

In many countries there is also an observable trend towards restricting the freedom of information in different fields and thus denying basic human rights to the mass media and to citizens in general. Across the world, recent years have witnessed an upsurge in secrecy and censorship (see Demac, 1988; Curry, 1988).

A basic problem with this recommendation on the mass media is that it overlooks the fact that the media themselves are often part of the problem. They are integrally linked to political and economic interests that may have little to gain by exposing human rights violations. Their professional codes of news production may often fail to select human rights issues as newsworthy or refuse to accept the promotion of human rights as a legitimate task. In fact, the media themselves may violate human rights whenever their reports are ethnocentric, racist or sexist, or whenever they apply discriminatory employment policies (Hamelink and Mehra, 1990).

The proposed right to communicate has not been codified. A consensus on its inclusion in international human rights law has not been reached and it remains unclear whether it should be defined as a new emerging concept (part of a new generation of collective or solidarity rights) or whether it is already implied in earlier information rights, and needs implementation, rather than codification. The further development of the right to communicate would at present seem to be paralysed by this controversy.

International cooperation

Section V of the MacBride Report's conclusion includes the following proposals:

> We recommend the progressive implementation of national and international measures that will foster the setting up of a new world information and communication order. The proposals contained in this report can serve as a contribution to develop the varied actions necessary to move in that direction.

> International cooperation for the development of communications be given equal priority within other sectors (e.g. health, agriculture, industry, science, education, etc.) as information is a basic resource for individual and collective advancement and for all-round development. This may be achieved by utilising funds provided through bilateral governmental agreements and from international and regional organisations, which should plan a considerable increase in their allocations for communication, infrastructures, equipment and programme development. Care should be taken that assistance is compatible with developing countries' priorities.
> Consideration should also be given to provision of assistance on a programme rather than on a strict project basis.

> The close relationship between the establishment of a new international economic order and the new world information and communication order should be carefully considered by the technical bodies dealing with these issues. Concrete plans of action linking both processes should be implemented within the United Nations system. The United Nations, in approving the international development strategy, should consider the communication sector as an integral element of it and not merely as an instrument of public information.[18]

In short: the commission recommends the establishment of a New World Information and Communication Order and the improvement of multilateral assistance to communication development.

The assessment of the fate of these recommendations is relatively easy. Neither a new international information order nor a New International Economic Order came into being, and even the acronyms NIIO and later NWICO have practically disappeared from the multilateral debate. In 1980, the IPDC was established as a forum for technical assistance but never became a genuine multilateral fund and continues to struggle with a shortage of finance.

Since 1987, the Centre for Telecommunications Development has been operational within the ITU. This initiative resulted from the recommendations of the so-called Maitland Commission,[19] which suggested the need for support to the developing countries for the development of their telecommunication infrastructures. The centre has been seriously handicapped by the fact that little support has been forthcoming.

In 1979, the United Nations Conference on Science and Technology for Development (UNCSTED, Vienna) resolved to establish a fund to finance the strengthening of the scientific and technological capacities of developing countries. In 1987, the fund-raising activities were aborted since no funds were forthcoming.

Among the explanatory factors is the problem that governments in both developed and developing countries tend to award low or no priority to communication development. National governments in the developing countries can obviously play an important role in the struggle against 'information famine'. More often than not, however, they accord the highest priority to such common development projects as industrialization, the building of harbours and roads, hospitals and airports, and neglect the development of communication.

Only a few countries have an allocation of public funds for communication development in their national five-year plans. This is particularly damaging to communication development in deteriorating economies. In such cases, the low priority areas are among the first victims of cuts in the national budget. In many countries the small libraries established in the 1970s were a dramatic example of disintegration as soon as the economic decline in the 1980s set in.

In addition to this, the donor-country governments in general give low marks to the communication sector. On average, West European countries reserve in their public development aid programmes less than 1 per cent for communication projects. Apparently, the communication development issue does not provide the politicians with the image potential that might move them to a more generous position.

Discrepancy between recommendation and reality

Taking five essential areas of concern one can establish that the recommendations that represent the core concerns of the MacBride Report have not been effective. This can be explained by the inadequate assessment by the commission of the politico-economic and socio-cultural realities for which the recommendations were designed. This conclusion, evidently, enjoys the privilege of hindsight. One could argue in defence of the commission that times have changed and that the lack of implementation is less the fault of the recommendations than of the evolving realities of the 1980s.

This argument makes sense in so far as the recommendations were not in themselves impossible propositions and, in fact, largely consequences of principles adopted in earlier debates. However, one could also maintain that – taking hindsight into consideration – there were inadequacies in the structure of the recommendations that made their ineffectiveness almost inevitable.

Four considerations support this position. These are the assumed clarity of principles, the lack of analysis of existing policies, the addressees of the recommendations and the 'wise men' approach to problem solving.

Principles

As the report states with regard to the aim of the recommendations: 'the time has come to move from principles to substantive reforms and concrete action' (UNESCO, 1980a: 253). This seems to assume that we have clarity on principles. This, however, can be questioned. By way of illustration, I shall use the cases of such principles as human rights, cultural identity and the new information order.

Human rights   In order to move from human rights principles to action, it would be useful to understand which interpretation of such principles is adopted. This is pertinent since if one adopts the common liberal interpretation of human rights, it may well be that one hampers rather than facilitates the resolution of such problems as 'information famine'.

The basic assumption of this interpretation is that freedom of expression as such is a given right and that the main regulatory task is to provide a sufficient level of protection against the danger of interference by the state. This assumption glosses over the fact that in the reality of unequal societies, this freedom does not exist for everyone. In almost every society, individuals and peoples are silenced. Therefore, the right to freedom of expression would have to rather focus on the provision of access to the public expression of opinions than on the prevention of restricting opinions.

The liberal right to freedom of expression does not imply that everyone acquires equal access to the means of expression. An important element is that the freedom of information in the liberal tradition is not directly linked with the principle of equality. As a result it offers insufficient support to the 'information-poor', who claim that their freedom of information can be realized only when adequate means of expression are available. The liberal interpretation does not favour the use of preferential measures ('positive discrimination') in situations of social inequality.

Cultural identity   This identity principle shows up on many pages of the MacBride Report without any proper definition. The usefulness of the principle is taken for granted and the analytical concerns are directed to such questions as, how is cultural identity threatened and how can it be preserved and developed? However, it can be argued that the principle is inadequate and, indeed, misleading.

I said earlier that the principle is based upon untenable assumptions about the possibility of isolating an identifiable set of features that would refer to 'what a culture is' and the convergence of a series of characteristics into the recognizable identity of a collective subject. These assumptions lead us into several problems.

When we accept the notion that a collective subject has an identity, we have to accept a generalization in which judgements are applied to all individual members of the collective. If the same categories are used for members of a group, however, they are perceived as more alike than they really are. This distortion seriously inhibits differentiated perception and thinking.

Through this approach, we might also fail to understand that what is referred to as cultural identity is imposed upon a collective subject for mere control purposes. The usage of the principle can be instrumental to the dominant distribution and execution of power. Another problem is the exclusive focus on the contents of culture ('what a culture is'), which neglects the more important problem of how people develop their cultural responses to the environment. Focusing on cultural identity neglects the more pressing problems of cultural development, i.e. the social process in which people make their cultural choices (elaborated in Hamelink, 1989b).

New information order   The MacBride Report supports, with some qualifications, the Third World case for a new information order. The commission, however, does not provide a clear understanding of the interpretation of this principle. Are we dealing with the principle as it was initially coined by the non-aligned nations? Is the proposed new information order the corollary to the new economic order that the developing countries demand? Does the commission adopt the strategic changes that took place in 1978, by which the original principle was replaced by its reformulation as a new, more just and effective world information and communication order?

Does the commission accept the implicit shift from a fundamental challenge to existing interests to a programme for the transfer of resources? Whose new order is recommended? The new order could also very well be the global order as envisaged by the transnational corporations in their cosmetic responses to Third World demands. The commission is certainly unclear about the relation between a new information order and a new economic order, and this could very well turn out to be the major obstacle in achieving a fundamental reordering of informational relations in the world.

Existing policies

In the MacBride Report, as in the reports by the UNESCO intergovernmental conferences on communication policies, there is the proposal to formulate national policies without taking serious account of the fact that many countries already have an explicit communication policy. Most countries have a broad range of explicit legislation on constitutional, civil and penal law that, taken together, certainly shape a national policy that either facilitates or hampers the development of communication.

The relevance of such existing policies could be demonstrated in the field of copyright law, which has a crucial impact on the development of local publishing and music industries, the protection of local folklore and the access to foreign cultural materials. In several developing countries, current forms of copyright legislation do restrain the development of an indigenous publishing industry. In cases where these countries are not net exporters of mass culture, a complete enforcement of their copyright law would inevitably mean a drain on the country's scarce foreign currency reserves.

With too much emphasis on the formulation of policies, one may miss the critical analysis of existing policies and bypass the need to radically change these.

The target audience for the recommendations

Out of the total of 82 recommendations, some 48 are addressed to national political actors (countries, policy-makers, societies). Twelve are directed to the multilateral bureaucracy (for example the UNESCO Secretariat). The professional community (journalists, media) is addressed 17 times and the business community only once. Most of the recommendations address the political community that by and large does not respond. To some extent this could have been foreseen, since this community very much has its own agenda and often tends to support multilateral initiatives because of their symbolic significance. These actors tend to be relatively closed against anything imposed upon them from outside. Although the political community is primarily expected to accommodate the social concerns of its clients, in the actual political process the political elites have become relatively independent entities demonstrating a lack of interest in their clients. Yet another problem, often underestimated, is the politician's preference to avoid taking decisions and spending a relatively large amount of energy in getting items off rather than on to the institutional agenda.

The bureaucracies of the international organizations are indeed a likely target for such recommendations as made in the MacBride Report, yet the institutional structures of these organizations develop their own agendas over time, with specific emphases and preferences. This renders them relatively closed to externally generated propositions.

The professional community is a complex entity to address. By and large, it represents a very diffuse and incoherent set of actors who may also have antagonistic interests. For example, addressing the mass media, it is not clear who the intended audience is: the media owners, the media managers, the media producers?

In spite of several critical comments directed at the commercial community in the final recommendations, the business actors, when mentioned, are treated rather generously. The largest community of actors in information worldwide consists of the numerous non-professional small users: the ultimate clients. They use telephone lines, buy recorded music, read newspapers or watch television and listen to the radio. They are affected by information, both national and international, in a variety of ways. What they all have in common is that they are usually ignored in the proposals that supposedly are ultimately to their benefit.

Ad-hocracy
It has become common practice to appoint 'wise men' commissions for the treatment of serious social problems. Just like the MacBride Commission and the Maitland Commission, there have been in other fields the Brandt Commission, the South Commission and the Brundtland Commission. The establishment of such commissions would seem to reflect a longing for the old belief in wizards who have the mysterious power to wave their magic wand to solve perplexing problems.

Addressing the world's most pressing issues through ad hoc groups of experts also suggests that social problems, in essence, are ahistorical and apolitical. The temporary nature of the problems' analysis and resolution ignores the processual quality of fundamental social problems. It cannot take into account that social reality is constantly shifting and changing. Delivering the recommendations while the commission is being dissolved also seems to suggest that there is no responsibility beyond the proposals, and it denies the inevitable problem that many proposed solutions may create other, maybe even more serious, problems. The efforts spent in these commissions to produce consensus recommendations also quite deceptively ignore the basic political character of important social issues. This makes all proposed resolutions contestable in the light of the divergences in value systems that exist in the real world.

On top of these more principled considerations, there is the trivial logistical reality that these commissions consistently have too little time and too few resources to do a decent piece of work.

Recommendations formulated for the 1990s

If one were to formulate recommendations for the information debate in the 1990s and beyond – with the benefit of hindsight – three areas would need to be highlighted.

The research agenda for the post-NIIO/NWICO era

Although the plea for more research tends to become the inevitable ritual dance at the end of academic contributions, little progress can be made in the international information debate if we continue to misunderstand very basic principles. Therefore, the research community, hopefully strengthened with new intellect and insight, should take another look at the conceptual essence of the debate.

Secondly, serious critical analysis is needed of existing implicit and explicit communication policies and their significance for such objectives as one may recommend for social communication. Such analysis would identify how existing regimes and structures help or hamper the development of communication.

We need, in addition, a far better understanding of the decision-making processes in the international politics of communication. The field of communication research and that of policy studies should finally initiate some forms of exchange. This is particularly pertinent with regard to developing modalities for more efficient involvement of the community as the ultimate client in these processes.

The client community

It is inevitable that recommendations that would be relevant for years to come have to address concerns of the largest community of communication users. This community comprises the millions of citizens across the globe that watch TV, read newspapers and magazines, buy recorded music and listen to radio.

Since the political, bureaucratic and business communities routinely suggest that their clients (the citizens, the peoples, the consumers) are the ultimate beneficiaries of their efforts, ways have to be found to involve this client community. The world's small communication users, although a heterogeneous entity, are in different ways confronted with concerns about the variety of content in the mass media, the representation of diverse social interests, the access to information, the price of telecommunication services, or the quality of information sources.

Standing commission
Reflection on the problems of communication in the modern world needs to be a continuous process. There should be a constant monitoring of worldwide information processes by a body where problems can be analysed, suggestions offered, realities observed and interpreted. The ad-hoc commissions of the past decades can no longer provide the insights we need in the accelerating complexities of the twenty-first century. The most productive conclusion from an assessment of the MacBride Report could be that another international commission is needed, but this time as a critical monitoring forum that refrains from final reports, but as a standing committee that regularly publishes reports about ongoing reflections on policy changes that are needed.[20]

Summary

The MacBride Report is the key document in the international information debate that took place in the 1970s. The effectiveness of the MacBride Commission's 82 recommendations in several crucial fields, such as communication policies, technology, culture, human rights and international cooperation, can be tested. This assessment leads, by and large, to the conclusion that the ensuing developments in the real world have been very different from what the commission saw as desirable.

This discrepancy is due to the inevitable changes in the reality of international and national development, but should also be accounted for by basic shortcomings of the report. Fundamental principles were taken for granted; wrong choices about major addressees were made; existing communication policies were ignored; and the commission's work itself revealed an inadequate understanding of social reality.

With the benefit of hindsight, a number of new recommendations can be proposed that might repair some of these shortcomings. However, it is a sobering thought that sooner or later, with the benefit of even more hindsight, these well-intended post-MacBride proposals may demonstrate new weaknesses once again.

Notes

1. *Declaration on Fundamental Principles concerning the Contribution of the Mass Media to Strengthening Peace and International Understanding, to the Promotion of Human Rights and to Countering Racialism, Apartheid and Incitement to War.* Final text adopted at the 20th session of the General Conference of UNESCO, Paris, October–November 1978. UNESCO document 20 c/20 Rev. 21 November 1978.

2. International Programme for the Development of Communication (IPDC), established at the 21st session of the General Conference of UNESCO, Belgrade, 1980.

3. The UN Conference on Freedom of Information formulated normative standards for the mass media in its resolution 1, paras 5 and 7; resolution 2 and resolution 35. By way of illustration, resolution 2 'appeals vigorously to the personnel of the Press and other agencies of information of all the countries of the world, and to those responsible for their activities, to serve the aims of friendship, understanding and peace by accomplishing their task in a spirit of accuracy, fairness and responsibility'.

4. UNESCO resolutions addressing norms of conduct for the mass media: thirteenth General Conference, resolution 6.21, 1964; fourteenth General Conference, resolution 10, 1966; fifteenth General Conference, resolution 9, 1968; sixteenth General Conference, resolution 4.301, 1970. The last of these resolutions, for example, addresses the questions of public information and the promotion of international understanding.

5. Illustrations of declarations evolving into treaties are, inter alia:

> Declaration of legal principles governing the activities of states in the exploration of outer space, UN General Assembly, 1963 = Treaty on principles governing the activities of states in the exploration and use of outer space, including the moon and other celestial bodies, 1967.
>
> Declaration on the elimination of discrimination against women, UN General Assembly, 1967 = Convention on the elimination of all forms of discrimination against women, 1979.

6. Illustration of a declaration evolving into international customary law: Universal Declaration of Human Rights, UN General Assembly, 1948.

7. Illustration of a declaration generally referred to as binding and legally significant: Declaration on the granting of independence to colonial countries, UN General Assembly, 1960.

8. Illustration of a declaration too controversial for strong legal significance: Declaration on the establishment of a new international economic order, UN General Assembly, 1974.

9. On the role of the mass media, strong prescriptions are contained in:

the recommendation concerning education for international understanding, cooperation and peace and education relating to human rights and fundamental freedoms (UNESCO, 1974), approved by 76:5:15;

the recommendation on participation by the people at large in cultural life and their contribution to it (UNESCO, 1976). Approved by 62:5:15;

the declaration on race and racial prejudice (UNESCO, 1978). Approved by acclamation.

10. Amadou Mahtar M'Bow at the 19th session of the General Conference of UNESCO on 30 November 1976. UNESCO document: 19C/INF.23, pp. 6–7.

11. International Commission for the Study of Communication Problems, (UNESCO, 1980a), Recommendation 1, pp. 254–5.

12. Ibid., Recommendations 24, 25 and 27, p. 259.

13. International Commission for the Study of Communication Problems (UNESCO, 1980a), Recommendations 28 and 29, pp. 259–60.

14. *San José Mercury News*, 28 January 1990: 6A. In the statement, reference was made to the company's cultural conquest.

15. This information was given to the author during a visit to various newspapers in India in September 1989.

16. International Commission for the Study of Communication Problems, (UNESCO, 1980a), Recommendations 52, 53 and 54, p. 265.

17. Herman and Chomsky (1988). This book offers, among other cases (such as comparative studies on the newspaper coverage of the elections in El Salvador, Guatemala and Nicaragua), a comparison between the treatment in the mass media of the murder of Jerzy Popieluszko, the Polish priest, and the priests murdered in Latin America.

18. International Commission for the Study of Communication Problems, (UNESCO, 1980a), Recommendations 66, 67 and 68, p. 268.

19. Independent International Commission for World-wide Telecommunications Development (chaired by Sir Donald Maitland). The 1984 report of the Maitland Commission was called *The Missing Link* (see Glossary).

20. This forum would obviously need independent and interdisciplinary expertise and it could no longer be a wise men's club; it would of course have to reflect the reality of the male/female ratio in the world.

5

The Western World and the
NWICO: United They Stand?

Colleen Roach

Background

The origins of the New World Information and Communication
Order (NWICO) are commonly traced back to the founding of the
Non-Aligned Movement in 1955 and the decolonization struggles
waged in Asia and Africa in the 1960s. It was, however, not until
the decade of the 1970s that a clear articulation of the demands for
a new world order were voiced by Third World leaders and
intellectuals. In 1973, at an historic Non-Aligned summit in Algiers,
a call was launched for a global restructuring of economic relations
with the industrialized world: a New International Economic Order
(NIEO). Although some Third World intellectuals, such as Samir
Amin, never viewed the demands for better terms of trade, debt
relief and increased foreign aid as truly radical (Amin, 1976, 1977a),
the NIEO nonetheless met with stiff resistance in the United States
(Laszlo et al., 1980). The US government and American-based
transnational corporations, which by the 1970s were more powerful
global actors than many countries in Africa, Asia or Latin America,
strongly opposed the notion that the global order was not as it
should be.

The Algiers summit also went down in history because it firmly
placed on the international agenda a subject that to this day
continues to inspire myriad books (including this one), debates and
arguments: cultural imperialism.

According to a famous quotation from the Economic Declaration
adopted at the Algiers summit:

> It is an established fact that the activities of imperialism are not confined
> solely to the political and economic fields, but also cover the cultural and
> social fields, thus imposing an alien ideological domination over the
> peoples of the developing world. (Jankowitsch and Sauvant, 1978: 226)

That economic and cultural concerns were *both* paramount issues at
the Algiers summit is highly significant: the later call for a NWICO

would be taken as inseparable from the NIEO by its proponents, a connection that was certainly not lost upon the Western powers.

Three years after the Algiers summit, another North African capital, Tunis, played host in 1976 to the Non-Aligned media seminar where the term 'New International Information Order' was first pronounced:

> Since information in the world shows a disequilibrium favouring some and ignoring others, it is the duty of the non-aligned countries . . . to change this situation and obtain the decolonization of information and initiate a new international order in information. (Information in the Non-Aligned Countries, 1976: 30)

Several of the most important people involved in the NWICO were influential in shaping the Tunis agenda: Mustapha Masmoudi, who would emerge as the most visible leader of the movement; the Peruvian Gernán Carnero Roque, who represented the more radical Latin American element; and Kaarle Nordenstreng, who would later become president of the International Organisation of Journalists (IOJ).

The most important aspect of the seminar, however, was its tone: radically anti-imperialist. The report of the seminar, *Information in the Non-Aligned Countries* (1976), is replete with references to the fight of the developing countries 'for their liberation from all kinds of neo-colonialism and imperialist oppression' (p. 25) or the 'imperialist considerations' that 'have deprived them of their sovereign right to the free use of their natural resources' (p. 26). Most importantly, the denunciation of imperialism acting through the media and culture was an important leitmotif at the Tunis meeting. The following citations, also taken from the report, are representative of the language of the seminar:

> the peoples of developing countries are the victims of domination in information and this domination is a blow to their most authentic cultural values, and in the final analysis subjugates their interests to those of imperialism. (p. 26)

> The colonialist, imperialist and racist powers have created effective means of information and communication which are conditioning the masses to the interests of these powers. (p. 41)

In 1976, with an African Director-General at its helm, the main UN agency responsible for international communications, UNESCO, also lent its considerable intellectual prestige to the call for the 'decolonization of information'. Amadou Mahtar M'Bow of Senegal represented the global realignment of forces that – at least temporarily – allowed the Third World a greater voice in international affairs. M'Bow made the struggle for a NWICO a personal and organizational priority of UNESCO.

At successive general conferences and specialized meetings held to assess the state of information imbalances, Third World complaints at UNESCO came to crystallize around several key areas: news flow, television flow, advertising, and communications technology. Although none of the UNESCO research published on these topics nor the various UNESCO communications resolutions of the 1970s and 1980s adopted the strong anti-imperialist language of the Non-Aligned Movement, they clearly challenged the prevailing Western wisdom on the 'free flow of information' doctrine. UNESCO research and meetings gave voice to Asian, African and Latin American complaints that they were almost completely dependent on the Western agencies for news from both inside and outside their own regions. The critique of US domination of TV exports and transnational advertising brought home to the West that in many ways the NWICO movement was an attack on capitalism: it was not only the values of a consumer society that were felt to be 'alien' to many non-Western countries, but also the transnationalized economy represented by Western TV shows and advertisements.

The conundrum of communications technology illustrated the complexity of the Third World position. Third World needs and demands were predicated upon a fundamental contradiction: anxious that the promised leap into the 'information age' could only be orchestrated via the high technology of satellites and computers, the 'global village' of Marshall McLuhan and Arthur C. Clarke nonetheless sparked new fears of ever more sophisticated forms of cultural and economic domination.

Mention of McLuhan reminds us that the NWICO has been not only a movement based on the material reality of satellites, news dispatches and TV shows, but also a debate of ideas on the very nature of communications and development. In the ideological fray of the 1970s, the academic work of writers such as Daniel Lerner (1958) and Wilbur Schramm (1964) did battle against the 'cultural imperialism' school, with the most widely circulated works from a Marxist perspective being those of Herbert Schiller (1969, 1976) and Armand Mattelart (1974, 1979). A host of other writers, mainly from Latin America, were also part of the 'cultural imperialism' vanguard: Pasquali (1963, 1967), Beltrán (1974, 1976), Bordenave (1976) and Kaplún (1973). For many in the Third World, their 'lived experiences' did not validate the messages of mainstream American communication scholars: Western communication models were not helping their countries along the road to economic and social advancement.[1] Instead, the message of the 'media imperialism' school resonated with a greater truth: since at least the end of the Second World War, Western communication practices had been part of a burgeoning military-industrial complex that assured the global hegemony of the United States, its allies and transnational corporations.

From the mid-1970s until the mid-1980s, the polemics over the new order pitted the Third World and supporters of the NWICO in Eastern Europe against the United States and its Western allies. Throughout this period an intensive attack was launched against UNESCO and the NWICO by a coalition of US-led Western forces including media, governments and private sector interest groups.[2] The culmination of the offensive was the US withdrawal from UNESCO in 1984, followed by that of the United Kingdom one year later.

The 'Western' factor in the NWICO debate: preliminaries

The answer to whether or not there was a 'Western' response to the NWICO must begin by dealing with a larger question: the degree to which this movement was itself a response not just to US hegemony, but also to that of other Western powers. First of all, there is no question but that the reality of post-war US domination of media markets in most parts of the world shaped the contours of the NWICO movement. Secondly, it is also beyond doubt that because of its historical experience of US cultural domination, of all the regions in the Third World, Latin America played the most important role in promoting the NWICO.

However, the attention paid to US cultural domination and the Latin American response has almost completely overshadowed any focus on that of other Western powers, or resistance in other regions of the world. The French colonial experience offers a case in point. In the brief history of the NWICO movement summarized above, it is striking that the two most important early meetings relating to the new order took place in North Africa and that both of the two most visible leaders – Masmoudi and M'Bow – were from former French colonies.

Although it would be hazardous to contend that one colonial power (e.g. France) had worse cultural effects than another (e.g. United Kingdom), one *could* argue that the heavy-handed French attempts at cultural assimilation of their colonies had some relationship to the virulence of the Algiers declaration (especially since this country had only a short time before fought off the French in an extremely bloody war of national liberation) or to the sentiments of a Masmoudi or a M'Bow. The pervasiveness of French cultural colonialism has been commented on at some length by African writers. Walter Rodney's classic *How Europe Underdeveloped Africa*, for example, refers to the term used by France's Ministry of Overseas to refer to its colonial subjects: 'Overseas Frenchmen' (Rodney, 1972: 216). A Francophone African who *does* venture onto the field of comparative colonialism has a very unfavourable judgement of France's 'expansionist mission in Africa':

> unlike some of its Western counterparts, France has never made a secret of its desire to 'frenchify' any developing country where it has had the opportunity to exert influence of any kind. Where others have preferred a more subtle approach, France has appeared rather blatant and aggressive. (quoted in Nyamnjoh, 1988: 81)

Any reference to the cultural consequences of French colonialism is incomplete without mention of another classic: Frantz Fanon's *The Wretched of the Earth* (1967). Produced during Algeria's national liberation struggle in the 1960s, Fanon's writings sounded the depths of the psychological and cultural degradation of France's 'other': the colonial subject. Fanon's experience in North Africa made him see colonialism as the 'systematic negation of the other person' that 'forces the people it dominates to ask themselves the question constantly, "In reality, who am I?"' (Fanon, 1967: 200).

Mention of 'the French connection' allows us to contextualize the topic of 'the Western world and the NWICO' within a larger historical framework than that provided simply by 'US cultural imperialism'. Although some of the early scholarly literature on media imperialism (such as the work of Tunstall, 1977; Smith, 1980; and Boyd-Barrett, 1977) did make reference to the cultural influence of France and Britain in their respective colonies, these works had virtually no effect on the press coverage or policy discussions of the NWICO, which has largely gone down in history as a struggle between the United States and the Third World.

Lastly, before moving on to the specifics of the Western response to the NWICO, it should also be noted that 'Western' in this chapter refers, first of all, to the positions adopted by a certain number of countries felt to be representative of the Western world. In addition to the United States, this will include the United Kingdom, the then Federal Republic of Germany, France and Canada, with particular attention being paid to the latter two countries. Secondly, we are limiting ourselves to the 'official' Western position on the new order: that of governments, the establishment press and private sector interest groups.

The subject of another article could well be the way Western intellectuals and even institutions provided both conceptual and practical momentum for the NWICO. In North America, for example, one thinks not only of the contributions of Dallas Smythe (1981) and Vincent Mosco (1979, 1982), but also of early content analyses done in the 1960s that were critical of American media complicity in US foreign policy in Latin America (Bernstein and Gordon, 1967; Houghton, 1965). In the UK, the early critical work done on Western communication models by researchers such as Peter Golding (1974) at the Leicester Centre for Mass Communication Research also comes to mind. France contributed not only Althusser's (1971) conceptual work on ideology but also a generation of activist writers won over to 'tiersmondisme', such as Jean-Paul Sartre (who wrote the preface to Fanon's work). The Friedrich-Ebert-Stiftung Foundation in Germany has undertaken a number of activities that have earned it the reputation of a 'pro-NWICO' defender. In the late 1980s, for example, it began subsidizing the translation into German of dispatches from the Third World news agency, Inter Press Service (IPS).

The 'Western' response to the NWICO

Determining whether or not there was a 'Western' response to the NWICO involves several related questions. First of all, what was it that the NWICO threatened or was perceived to threaten in the Western world? Secondly, how did 'the West' respond to the reality or perception of this threat? Thirdly, is it not an erroneous amalgamation to speak of the 'US/Western' response to the NWICO? That is, did different Western countries not fashion substantially divergent responses to the issues and demands raised by this movement? The following remarks attempt an integrated response to these queries.

A chronological reminder: the information society

One of the most enlightening publications on what the United States feared from the NWICO is to be found not in a Congressional document or academic treatise, but in a short book review of a volume promoting national information sovereignty edited by Kaarle Nordenstreng and Herbert Schiller (1979). The review was written by Daniel Lerner in *The Public Opinion Quarterly* (1980). Lerner, whose communication and development paradigm was one of the principal targets of the NWICO movement, ridicules the two authors for contributing absolutely 'nothing' to research or theory and lambasts them for supporting the 'outdated' concept of national sovereignty. In the following passage, he zeros in on the real menace of their work:

> The clearest impact of New Left activity was on international communi-
> cation policy. Their vigorous support of the Soviet-led campaign against
> 'free flow' doubtless helped to build the massive majorities that defeated
> the U.S. in both the U.N. and UNESCO. Given the New Left 'analysis'
> which dictated that all 'policy thinking' must derive from opposition to
> official U.S. positions, it was obvious that 'free flow must go'. (Lerner,
> 1980: 132)

The most important part of this message is what comes first: the
impact of the New Left (i.e. Marxist writers like Schiller and
Nordenstreng) on international communication policy-making.
Here, one must fill in certain spaces behind the deductions of
Lerner, who must have represented some degree of high-level policy
thinking in the United States. The fear that Third World countries
would adopt communication policies promoting national sovereignty is linked to the pro-Soviet and anti-free-flow dimensions of
the new order, both of which are, in turn, linked to the basis of the
perceived threat: government control of the media.[3]

These three factors – threats to free flow, the Soviet–Third World
alliance, and the supposed promotion of government-controlled
media – provide us with a barebones outline of why the 'Western
world' should react harshly to the NWICO demands. As background, one could also add the renewed Cold War context of
international relations during the late 1970s and early 1980s.

However, the above sketch of the West's apprehension regarding
the NWICO is incomplete. For one thing it does not account for the
fact that since many Western countries, including all of those under
consideration (United Kingdom, France, Germany and Canada)
had media systems with varying degrees of government intervention,
their allergy to 'government controlled' media should not have been
as severe as that of the United States. Secondly, there is the question
of the well-known contradictions among the Western allies, which
we shall also briefly examine. Here, we are referring to countries
such as France and Canada, which rallied around 'free flow' in
UNESCO, but sang a different tune in other fora.

In order to understand why the West should present a united
front on the new order, one must bring into the picture another
movement conterminous in time with the NWICO: the information
society. Just as the groundwork for the NWICO's emergence in the
1970s was being laid in the national liberation struggles of the 1960s,
so economic developments of the 1960s paved the way for the
notion of a 'new' society in the 1970s, to wit the 'information
society'.

As with most crises in contemporary capitalism, events in the
United States foreshadowed the shape of things to come throughout

the entire Western world. Although the 1960s has often been portrayed by anthropologists and sociologists (cf. Mead, 1970; Gitlin, 1987) as an era of 'affluence', in reality significant structural changes were already well under way. That the 1960s signalled the beginning of the end of America's post-war pre-eminence was underscored in Paul Kennedy's acclaimed economic history, *The Rise and Fall of the Great Powers* (Kennedy, 1987). Kennedy notes that it was 'from the 1960s onwards' that the United States began to lose its imperial economic strength, as would become evident in the 1970s and particularly the 1980s (Kennedy, 1987: 432).

The answer to the impending economic crisis was (in addition to the Vietnam War) the promotion of another society and economy: the information society or the information economy. As William Leiss (1984) has shown, it was during the 1960s that the early conceptual work on the information society was carried out, much of it financed by large corporations such as IBM. But it was precisely during the 1970s that much of this work came to fruition in a series of well-known works, of which the most important were Daniel Bell's *The Coming of Post-Industrial Society* (1973) and Marc Porat's *The Information Economy* (1976). Here the synchronicity of events is particularly fortuitous: as noted previously, 1973 and 1976 were also key years for NWICO developments.

The 'information society' (closely connected to Bell's 'post-industrial society') represented both a domestic and an international project. On the domestic front, it aimed at creating a service-based economy heavily reliant on information technology and a managerial class of technocrats. On the international level, in addition to its strong anti-Marxist tones (which served as a nice counter-attack on the media imperialist school), there were two aspects of relevance to the NWICO. First of all, the information society was to be exportable to developing countries so that they could supposedly 'leap-frog' over the industrial stage of development into the post-industrial era (Reddi, 1986). Secondly, the Third World was viewed as a source of new markets for Western-based communication TNCs. Since government-run communication systems would threaten this private sector expansion, the spectre of state-run, Soviet-style media was intolerable.

There is a plethora of policy literature of this period referring to the importance of media and information technology markets for the prosperity of the United States. A few citations will illustrate our point. In 1968, the Conference Board, an organization representing the most important US corporations, issued a report stating that 'political and financial competition for the possession and control of information would increase dramatically as a consequence of the technological explosion in data gathering. Information as distinct from property or energy will be an indication of social wealth and power' (Silk, 1973: 47). Reports of the Conference Board issued in 1972 not only continued to emphasize the economic significance of information, but also called for a national effort to use communication technology to advance US business interests globally (The Conference Board, 1972). A US Department of Commerce report entitled *Long Range Goals in International Telecommunications and Information* highlighted similar goals: free flow of information, information flow to developing nations, and a free and competitive market-place for telecommunications equipment (US Congress, 1983: 11).

It was very clear how the US concern for media and telecommunication markets became a major aspect of the US response to the NWICO at UNESCO. In addition to the previous citations produced in policy-making arenas running parallel to the NWICO debate, there was a host of other similar declarations made by US officials that directly responded to concerns raised at UNESCO. In Congressional hearings on UNESCO in 1981, for example, the late Sarah Power, a high-ranking State Department official, made a very typical assessment of the stakes of the NWICO battle:

> I might remind this body that the information industry is now the second largest export enterprise in the United States. Its foreign sales a year ago were estimated at approximately 75 billion dollars. (Power, 1982: 115)

In 1978, precisely the same year that John Eger (another former high-ranking government official) coined the term 'information war' (Eger, 1978), the United States launched its most important initiative at UNESCO based on the expansionist needs of the information society: the International Programme for the Development of Communication (IPDC). The significance of IPDC in the US strategy for the NWICO has already been analysed by several writers (Nordenstreng, 1984; Pendakur, 1983). In sum, the US proposal was designed to divert attention from what might be termed the more radical, ideological, or even 'anti-imperialist' bent of the NWICO movement. Instead of negotiating over questions of global inequity, domination, dependence and ideological conditioning, the aim was to reduce the NWICO to a question of communications 'aid', with an emphasis on technology transfer.

Power's summary of the goals of the IPDC is to the point: 'This new mechanism [the IPDC] institutionalizes the shift away from the unhelpful ideological debate and into constructive development work' (Power, 1982: 117–18). The same point was made by others who were more genuinely in sympathy with the Third World, such as Gunnar Garbo, the first head of the IPDC Council. In 1983, Garbo described the 'bargain' that had been struck between the West and the pro-NWICO forces: 'Western countries indicated that if ideological questions could be set aside, there existed a willingness to increase the financial contributions to the building up of communications capacities in developing countries' (Garbo, 1983: 4).

Our argument up to now may be summarized as follows. Two parallel movements, the NWICO and the information society, developed during the 1970s and the 1980s. Insofar as the United States was typical of the Western world's answer to Third World demands, one could say that the West responded by promoting the information society, that is, expansion of global communication markets.

The 'West': monolith or myth?

In order to generalize our argument, it should be shown, first of all, that other Western countries did indeed support the United States in its defence of free flow and freedom of information, and its attack on government-run media, that is, that there was in this sense a 'Western' position on the NWICO. Secondly, it should also be demonstrated that the notion of the 'information society' was accepted by other Western countries such as France, the United Kingdom and Canada.

Although there is a dearth of writings on the Western positions on the NWICO – other than that of the United States and, to a certain extent, Canada – available literature strongly suggests a closing of the ranks. The case of France, particularly as manifested at two UNESCO general conferences, illustrates the unity of the Western world.[4] The 1978 General Conference in Paris took place when the NWICO polemics were at their height. The contentious UNESCO Mass Media Declaration (often referred to as the 'NWICO Declaration') was finally adopted after six years of prolonged disputes over clauses supposedly sanctioning state-run media (Nordenstreng, 1984).

The French position on the NWICO, as reflected at this conference, may be summarized as follows. The free flow of information was strongly defended by the government as well as the press and the main press owners' association. Freedom of information and freedom of the press were the other major components of what was regarded by the French as 'universal' Western assumptions about the media, which were contrasted with the highly objectionable statist media principles of the Soviet bloc. In line with this thinking, the Mass Media Declaration was presented by the French press and delegates to the conference only in terms of the 'government control' question, in spite of the fact that its 11 different articles dealt with a host of issues ranging from the role of the media in promoting peace and human rights to the protection of journalists. Since the final text of the Mass Media Declaration eliminated the clauses interpreted as sanctioning state 'responsibility' for the media, its passage was presented as a victory for 'the West'. As for the Third World, in spite of the tradition of 'tiersmondisme' among French intellectuals, the French press showed remarkably scant sympathy for its demands for change in the global communication order, not even bothering to present its views. US/Western proposals for aid were largely endorsed by French officials and the press (Roach, 1979).

The French stance on the NWICO at the 1980 General Conference (known as the 'Belgrade Conference') confirmed the trends cited above. The government spokesperson continued to take a stalwart position on free flow, presenting it as the major plank of the French platform. Substantive NWICO discussions in Belgrade revolved around the MacBride Report (officially presented to member states) and the IPDC. French delegates and the press kept to the 'government control' framing of the NWICO in their treatment of the report, which was generally treated as sanctioning state control of the media (with no evidence to back up this assertion). The IPDC was highlighted as a programme to help the developing countries with technical aid and financial assistance (Roach, 1981).

Generally speaking, the United Kingdom was even more virulently anti-NWICO than France. From the earliest days, Western press institutions based in the UK and British journalists had played important roles in leading the attack against UNESCO and the NWICO. Thus one of the first and most vehement critics of UNESCO was the *Sunday Times* journalist Rosemary Righter, who published one of the earliest broadside attacks on the NWICO (Righter, 1978). The International Press Institute, with which Righter was affiliated, was one of the principal Western 'free press' organizations that initiated and sustained well-publicized attacks against UNESCO, very much in the Cold War vein. British press representatives were also out in force at the two US-initiated meetings of the 'free world media' held in Talloires, France, in 1981 and 1983.

A study of the British press coverage of the NWICO debate in 1980–81 by Sparks et al. (1993) found that it matched its American counterpart in bias and distortion. The NWICO was essentially framed within a Cold War context that highlighted the role of the 'Communists' in supporting UNESCO, and the latter's attempts to 'shackle' the free press. The following quotation was taken as representative of the over-simplified British view of what the authors stress was a highly complex issue: 'The essential argument has always been that between state control and private control of information and the media, with the communist bloc favouring the former and the Western bloc the latter' (*The Times*, 23 April 1980). A curious revelation of the totality of the 'Western bloc' mentality was also highlighted in the study: British identification with the United States was so complete that the US was cited as an actor in the debate even more than the home country (Sparks et al., 1993: 15–16).

At the 1980 General Conference, the remarks of the British delegation on a proposed resolution on the NWICO (which, in its final version, was a finely tuned compromise between Western and Third World concerns) also underscored the unity of the 'Western' position. The very idea of such a resolution was rejected out of hand. For the British delegate, the principal matters of concern were 'free circulation of information' and 'freedom from censorship and arbitrary government control' (Voices of Freedom, 1981: 64–5).

Finally, it was the 1984 announcement of the United Kingdom's intention to withdraw from UNESCO that indicated most clearly the strength of the British aversion to UNESCO's pro-NWICO activities. In the letter sent by the British to the Director-General in 1984, announcing a high-level government review of UNESCO, the organization was taken to task for concerning itself with 'political controversy', notably through its 'involvement with communication and media issues'.[5] At a press conference on his government's action, an official stated that Britain opposed 'dangerous tendencies among certain member countries that are trying to impose non-democratic values on the so-called communications programme' (*International Herald Tribune*, 6 April 1984). In November 1984, when the British government announced its intention of withdrawing from UNESCO in a year's time, the then Prime Minister, Margaret Thatcher, singled out the organization's attempts 'to prevent freedom of speech and freedom of the press' as a prime reason for this action (Associated Press, 21 November 1984).

Although Becker has characterized the Federal Republic of Germany as deliberately taking a more 'low profile' position on the NWICO than its more vocal allies (Becker, 1986: 55–6), available information does indicate a meeting of the minds. A German official summarized the UNESCO Mass Media Declaration within a context solely related to Western notions of freedom of the press, and congratulated the 1978 UNESCO General Conference for rejecting a text that would have established state supervision of the media (Bruck, 1979: 65).

At the 1980 General Conference, the West German delegate was reported by AFP (Agence France Presse) as stating that because of past events, his country 'had a sense of the importance of a press free of state control' (Roach, 1981: 181). A working paper on the NWICO's consequences for German development policy, prepared by the government in 1978, adopted the quintessential American position, linking the establishment of freedom of information to Western communications assistance (Federal Ministry for Economic Cooperation, 1978: 607).

The Canadian case[6]

The Canadian position on the NWICO is of special interest because if there had been a 'renegade' in the Western ranks it probably would have been Canada, given that its intellectuals and bureaucrats have long criticized the cultural domination of the United States.[7] The official history of Canadian communication policy has been marked by innumerable reports and task forces criticizing dependence on US media products, from the Aird Commission Report in 1929, warning that Canada was fast becoming a satellite of American broadcasting, to two government reports issued in 1985 and 1986 calling for reductions in US programming.[8]

It is not very difficult to find statements by Canadian officials echoing Third World complaints against the United States, such as Prime Minister Mulroney's criticism of American media treatment of his country:

> To be blunt, the American media has decided Canada doesn't matter – and we've been treated accordingly. Canada is seldom deemed newsworthy in the United States . . . Largely as a result of media inattention, lack of knowledge, misconceptions and stereotypes about Canada among American politicians and the public still abound. (*Presstime*, May 1984)

More recently, Mosco (1993) has analysed how US cultural domination was replayed to the detriment of Canada in the Free Trade Agreement.

The parallel nature of the cultural concerns of Canada and the Third World was apparent to a number of Canadians involved in the NWICO debate. Thomas McPhail, who supported the NWICO in the early 1980s, noted this parallel:

> the continuing struggle that Canada has had in protecting its broadcasting system from US control and in Canadianizing its cultural industries is very similar to the objectives of Third World countries in their call for a NWICO. (McPhail, 1982b)

The similarity between Canadian and Third World criticism was also made explicit by a well-known Canadian media official and scholar at the 1983 UN/UNESCO Round Table on the NWICO. John Meisel, former head of the Canadian Radio Television Commission, stated that his country was in the 'front lines' of the NWICO battle because of its constant struggle with the United States to preserve its own cultural identity (Roach, 1983). The Canadian Commission for UNESCO noted in one of its bulletins that 'Canada shares with the industrially developing nations the experience of having its culture pressured by the mass media of its powerful Southern neighbor' and pointed to legislative attempts to ensure local content on television (Canadian Commission for UNESCO, 1986: 4).[9] The commission even went so far as to give Canada credit – erroneously as far as I can determine – for first introducing the term 'new information order' at a 1969 meeting in Montreal of the commission.[10]

The irony is that in spite of this apparent sympathy for Third World demands in certain sectors, in spite of its own public system of broadcasting that would seem to preclude falling into the dichotomous 'government control' camp, and in spite of its long history of US cultural domination, Canada was clearly one of the strongest allies of the United States in the NWICO debate. A Canadian speech made at the UNESCO General Conference in 1989 shows that Canada's absent ally could rest assured that its position was well represented: freedom of the press, free flow of information, a commitment to 'practical' communication activities, and a moratorium on so-called ideological debates:

> First, Canada believes strongly in the freedom of the press, the principles of freedom of information and of the free flow of information . . .
> Second, Canada realizes . . . that there are serious gaps in terms of availability of media and information technologies . . . What is needed now are practical and feasible projects aimed at ameliorating the substantial gap.
> In conclusion, Canada's position is therefore that priority should be given to freedom of the press, that UNESCO should avoid ideological battles, and take a practical approach towards finding solutions to the disparities which exist. (Canadian Delegate to UNESCO's General Conference, 1989: 1,2,8)

Other contradictions in the Western camp

In spite of Canada's support for the US stance, the contradictions in its position did not go unnoticed in the United States. Nor was

Canada alone in its opposition to American policy outside of UNESCO. Already in 1980, a Congressional report sounded a very critical note on the actions that various allies in the West were taking 'for the benefit of their economies' and 'national sovereignty' in an area of vital interest to the United States: transborder data flow (TDF). The report, which singled out Canada and France, summed up the situation in alarmist tones: 'These policy development efforts by major trading partners are in sharp contrast to United States actions and deserve the most careful scrutiny by the United States' (Committee on Government Operations, 1980: 32).

France has often been one of the most virulent critics of the United States, with French officials not uncommonly even resorting to the term 'imperialism' to attack American hegemony. French concern about computers and TDF dated at least as far back as the publication in 1978 of the famous Nora–Minc Report, which criticized IBM dominance of the European market, and called for a concerted 'national plan' for France (Nora and Minc, 1980). The US Congressional study previously cited noted that a 1980 report to the French government on TDF suggested that 'the world needed to move away from the principle' of free flow. An ominous passage in the French document was cited:

> Other complementary values cannot be ignored, i.e. the responsibility of sovereign states, the balance of advantage to be derived from mutually profitable trade, and respect for the diversity of peoples and cultures. (Committee on Government Operations, 1980: 33)

Although not as rancorous as the French, there were occasionally other critical Western voices. For example, officials from the former Federal Republic of Germany or a Scandinavian country such as Sweden might also criticize aspects of free flow or the inconsistency of the American 'government control' argument. But the question to ask is: what do these contradictions mean? Do they indicate that the Western world was, in fact, divided in its position on the NWICO? This is hardly arguable, since most of the 'contradictions' are based on criticism levelled at the United States outside the principal NWICO fora where, as we have seen, there was virtual unanimity in the Western position: defence of 'free flow' and freedom of the press, use of the 'government control' argument, and support for 'practical' solutions to the more 'ideological' (i.e. radical) demands of the Third World.

Thus, what is clear is that the contradictions did *not* mean Western support for the Third World position, especially if the latter is understood in its radical, ideological sense, that is, as a challenge to Western media/cultural hegemony. There is precious little evidence, for example, that the French rhetoric about 'cultural sovereignty' or 'cultural imperialism' has ever meant anything more than concern for the French TV/film industry or an opening of its markets to more programmes from Western Europe. In a study of a year's programming from the six French channels operating in 1990, Jean Devèze found that TV imports from countries other than the United States and the members of the Common Market had only a 'symbolic' presence: 'The total of these programs from regions of the world where more than ¾ of humanity lives accounted for only 5% of total programming and 9.2% of the total non-French programs!' (Devèze, 1990:5). In noting the virtual absence of TV programmes and films from Asia, Africa or Latin America, Devèze remarked: 'An example that is almost a caricature illustrates this general deficit: only one Indian programme was shown during an entire year, when this country is the number one film producer in the world!'

France is undoubtedly not alone in its hypocrisy: it is doubtful if any of the other Western countries that criticize free flow and cultural imperialism have adopted broadcasting policies that balance their flow of programming to the Third World with reciprocal exchanges.

Back to basics: the information society redux

Although the contradictions cited above do not indicate a fissure in the Western position on NWICO, they do, undoubtedly, point in a certain direction. This direction leads us back to an earlier argument: that it is impossible to understand the political economy of the Western response to NWICO without referring once again to the information society.

If the Western world in general embraced the concept of the information society this would not only offer a reason why it was united in its stance on the NWICO, but would also provide an explanation for some of the contradictions cited above. Here, I am adopting a line of reasoning put forth by Melody and Samarajiwa (1986) to explain why Canada fully embraced the free flow doctrine at the international level, while adopting a rhetoric and policy designed to protect the cultural and economic stakes of its media/communication markets. The authors see this seeming contradiction as a real-world pragmatism: its defence of 'free flow' not only had the advantage of serving its most important ally's political interest, but also meant that Canada could use 'free flow' for the same purpose as the United States: to gain entry into information markets in the developing world.

Canada has indeed been one of the earliest and strongest supporters of the information society concepts (Leiss, 1984; Collins, 1986: 291). The 1981 Department of Communication Report *The Information Revolution and its Implications for Canada* offers an endorsement that was quite typical in information policy-making circles: 'Like the industrial revolution, the information revolution is unavoidable. Consequently the objectives of public policy should be not to prevent the revolution from occurring, but rather to turn it to our advantage' (cited in Leiss, 1984: 2). Embracing the information age in Canada means the same thing as in the United States: a view to foreign markets. Nowhere is this more evident than in the promotional publications of Canada's main development aid organization, the Canadian International Development Agency (CIDA). In the spring-summer issue of its 1986 bulletin (*Development*), CIDA even coined a new term: 'teledevelopment'. An article with this word as its title shows that the United States and Canada share more than a border:

> Telecommunications is both a vital global activity, linking the world's nations and peoples, and an essential tool for economic and social development. The global market in telecom equipment, currently more than $80 billion annually, is expected to double in the next decade. (*Development*, Spring-Summer 1986: 46)

France is another excellent example of a Western country that wholly embraced the notion of the information society, having also introduced into the technology lexicon a new term: 'informatique'. Subsequent to the publication of the Nora–Minc report in 1978, there was a host of government initiatives aimed at nothing short of a technological blitzkrieg of French society, whose tanks were to be computers, fibre optic, and the famous 'mini-tel' screens. By the late 1970s, 'l'informatisation de la société' was both slogan and reality.

Needless to say, France's rush into the information society, like that of Canada and the United States, was also buoyed by the prospect of winning foreign markets, as was evident in François Mitterand's 'World Communication Charter' promulgated in 1982. Although the rhetoric was that of 'partnership' with developing countries, researchers such as Mattelart have noted the difficulty of reconciling two objectives: winning foreign markets and building a global economy that does not exploit the Third World (Mattelart, 1982: 22).

The best statement of France's grandiose goal of becoming an informatics superpower, especially in the Third World, was Jean-Jacques Servan-Schreiber's treatise *Le Défi mondial* (Servan-

Schreiber, 1980) and the subsequent founding in 1982 of a 'World Centre for Computer Sciences and Human Resources'. In Schreiber's tome, one finds arrayed all the stock arguments for bringing the Third World into the era of the information society: the communication technology = development equation, the leap-frog theory of development and, of course, buttressing both these ideas, calls for technology transfer emanating from the Third World itself.

Not all of the Western world rushed onto the information society bandwagon as early, or as fervently, as the United States, Canada and France. The UK was perhaps more of a laggard than others (Collins, 1986: 293), which would probably explain its lack of criticism of the 'free flow' doctrine. But there can be no doubt that information society thinking has been a hallmark of the Western world since the 1970s and that this reality was not unconnected to its strategy *vis-à-vis* the NWICO.[11]

The conundrum of communications 'aid'

The above analysis leads to an obvious conclusion: the West was united in countering the NWICO demands with supposed offers of communications 'aid' and technology transfer. The following points relating to this strategy are of particular relevance: (1) the idea of heading off the more radical demands of the Third World with offers of aid and technology was floated in the earliest stages of the NWICO debate; (2) the call for communications aid was largely a rhetorical device, since little new multilateral assistance has actually been forthcoming; and (3) the strategy at UNESCO was played out within a larger context: attempting to use the UN system as a vehicle for gaining increased market entry into the Third World.

Barely one year after the call for a NWICO was launched, the Kroloff–Cohen (1977) report on the NWICO to the US Senate waxed extremely enthusiastic about the possibility of the new order opening up new markets. The tone of the report was cynical but clear: 'getting a system of usable and useful telecommunication equipment . . . is so attractive to LDCs' [least developed countries] problem solving that it's like eating a peanut. The user can't eat just one' (Kroloff and Cohen, 1977: 22). The authors also issued a prescient warning of the shape of things to come: although the US government had promised extensive aid to the Third World, already in 1976, the only follow-up had come from a private press group.

The story of what happened with the IPDC is by now a familiar chapter in the NWICO history: the United States used the ploy of aid to ward off radical demands for change, but then gave virtually nothing unless one counts the contributions it made for projects of its own choosing ('funds in trust') which, in effect, circumvented the multilateral framework of the programme.

Based on early IPDC documents, Norway and France were the only Western countries that made sustained substantial contributions to funds that the IPDC itself controlled (the 'Special Account').[12] (More limited contributions from the West came from countries such as Finland, Italy, Sweden and Switzerland. Japan, if included in the 'West', was one of the largest contributors to the IPDC) (UNESCO, 1991b: Annex 1). Although Canada made two sizeable donations to the IPDC in its early stages, it then desisted, preferring to channel its aid through the CIDA or the private sector.

In 1984, the International Telecommunications Union (ITU) estimated that it would need $12 billion a year in telecommunication investments if the developing countries were to expand adequately in this area (ITU, 1984: 57). Just how meagre aid to the IPDC has been is underscored by noting the total funds it had available in its 'Special Account' from 1981 to 1990: a mere $20 million (UNESCO, 1991b: Annex 1).

In spite of the lack of funds, recycled rhetoric equating telecommunications with development (a new version of the old 'media = development' slogan of the 1960s) flourished in the 1980s. The year 1983, designated World Communications Year by the United Nations, brought fresh evidence of the world community's concern for linking telecommunications to development. The ITU and the Organization for Economic Cooperation and Development (OECD) published a major study entitled *Telecommunications for Development* (OECD/ITU, 1983) and the ITU established the Independent Commission for Telecommunication Development, known as the Maitland Commission. Although both the OECD/ITU study and the report of the Maitland Commission (ITU, 1984) reviewed the relevant literature and admitted that there was no clear cause–effect relationship between telecommunications and development, it would be naive not to see that both entities presumed otherwise. The Global Centre for Telecommunication Development, set up by the Maitland Commission, fared little better, however, than the IPDC. In spite of the fact that the ITU's centre had not been preceded by 'ideological' conflicts, as Robert Stevenson noted, 'donor aid to support telecommunication development has not followed' (Stevenson, 1990: 6).

Any increase in Western 'aid' has therefore most likely been on a bilateral basis. 'Bilateral aid' (the watchword of the 1980s) not only has the advantage of being targeted to countries and projects that support free market mechanisms but also can fulfil a definite economic agenda. Put simply: almost all bilateral aid is 'tied aid' (Wood, 1986: 14), so not really 'aid' at all.

Since developing countries themselves are increasing their own investments in telecommunications – estimated by Stevenson at $8 billion a year as early as 1983 (Stevenson, 1990: 6) – lacking the wherewithal for largesse, the UN agencies can still play a vital role for the West: they can serve as high-tech market-places. In 1984, one of the principal arguments used by US transitionals to lobby against American withdrawal from UNESCO was precisely that of losing markets in the Third World if the United States cut itself off from the organization (The Conference Board, 1984). In the same vein, when the United Nations Association of the United States (UNA) lobbied for re-entry in 1989, it stated that UNESCO was now emerging as a 'clearing house for information on the new technologies' and that, were it not present, the United States would lose out to European and Japanese telecommunication giants (UNA, 1989: 11, 14). A detailed study of the Maitland Commission's report revealed a similar strategy for the ITU; the Commission recommended that the UN agency also serve as a marketing vehicle for telecommunication equipment suppliers (Mosco and McAllister, 1986: 125).

Conclusion

In this chapter I have answered the query: 'was there a "Western" response to the NWICO' with a definite 'yes'. I have privileged a general political economy approach since it provides the best answers to the queries posed herein. The 'Free Flow vs Government Control' banner could not have been carried so high by so many countries in the West (given their history of state intervention in the media and the opposition of many of them to 'free flow') if it did not serve their own economic interests.

The only Western countries that might have had a different policy of economic self-interest in this debate were the Scandinavian nations, which are usually acknowledged to distribute more multilateral and less 'tied' aid. However, in my research I did not find any evidence that the 'official' Nordic actors took substantially different positions on the NWICO than their homologues in the Western world. In fact, during the 1980s, certain Scandinavian countries even rivalled the United States in their virulent support for Western doctrines. Among seasoned observers of the diplomatic circuit, it was widely acknowledged, for example, that in the 1980s Denmark (which made only a small contribution to the IPDC 'Special

Account' in 1990) was one of the staunchest supporters of the 'free flow' position.

However, the Western world could not have responded as it did to the NWICO without the participation of the national elites of the developing countries. Although one must be careful not to fall into the 'blame the victim' syndrome, it is obvious that Western offers of 'aid' and technology did not fall on deaf ears. Although co-optation of Third World leadership is an old story that predates the NWICO battle, there is no doubt that the Non-Aligned militancy of the 1970s was met by renewed and deliberate sorties on this front. In 1975, *Foreign Affairs* (the leading foreign policy journal in Washington) published a very revealing article entitled 'The United States and the Third World: A Basis for Accommodation' (Farer, 1975). The author states that the United States should rely on its own history of 'the creaming off and co-optation of the natural elite of the working class' to do the same thing in the Third World: 'Is the present struggle between the classes of nation-states not susceptible to mitigation by the employment of an analogous strategy of accommodation . . . Third World elites are even less committed to human equality as a general condition of humanity than we are' (Farer, 1975: 92).[13]

My final comments relate to the relevance of the 'communication and development' paradigm in the Third World and the 'information society' model in the world at large. People in the Third World should take a hard look at what so-called 'aid' has wrought in their countries. Many requests for aid are still based upon '(tele) communications = development' thinking, without acknowledgement of the fact that in an early stage the NWICO movement challenged this paradigm as being part and parcel of continued Western exploitation of the Third World under the guise of so-called 'modernisation'. Many UN reports, admitting that development specialists cannot state with certainty how – or even if – the equation is valid, attempt sophisticated statistical correlations between various indices of development and telecommunications. Shouldn't we, instead, ask some very simple questions, beginning with the query of the 1970s: 'Development for whom?' We could then move on to a few other basic questions: Have communications 'aid' and investment in this sector increased in the Third World over the last 20 years? Are the vast majority of people living in these countries better or worse off today? At a seminar on the NWICO held in London in 1990, Golding sounded a similar note. He stated that if researchers were to 'go back to the basics' of a 'political economy of North–South relations' they would find that by almost any measurement of economic or social progress, 'the 1980s were the "lost decade" for the developing countries' (Golding, 1990: 3).

Lastly, I have argued here that the Western response to the NWICO was very much related to what first the United States, and then others, saw as an answer to their economic crises: the information society. But I have not argued that this response has worked. The United States may be a very unhappy harbinger of things to come throughout the capitalist world. A 'back to basics' approach is, again, instructive: by any index of social and economic well-being, the vast majority of Americans fared very poorly in the 1970s and 1980s, and there is no sign that the 1990s are any better.[14] In short, the information society has not delivered the goods.

Notes

1. There is an enormous NWICO literature challenging the dominant Western communication models. For some of the important titles, see Roach's bibliography (1986).

2. The following works deal with the US attack on UNESCO and the NWICO: Coates (1988); Giffard (1989); Mehra (1986); Preston et al. (1989); and Roach (1987, 1990).

3. For an analysis of the role of the 'government control' argument in the NWICO debate, see Roach (1987).

4. Most of the information on France in this section is taken from two reports written while working and studying in France (Roach, 1979, 1981).

5. Letter sent by Timothy Raison of the Overseas Development Administration, dated 2 April 1984.

6. My research on Canada was greatly assisted by Susan Chadwick, graduate student in the Sociology Department, Queen's University, Kingston, Ontario.

7. For a sampling of this literature, see McPhail (1981), Smythe (1981) and Pendakur (1984, 1991).

8. The two reports were: Canadian Broadcasting Corporation, *Let's Do It: A Vision of Canadian Broadcasting* (1985), and *The Report of the Task Force on Broadcasting Policy* (1986).

9. The Canadian Commission for UNESCO, located in Ottawa, is at present one of the best information sources on the NWICO. Another bountiful source of information is the archive of Betty Zimmerman, the Canadian member of the MacBride Commission, housed in the library of the School of Journalism, Carleton University, Ottawa.

10. The statement that the NWICO term was first pronounced on Canadian soil is presented in two documents of the Canadian commission: its *Bulletin* no. 5, December 1986; and a *Chronology of UNESCO Information and Communication, 1985–1986.* However, I have not found any evidence of this based on the report of the Montreal meeting. Although the term 'new order' was being used in Non-Aligned circles before the 1970s (Singham and Hune, 1986), every book and document on the NWICO dealing with its origin that I am familiar with traces the actual term back to the 1976 Non-Aligned media seminar in Tunis. Having said this, many chronologies of the NWICO do begin with the Montreal meeting since a number of the concepts associated with the movement, such as the call for 'two-way flow', were first introduced here.

11. Support for the connection established between the NWICO and the West's move towards the 'information society' was offered by a former UN official. In 1990, Thérèse Paquet-Sévigny, then the UN Under-Secretary-General for Information, wrote the following: 'Over many years, the international debate on information and communication did not result in agreement on a common approach. I wish only to refer to some of the discussions, for instance, *on concepts of a new world information order, which in the eyes of many actors in the field of communication have harmed international efforts to construct a world-wide information society*' (Paquet-Sévigny, 1990: 16; my emphasis).

12. Norway has, by far, topped the list of contributors. As of 1990, it had contributed US$ 7,130,126 to the IPDC Special Account. France's contribution for the same period (1981–90) totalled US$ 1,370,215 (UNESCO, 1991b: Annex 1).

13. Some of the recent literature on the NWICO sees the national elites as having been one of the principal problems with the movement thus far. This critique is often linked to the call for a genuine grassroots NWICO (cf. Sparks and Roach, 1990).

14. There is a number of excellent books documenting how the Reagan–Bush era in America was one of social decline. See, for example, Mattera (1990).

6

From Optimism to Reality: An Overview of Third World News Agencies

Mohammed Musa

The process of decolonizing the information sphere in many Third World countries is part of a wider struggle for self-determination. The anti-colonial struggle of the early nineteenth century has led to two significant yet dialectically related developments. First, the growth of a nationalist press in many of the colonies and the subsequent involvement of foreign press ownership to neutralize or contain the activities of these nationalist presses as in some of the colonies like Ghana, Nigeria and India. Secondly, the creation of a ready-made market for the Western news agencies that stepped in to provide foreign news to these emerging media clients.

The trend whereby the news media in the new nations gradually became dependent on foreign agencies for their material was seen as inimical to the former's commitment to self-determination. The activities of the foreign news agencies that produced news with a Western perception and aimed primarily at a Western audience came under increasing attack from the Third World countries. Among the criticisms levied against the news content of the foreign news agencies was that more was heard about the advanced Western powers than about the Third World, and that even the little that was reported gave a distorted version of their (Third World) realities.

Indigenous news agencies (national and regional) have emerged in various parts of the globe. While several factors could be advanced to account for the emergence of news agencies in the Third World – from popular concern among Third World citizens for their right to self-determination, through cultural nationalism among the dominant classes of newly emergent nations, to their quest for a better share of resources within the existing international political economy, and so on – all have been galvanized and channelled by Third World ruling elites in the form of agitation for a new international information order.

The agitation, however, has focused largely on the subordination of the emergent nations to the advanced industrialized countries in the spheres of technology, information and culture, i.e. news and entertainment material. In the cultural/informational sphere, the contention at the quantitative level revolved around the vast and overwhelming flow of media programmes, news and information from the advanced Western countries to the emergent nations, especially from the beginning of the nineteenth century. The uni-directional character of this flow was criticized since it had not been complemented by a significant counter-flow. The contention further held that this uni-directional tendency was not incidental but had fundamental links with the old or collapsing framework and reflected the metropolitan hegemonic status. Most of the detailed studies in the past have focused mainly on entertainment material like television and radio programmes, records and films (see for example Varis, 1973; Schiller, 1976; Hamelink, 1983; Tunstall, 1977; Lee, 1980; and Fejes, 1981). The conquering effect of such imported cultural artefacts on the culture of indigenous populations has continuously attracted concern. Subsequent studies on news as a cultural/ideological form have emerged along similar lines.

Such concerns, however, are not without a qualitative dimension. Particularly obtrusive was the question of the content or nature of such news and information products, which were seen to reflect a negative picture of Third World reality. Such information displayed a near fascination with crime, scandal, disaster, political strife or unrest, and at best sports (see for example Samarajiwa, 1984; Ansah, 1985). Subsequent concerns at the qualitative level also focused on the distribution of communication hardware, i.e. technology and its operational modes, as well as the issue of professional ideology transferred through training and so on (see for example Mattelart, 1980; Schiller, 1976; Hamelink, 1983, 1984; Golding, 1977).

Earlier detailed studies on international news flow were more especially concerned with the role of international news agencies such as Reuters, Associated Press (AP), United Press International (UPI) and Agence France Presse (AFP). Such pioneering studies are the works of Harris (1978, 1985) and Boyd-Barrett (1980). Both have validated Third World claims of dominance and negative news by the international news agencies.

Commitment of Third World ruling elites in the agitation for a new international order was given an increasing stimulus by the discovery that their destiny in the post-independence period was subject to the dictates of a system of global market relations ema-nating from the centres of international capitalism over which they had no control. In this regard, the contention further held that the negative and unbalanced information about the Third World (as disseminated by the international media) was primarily produced to serve a commodity-oriented Western audience. A supportive framework for this was provided by the free flow of information doctrine advanced by Western interests under US hegemony. This free flow was seen as an essential component of the transnational system.

But because the theoretical framework that shaped the debate led to a focus on the relationship between Third World countries and the advanced Western countries, the recipe put forward to end Third World subordination, thus guaranteeing a new order, was one that emphasized, among others, the establishment of indigenous news sources in the Third World countries.

The NWICO debate and Third World optimism

While it has become the norm to trace the origin of the New World Information and Communication Order (NWICO) agitation to the 1973 Non-Aligned summit in Algiers, the actual genesis of this agitation predates this summit. The agitation for an equitable flow of news across national borders is part of, and has its roots in, the struggle of the nations of Africa, Asia, Latin America and later Eastern Europe for their rights to self-determination. In this process, genuine attempts were made to counter the information disseminated by the colonial media of radio, news agencies and the press. These include the use of vernacular press, pamphlets, theatre, churches and mosques and other places of worship which played an instrumental role in raising public consciousness about the struggle for independence.

National independence in the Third World ensured, among others, the transformation of remaining struggles for the decolonization of vital sectors of social life to state platforms. In this light, the Non-Aligned Movement (NAM) drew up a charter for a 'New International Economic Order' (NIEO) which was approved at a special session of the UN General Assembly in May 1974. Moreover, NAM member states recognized information as a vital component of all economies and thus saw the struggle for a New International Information Order (NIIO) as integral to that of the NIEO. The 1973 Algiers summit resolved that to achieve a New International Economic Order, member states would have to 'take concerted action in the field of Mass Communication . . . in order to promote a greater interchange of ideas among themselves'. The resolution aimed to achieve a free flow of information among NAM member states, and the birth of the Non-Aligned News Agency Pool had its roots in this resolution.

The continuing emergence of new nations, and the right of participation in international fora that independence has guaranteed such states, enabled them to use their franchise in challenging Western dominance and global inequalities, especially in the spheres of information and economics. Algeria's initiative at the sixth Special Session of the UN General Assembly resulted in the adoption of two important resolutions on the need for the establishment of a new international order in both information and economics, and also a 'programme of action' for attaining these. Regional and international organizations such as the Organization of African Unity (OAU), the Non-Aligned Movement, the Arab League and the Caribbean Free Trade Association (CARIFTA) not only gave strong backing to the proposal but also preached the gospel of NIEO and NWICO as effective steps toward consolidating the gains of independence and putting the new nations firmly on the path of development.

This concern with their disadvantaged position within the existing international political economy has been a major focus for Third World ruling elites since the 1970s. Whereas the early 1960s was a period characterized by concern with the indispensability of Western media form and content as an essential recipe for development, subsequent years saw a reconsideration of this position and, in its place, an outcry against the activities of Western media which led to agitation for the New World Information and Communication Order.

Early academic research in international communications reflected a dominant Western concern with the way in which the expanding capitalist technology could better encompass the periphery nations in its orbit. The paraphernalia of modernization, of which communications technologies comprised one element, was seen as a defining feature of developed societies and its acquisition would, therefore, stimulate modernization and extract the periphery nations from their state of backwardness. The consequence of this ethnocentricity was not only the unquestioned acceptance of Western media form (technology and content), but also the scarce consideration of its limited relevance to emerging non-Western societies.

However, later studies (see for example Golding, 1974; Schiller, 1976; Harris, 1978; Hamelink, 1983) rejected this dominant Western position and agreed instead that the very position was faulty because it ignored the fundamental fact that underdevelopment is not just a backward stage of development but the structural outcome of the dynamic relationship between advanced and underdeveloped societies, a relationship characterized by the dominance of the former over the latter. In this regard, embracing Western form and content only exacerbates dependence and, in turn, increases rather than turns the table of underdevelopment. Moreover, communications cannot be separated from the wider sectors of political, economic and cultural relations within which they are located. Indeed, such communications cannot bring any positive change since they are merely a reflection at the ideological level of a particular set of relationships characterized by the domination of one sector over the other.

The key concept in the two dominant perspectives that have informed studies concerned with international communications (acquisition versus rejection of Western technology) is that of 'development'. By implication, both the NIIO and the NIEO are concerned with development in peripheral societies. An excursion into this debate has become a necessary starting point in this chapter, particularly since national and regional news agencies (the subject of our analysis here) are to a large extent seen as the outcome of this debate. In doing so, we shall reassess the major features of the agitation for a New World Information and Communication Order and examine why it has remained incapable of solving Third World information problems and general problems of underdevelopment.

While it is true that the policies and ideologies of the 'Development Decade' in the early days of independence failed to usher in expected modernization to the traditional societies of newly emergent nations of Africa and Asia, and that the strategy of import substitution industrialization adopted by Latin American countries only exacerbated their dependence on the industrialized Western countries (the United States in particular), concern about self-reliant national development became the major item on the agenda of dependency theory as a radical scholarship which was seen to provide a panacea to the problem that: 'The social structures of colonies, ex-colonies or neo-colonies are not the result of autonomous historic development, but they are determined by foreign hegemony and exploitation' (quoted in Lee, 1983: 179). Authentic national development was perceived as a possibility only through the countering of 'imported civilization' imposed by imperialism, thereby guaranteeing the right of the citizen to self-determination.

Most Third World commentators on the NWICO arguing from this centre/periphery perspective have directed attention to the fairness or unfairness in international media content that circulates negative words and images about the Third World, to the unidirectional flow of media material originating from the advanced Western nations, especially the United States and Britain, and to the tendency of submerging the cultures of recipient nations, thus leading to what is generally termed cultural imperialism (see Schiller, 1976; Hamelink, 1983, 1984).

The notion of cultural imperialism is central to the debate, where the phenomenon is seen as inimical to self-reliant development. At the empirical level, it has often been noted that the existing system of mass communication is dominated by transnational activities where the 'Big Four' international news agencies – AFP, AP, Reuters and UPI – and the major newspapers, television and radio companies, especially the transnational advertising network, as well as satellites, cable, trans-border data flow and so on, were established to serve the requirements of the old order.

The limitations of the NWICO debate, and its proposals, are glaring at both the theoretical and empirical levels. From the outset, an error is often committed by dehistoricizing the debate in the sense of tracing its origins to the formal stage in world fora such as UNESCO, the United Nations, etc., even though it predates the Second World War and forms part of a wider struggle of Third World people for their right to self-determination.

While we have observed how the cultural imperialism approach guides the debate, thus focusing on the role of transnational corporations (TNCs) in shaping communication between the Third World and advanced Western societies, we equally acknowledge that this model is an improvement on earlier communications and development models. These models define development within the realm of modernization or industrialization, especially by highlighting the role of TNCs in communication in the Third World. However, such a focus is still very limited and deceptive. For, among others, the approach neglects how imperialism has penetrated Third World societies and made of them imperialists also, and neglects the internal dynamics operating at both national and local levels that perpetuate and react against dependence. It also ignores the dynamic relationship that exists between the internal and the external forces in this process.

Underdevelopment can be defined within the dependency spectrum as an asymmetrical relationship between metropolis and satellite where dependence and exploitation become the main feature, with the satellite always at a disadvantage. This is a central theme in the debate and is why all proposals put forward appear incapable of solving the problem of Third World underdevelopment. Such proposals aim at removing this relationship of dependence without going further to address the primary contradiction: unequal access to resources within periphery nations. That is why, as will be shown later, even after the implementation of some of the proposals in the debate – more aid to the Third World in terms of media infrastructure, establishment of national and regional news agencies, ending the dissemination of 'negative' news by international media – the information gap among citizens of the Third World is far from removed. The domestic dimension of the new order has not been addressed.

To come to grips with the situation we need to identify and define the problem in proper perspective. This means going beyond indigenous news sources (forces of production) by looking at the distribution of the end product (the relation of production). For any incisive analysis of the new order, and therefore of development and underdevelopment in the Third World, one must look at both the productive forces and the relations of production, otherwise the analysis is bound to remain inadequate. Analysis could over-emphasize the productive forces, thus leading to the acquisition of more media infrastructure. Other questions remain unanswered and these have to do with content: who has access, who does not and who benefits? Indeed, the present situation in some Third World countries is one where media infrastructure is highly developed – in, for example, Mexico, Nigeria, Egypt and Brazil – but this has not rendered citizens better informed than they were a decade ago. The increasing phenomenon of privatization and commercialization of the media has turned high-quality information into an expensive commodity, making its availability a monetary function. Those who cannot afford to pay (and they constitute the majority) live in information poverty and, in the final analysis, a highly stratified information system emerges in which a few (because they can afford it) have access to high-quality information, while the majority live in a situation of information underdevelopment.

Finally, is the New World Information and Communication Order set to end this inequitable distribution of information (domestic and international) which leads to underdevelopment by resolving the primary contradictions in material life, or is it set to further develop the already developed classes in the Third World?

News agencies in the Third World: toward a typology

The need for self-reliance, to counter dependence on the news agencies of the superpowers, as well as the need to disseminate an undistorted version of their own experiences, led Third World countries to come up with national, and in some cases regional, alternatives.

Even though it appears easy to identify common factors as bearing responsibility for the emergence of these national and regional news agencies, it is curious that these agencies differ one from the other. Their varying characteristics and features, which at times raise questions as to their stated aims, can be gleaned from their purposes, patterns of ownership, services offered, functions and clients.

The end of the Second World War in 1945 has been recorded as a turning point in world history in the sense that independence struggles in many of the countries now referred to as the Third World gathered momentum. Motivated and encouraged by the independence of India in 1947, nationalists in various regions intensified their struggles against foreign domination, which resulted in the birth of many new nations. The continuing endeavours of the nationalists in these new nations were redirected not only to consolidating their newly won independence but also to expressing nascent national energies through the establishment of some national symbols. The flag of independence, a national anthem and a seat at the United Nations were followed by the setting up of icons of nationalistic establishments such as new airports, national television and radio stations, and a national currency. Early presses, in the form of missionary or nationalist publications, and some foreign presses had existed in most of these new nations. Radio, as the oldest and widest form of broadcasting – which in some places began life as relay systems for the mother country's broadcasting system – provided the infrastructure for the establishment at independence of national radio, which also became a leading client of the news agencies.

However, when they emerged in the Third World, news agencies were characterized by both differences and similarities. The differences were inevitable, bearing in mind the very specific way in which each of them emerged to confront a uniform problem.

Boyd-Barrett (1980), for example, has attempted to differentiate between news agencies other than the international news merchants that belonged to the nineteenth-century cartel. He was able to identify and distinguish between intermediary news agencies, international intermediary news agencies and national news agencies. Differences among news agencies, he observes, represent 'different points on a continuum, which itself is made up of different dimensions'.

In his categorization, he termed as intermediary those news agencies whose scale of international operation is smaller than that of the international news agencies and whose activities are confined to specific and limited geographical areas. Since they only maintain a sizeable overseas reporting staff in relation to the 'Big Four', they rely on the latter for news reports on areas in which they are absent or deficient. Such agencies serve fewer foreign clients than the 'Big Four' and their focus is often their domestic home markets whose news requirements they strive to meet. They are intermediate because they are in between the big international news agencies and the average national agencies. Such intermediate agencies, according to Boyd-Barrett, are represented by DPA of West Germany, Japan's Kyodo, Tanjug of Yugoslavia, ADN of East Germany and EFE of Spain.

In this kind of categorization what is labelled as international intermediary news agencies are mostly the regional news agencies which evolved from the 1970s onwards. They are not associated with any specific national base and they involve the cooperation or pooling of many different national agencies in meeting the news requirements of particular regions or certain categories of country. Among these are the Non-Aligned News Agency Pool, the Caribbean News Agency (CANA), the Pan-African News Agency (PANA), LATIN and the ASIN-Latin American and Caribbean news exchange pool that was set up in 1979.

The third category is the national agency which also has a very limited number of overseas correspondents and foreign markets, if any. It mostly exchanges its services with other foreign agencies including the 'Big Four' and aims primarily at its domestic audience. In many cases, the principal function of the national news agencies is the redistribution of news from the 'Big Four' to local subscribers.

At the bottom of the continuum there is yet another large variety of smaller services, mostly specializing in a particular product like features, economic news or news photos. Some of them, like the syndicated services of some major US dailies, are patronized by quite a number of foreign clients.

My contention in this chapter is that this typology is not exhaustive in the sense that it has a tendency to imply that all the so-called 'average national news agencies' of the Third World are the same, for the fundamental reason that they are national. If the argument is carried further, then it will be implied as well that all the intermediary news agencies could also be the same, for the major reason that they are mainly concerned with some regions, areas or issues. By the same implication, CANA, with all its private interest concern, could be put in the same category as the Non-Aligned News Agency Pool, the very model that CANA's major owners (private Caribbean newspapers) rejected for their own agency.

Being intermediary, international intermediary, national or syndicate, therefore, describes these agencies only at a general and simple level. For this reason, I want to look at other features of the agencies and add that beyond or in addition to the present description and categorization they could also be alternative news agencies or extension news agencies. The main defining feature of the previous typology, where an agency is classified as intermediary, international intermediary or national, has to do with quantity, as it focuses on the geographical scope of the agencies' operations, total number of employees, etc. In our contention, an agency could be any of these and in the final count end up as either an alternative news source or an extension of existing news sources.

On the whole, an exhaustive analysis of types of news agencies in the Third World must break away from the traditional quantitative yardstick of appraisal or categorization. As observed earlier, the NWICO debate placed undue emphasis on the imbalance in news flow between the advanced Western countries and the Third World in terms of quantity, a problem whose solution was thought to lie in the provision of more media infrastructure. The fact that the analysis of quality of the transmitted news is not given the attention it deserves leaves the problem of information imbalance largely unresolved, despite the creation of indigenous news sources.

Determining the quality of the product disseminated by national and regional news agencies calls for a careful and detailed study of the historical forces surrounding the emergence of these agencies, their structure and organization (whether they represent a recreation of the dominant news agency framework or deviate from that), pattern of ownership and control, the journalistic tradition upon which they were established, stated purposes, function and the audience they serve. By doing this, we should be able to distinguish between alternative and extension news, between whether an agency is poised to disseminate alternative news, or whether it serves to provide more of the same type of news that has hitherto been provided by the 'Big Four'. Further research needs to be done along these lines.

The alternative news agencies

To talk of alternative implies deviation from a dominant model. In this context, the dominant established model is that of the 'Big Four' agencies that formed the nineteenth-century cartel. A Third World news agency could be an alternative news agency if the purpose for which it was set up, as well as its functions, is different from the dominant model. Take, for instance, the Non-Aligned News Agency Pool, which was set up in recognition of an existing information gap among member countries, thus making one of the agency's purposes that of bridging the gap quantitatively and providing a more qualitatively balanced and accurate picture of these countries. The agency functions differently from the 'Big Four' in the sense that it pools and retransmits news material from Third World news agencies among member countries. Instead of relying on and retransmitting 'Big Four' news material like other agencies, the Non-Aligned News Agency Pool retransmits domestic news material from the Third World news agencies which could serve as foreign news when used by another news agency. In this regard, both the Non-Aligned News Agency Pool and the Pan-African News Agency fall into the category of alternative news agencies, in addition to their status as international intermediary. At a general level, however, an agency could also be an alternative if it is self-reliant and does not depend on other agencies for news material. This, added to its alternative perception of what makes news, qualified Yugoslavia's Tanjug as an alternative news agency.

The extension news agencies

The term refers to those agencies whose stated purposes do not go beyond the familiar context of transmitting 'impartial', 'balanced', 'objective' and 'neutral' news reports. Since these are values that inform 'Big Four' journalism, the structuring of an agency along the same traditional lines makes such an agency a reinforcer of 'Big Four' news values. This is also true of functions; that is, when an agency is involved in retransmitting 'Big Four' newscasts because it is incapable of depending on its own staff. Many Third World national news agencies, as well as some regional services like CANA and LATIN, are extension agencies.

At the same time, a definitive classification of agencies depends on further detailed study of the historical forces surrounding their emergence, their structure and news production process, as well as analysis of their content.

The dimensions of agency news

In this section, I have analysed the content of news bulletins from a national news agency, the News Agency of Nigeria (NAN) during August, September and October 1987 as well as a regional news agency (CANA) in August, September and October 1988. My concern is with news types: what makes the news, which actors are covered and in which locations do they make news? This analysis applies to both domestic and foreign news. I have also tried to identify the sources of foreign news for both types of agencies, in view of the fact that the weak economic bases of these agencies do not allow them to maintain correspondents in all locations of the world.

News dependence

The first striking feature of NAN's foreign news bulletin is its dependence on Reuters as the major source of foreign news. Accounting for 33.2 per cent of NAN's foreign news stories, Reuters occupies first position as supplier of foreign news to NAN (see Table 6.1). Indeed, Reuters is ahead of the continental agency PANA, which comes second, accounting for 17.9 per cent of foreign news stories. China's Xinhua and NAN itself came third and fourth,

Table 6.1   *Distribution of NAN's foreign news source by agency (1989)*

Agency	Number of stories	%
Reuters	405	33.3
PANA	218	17.9
Xinhua	189	15.5
NAN	158	12.9
AFP	140	11.5
IPS	53	4.4
AP	46	3.8
TASS	5	0.4
UPI	4	0.3
Total	1218	100

accounting for 15.5 per cent and 12.9 per cent respectively of foreign news stories. To a large extent, it would appear that Nigeria learns of Africa from an African source, PANA, which largely retransmits stories from African national news agencies. However, as this writer observed during a production study in NAN (see Musa, 1989), the reality is that there are times when foreign desk editors turn to one of the 'Big Four' Western agencies for news on some African countries, either in search of 'more detail' and 'up-to-date' information when PANA copy arrives late, or in search of a more 'neutral' report on a sensitive issue. A typical example was the 1987 military coup in neighbouring Burkina Faso in which former leader Captain Thomas Sankara was murdered: editors on the foreign desk spent their time going through the AFP cast every hour to receive the latest 'neutral' reports on developments, believing that what came through PANA would come from the Burkinabe national agency, which would not be neutral.

Other reports on situations and events outside Africa continue to be heard from non-African sources. The little alteration, if any, that is made to such news stories by NAN editors who play the role of gate-keeper in this regard has to do with the replacement of terms such as 'terrorist' or 'extremist' in reference to liberation movements in Africa and elsewhere which are widely recognized as struggling for a just cause.

In Table 6.2, which shows regional distribution of story types in NAN's foreign news, it is clear that Africa comes first, with 659 out of 1,591 stories (41.4 per cent). This would lead one to expect PANA to come first as NAN's major foreign news source. Besides the reason cited above, there are another two possible explanations: NAN might have been using many stories from its correspondents in

Table 6.2 *Regional distribution of story types in NAN's foreign news*

Story type	Africa	Socialist	Third World	Advanced industrialized	Others	UN	All
Politics	222	31	90	85	62	9	499
Accident/disasters/scandals	51	27	73	54	13	0	218
Military	56	9	82	52	4	7	210
Development issues	131	8	15	18	3	0	175
Social service	50	12	8	9	29	6	114
Economics	54	8	14	17	11	0	104
Aid	50	0	18	27	1	0	96
Crime	18	28	15	25	5	0	91
Personalities	14	3	7	14	1	6	45
Science and technology	4	2	2	7	2	0	17
Religion	6	1	2	7	0	0	16
Culture and the arts	3	0	0	1	0	0	4
Sports	0	1	0	1	0	0	2
Total	659	130	326	317	131	28	1591

African countries; and the foreign desk editors may still have had greater preference for stories from, for example, Reuters than from PANA because of convenience of language; many PANA stories are disseminated in French, which then have to be translated into English, thus increasing processing time. A curious finding in terms of foreign news source distribution is the low number of stories used from the then Soviet Union's TASS agency and from the Inter Press Service (IPS) Third World news agency (for more on IPS, see Chapter 7). The finding is particularly curious in view of NAN's stated commitment to the New Information Order and alternative news (disclosed in an interview with NAN's general manager) and the commitment of both TASS and IPS to the same ideals. Perhaps the low rating for TASS was more deeply rooted than first appears and depended on the assumptions among NAN foreign editors about the image of the then Soviet Union, communism, propaganda and even the entire notion of news itself. Having internalized a Western ideology of journalism with all its accompanying definitions of news, many NAN journalists view any news form that deviates from these definitions as less acceptable. The belief that IPS is stronger on news to do with Latin America than with any other region could indicate that NAN only used IPS stories on issues referring to Latin America. The fact that Latin America is a momentary news centre and, therefore a less important news location for NAN could explain the lower relevance of IPS as a NAN news source.

In the distribution of CANA's foreign news sources, Reuters came first, accounting for 90 per cent of the former's foreign news (see Table 6.9, p. 139). Caribbeans only hear about the world from CANA as a second-ranking source, accounting for only 4.3 per cent of the total. Indeed, Reuters' monopoly in the region is so overwhelming that, with the exception of AP, one hardly notes the presence of any other agency.

Several factors could be responsible for the excessive dependence of CANA on Reuters for its foreign news. First, the extent to which CANA was modelled on Reuters was so great that belonging to the Reuters block contract was a condition for acquiring share ownership in CANA in its formative days. This implied a situation in which much of the ownership of CANA went to the private sector since traditional private media owners constituted a majority among block contract subscribers to Reuters. Secondly, the operating model set for CANA in its formative days was evidently Reuters, with whose services the negotiating team was satisfied.[1] In fact, the team recommended that Reuters should provide CANA's foreign news. Granted that this could have been due to economic reasons, since CANA could not then afford to have correspondents all over the world, the fact remains that the foreign news received from Reuters was to be retransmitted in unedited form, demonstrating the extent of faith shown in Reuters as well as its enviable position as the 'ideal' in news agency journalism. Thirdly, CANA was launched in 1976 as a private limited liability company, starting out as a six-month joint operation with Reuters, during which time the service was to be known as Reuters-CANA, and the first CANA chief editor and chief executive was Harry Mayers, Reuters' Caribbean editor.

The issue here is that both the structure and operation of CANA stood in contrast to the expectations of the region's political leadership which had first stimulated interest in a regional news agency. In the words of Jamaica's then Prime Minister Michael Manley in 1974:

> We cannot stop the metropolitan world from interpreting itself through the wire services. But we must recognise that the Caribbean, the Black World, has its own view of the world and needs to be aware of that view. (quoted in Cuthbert, 1980: 19)

The realization that the limited market base of the agency was reaching saturation point and that, therefore, the economic environment was becoming harsher, led the owners of CANA to look for a more viable revenue base. It was in this light that the agency acquired new communication technologies and began marketing Reuters' financial data file, which started yielding some profit for the agency. This exacerbated the extent of CANA's dependence on Reuters.

News focus

News focus has been an area of concern to Third World countries, reflected in their grievances expressed during the NWICO debate. For this reason, the content of NAN and CANA news stories was analysed with a view to determining the extent to which these agencies depart from the Western news agencies' pattern of news focus (for the CANA findings, see the section on CANA news, p. 138).

As the table on NAN's foreign news focus (Table 6.2, p. 129) shows, Politics as a category came first in all regions of the world. In Africa, Development issues came second, while Economics was marginally displaced to fourth position by Military. In the Third World as a region, Military comes second, with Accidents/Disasters/Scandals as a single category third. Of stories from the socialist countries, Crime was the second most important category, followed by Accidents/Disasters/Scandals. From the United Nations as a supranational arena, Politics dominated, while Military stories were the second most important, with Social Services and Personalities sharing third position.

A few observations emerge from these variations. For instance, they show that in the NAN news bulletin certain parts of the world are mostly associated with certain events. In this light, development issues are the second most important category in Africa. Most of these stories are sifted from other news agencies and, since PANA is NAN's major source of news on Africa, we see the former's policy reflected in the news content.[2] But even among what are considered development stories, there are interesting discrepancies, such as 'exchange of visits among leaders' which constitutes the highest single category. The contradiction of development journalism is that its categories are built on some simplifications and trivializations of the concept of 'development'. African ruling elites, for example, propagate the idea of visits between and among themselves as a necessary step toward the unity of the continent, Pan-Africanism and therefore development. That NAN could also operate with the same simplified notion of development exposes the tendency of the media to operate within a consensual framework: for instance, the African ruling elite is presented as the 'genuine' and 'legal' representative of the people and activities such as visits are portrayed as having the backing of the people. Such a tendency is in line with Golding and Elliot's discovery (1979) that the media tend to report more on activities that are visible and observable, and therefore dramatic.

That Military takes third position in African foreign news can be partly explained by Golding and Elliot's finding that the image of the Third World in international media is one of 'bullet before the ballot box', but also, and very importantly, by the increasing militarization of African politics whereby the military as an institution is occupying an increasingly dominant position in the power structure. An additional explanation for the prominence of military stories in the news had to do with increasing militancy in the activities of liberation movements in the front-line states of Africa at the time of the analysis.

Fourth ranking is Economics, even if the leading categories of economic news stories are reported within a political context. The single leading economic story type is 'Other Economic', including petroleum and big business. Since Nigeria is a member of the Organization of Petroleum Exporting Countries (OPEC) cartel, NAN monitors developments in the organization as well as fluctuations in petroleum prices worldwide, especially since this has implications for domestic policies.

The second most important economic category is 'International Trade and Tariffs', closely followed by 'Economic Performance', where the topic of the day was the extent of Third World indebtedness to international finance capital and institutions such as the World Bank and the International Monetary Fund (IMF). Issues that might have been expected to generate an equally crucial economic interest, such as the subordination of labour by capital and the attempt by the former to resolve this contradiction through picketing activities and the like, go unreported and when they are reported at all, the impression is created that ungrateful workers are disrupting the 'normal order' by engaging in strikes.

The image of the Third World that emerges from the data is that it is an area full of not just 'political' activities, but also full of military activities and disasters, scandals and calamities. Here again, there is a glaring simplification of the realm of politics where the most reported activities are those of the dominant actors involved in diplomatic activities, or of conflicts and crises. In the first case, news reports concern situations involving diplomats, while in the second ordinary people make the news in the context of negative happenings. This latter finding reflects Galtung's proposition that by virtue of his marginal position, the ordinary man is more likely to feature in the news when there is something negative to report (see Galtung, 1985).

In the advanced industrialized countries, just as in other regions of the world, Politics is the most important category, but while Accidents/Disasters/Scandals come second, this category is closely followed by Military. In NAN's news coverage, it is interesting to note that although all regions of the world record the highest figures in terms of coverage of politics, the region with the highest level is Africa, possibly because this is essentially an African service (Africa with 222 stories, Third World with 90, Advanced Industrialized Countries with 85, Socialist Countries with 31, etc.). The trend of simplifying political activities into political elite activities cuts across all regions with minor variations, in that the concentration is higher in peripheral regions than in advanced industrialized regions. Again, we are dealing with an African service in which there are more stories on Africa and the Third World. However, it is interesting to note that the foreign news agencies appear to have stopped, or at least reduced, their emphasis on the negative *per se* when reporting peripheral regions. Meanwhile, if PANA is the major source of news on Africa, NAN relies on the 'Big Four' agencies for news of other peripheral regions of the world and here Politics and Military are again the two most important categories.

Table 6.3   *Distribution of actor nationality in NAN's foreign news*

Region	Number of stories	%
Africa	322	31.3
Third World	232	22.5
Advanced industralized	193	18.8
Supranational	131	12.7
Others	84	8.2
Socialist countries	67	6.5
Total	1029	100

Actor focus

Analysis of the nationality of actors reported in NAN's foreign news (see Table 6.3) shows Africa as top of the list, with 322 out of the 1,029 cases reported and identified (31.3 per cent). Other regions of the Third World account for 232 or 22.5 per cent of the stories reported, while the Advanced Industrialized Countries come third, with 193 stories (18.8 per cent). The conclusions are that the emergence of Third World news agencies has had some positive impact on the quantitative pattern of international news flow in favour of previously disadvantaged regions, that NAN also favours African actors over actors from other regions, and/or that the international news agencies (which are also major sources of foreign news) are now responding by giving more coverage to the peripheral regions and their news makers.

An interesting feature of actor coverage in NAN's foreign news (see Table 6.4), is that the Minister/Government Official category appears as the most prominent in all regions, with a total of 265 appearances out of 1,420 cases, representing a level of 18.7 per cent. Head of State is second in all regions, with 166 appearances, or 11.7 per cent, while Others and Ordinary Citizens closely follow each other with 85 and 84 appearances (6.0% and 5.9%). Popular groups like Trade Unions and Pressure Groups each account for only 2 per cent. On the whole, there are more African actors reported, followed by those of the Advanced Industrialized Countries, the Third World, the United Nations and the Socialist countries in last position.

The domestic news: NAN covers Nigeria

It was argued at the beginning of this chapter that, among others, a major weakness of the NWICO debate has been its neglect of the domestic dimension of the information order. In an attempt to

Table 6.4 *Regional distribution of actor types in NAN's foreign news*

Actor type	Africa	Socialist	Third World	Advanced industrialized	Others	UN	All
Minister/govt official	130	26	53	43	13	0	265
Head of State	84	4	37	31	9	1	166
Others	31	9	12	26	7	0	85
Ordinary citizens	18	16	28	11	11	0	84
Group of nations	33	2	14	13	3	2	67
Regular dissident group	31	0	26	5	4	0	66
Other international bodies	36	0	4	21	1	0	62
Regular forces of state	13	3	23	15	7	0	61
Regular army	23	2	24	3	3	1	56
The United Nations	16	0	14	23	0	10	63
Academics/scientists	13	8	1	20	7	0	49
Ambassador/diplomat	20	3	9	9	1	0	42
Criminal	8	1	9	16	3	0	37
Non-legitimate opposition	10	1	9	10	4	0	34
News media/journalists	14	4	6	8	0	0	32
Industry/corporate official	10	2	5	7	7	0	31
Trade union/workers	8	1	3	3	16	0	31
Ruling party/military	16	4	3	5	2	0	30
Pressure groups	18	0	3	3	5	0	29
Religious bodies	7	0	8	9	2	0	26
Judiciary/judges	8	3	6	7	0	0	24
Legislature	11	0	5	5	1	0	22
Legitimate opposition	4	0	6	4	4	0	18
International govt orgs	6	0	4	5	2	0	17
Celebrities	2	0	2	9	0	1	14
Royalty	0	0	0	6	0	1	7
Sports figures	1	0	0	1	0	0	2
Total	571	89	314	318	112	16	1420

Table 6.5   *Setting of domestic news in NAN's news bulletins*

Setting	Number of stories	%
Urban	976	87.3
Rural	142	12.7
Total	1118	100.0

determine the domestic news coverage given to the Third World by the indigenous news agencies, the content of the domestic news bulletin disseminated by NAN was analysed.

News dateline

The dateline refers to the location of a news event, that is, the place from where the news is reported. Part of the aim of the content analysis of the NAN domestic news bulletin was to determine what images of Nigeria the agency disseminates to its clients by identifying the news dateline and focus, as well as types of actors that make the news.

The analysis shows that some 87 per cent of the news stories came from Nigeria's cities and urban areas, while less than 13 per cent were from the peripheral rural areas (see Table 6.5). The picture is of a massive imbalance, in which the urban centres – headquarters of government, finance capital, missions and embassies – are given prominence to the detriment of the rural areas where over 70 per cent of the country's population resides. This lopsidedness is reflected (and can partly have its roots) in the posting of journalists. There are more NAN journalists in cities than in rural areas, and the few posted to the rural areas often find themselves unable to communicate in the language spoken by the locals. This often leaves the English-speaking journalist alienated from rural dwellers. Stories that reach the NAN bulletin are partially determined, among others, by the ability of the news-maker to communicate in the journalist's language.

Story types

The data in Table 6.6 shows the distribution of domestic story types and reveals that Development issues is the most prominent category (36.4 per cent), Social Services is second (16.3 per cent), Politics is third (15.7 per cent), Economics is fourth (13.9 per cent), Crime is fifth (6.9 per cent) and Accidents/Disasters/Scandals sixth (4.7 per

Table 6.6 *Distribution of story types in NAN's domestic news by setting (%)*

Story type	Urban	Rural	Both
Development issues	29.2	7.2	36.4
Social services	14.0	2.3	16.3
Politics	14.8	0.9	15.7
Economics	12.5	1.4	13.9
Crime	6.5	0.4	6.9
Accidents/disasters	4.1	0.6	4.7
Personalities	1.3	0.1	1.4
Aid	1.2	0.3	1.5
Religion	1.2	0.1	1.3
Science and technology	1.0	0	1.0
Culture and the arts	0.5	0.1	0.6
Military	0.3	0	0.3
Sports	0.1	0	0.1
Total %	86.6	13.4	100.0

cent). What is interesting to note is not only which aspects of these categories are given most prominence but the narrow realm within which concepts like 'development' and 'politics' are defined. Development is defined as the observable activities of elite groups, especially government representatives and some corporate personnel, in activities like 'mobilization' campaigns, official launches, speeches at conferences or seminars, or the inauguration of new schools. Politics is also reduced to the observable activities of political parties and political elite actors.

Actor types
Actor distribution in domestic news reveals another imbalance, since over 80 per cent of those reported are urban actors, while only 12 per cent are rural (see Table 6.7). The Minister/Commissioner/ Government Official category ranks highest with 601 (or 35.7 per cent) of the 1,630 cases reported (see Table 6.8). The data also reveal that about 80 per cent of those reported are in urban centres. Heads of State/State Governors as a category comes second and the category of Ordinary Citizens is third. One possible explanation for ordinary citizens even coming third may lie in the fact that self-help projects undertaken by rural people (due to government neglect) are regularly covered as 'development' issues, as are 'mass mobilization campaigns', in which ordinary citizens are assembled and addressed on government policies. But, apart from these sectors,

Table 6.7   *Overall distribution of actor geography by setting in NAN's domestic news*

	Urban	%	Rural	%
Number of actors	1471	87.6	208	12.4

Table 6.8   *Distribution of actor types by setting in NAN's domestic news*

Actor type	Urban	Rural	Both
Minister/commissioner/government	496	100	596
Head of State/state governers	228	20	248
Ordinary citizens	86	31	117
Industry/corporate official	103	4	107
Judiciary	88	1	89
Academics/scientists	81	5	86
Trade union	62	6	68
Regular forces of state	55	8	63
Students	50	9	59
Entertainers	25	1	26
Traditional rulers	37	11	48
News media/journalists	28	1	29
Religious body/clergy	25	2	27
Regular army	15	0	15
Ambassador/diplomat	12	0	12
Military junta	9	1	10
Other bodies	9	0	9
Group of nations	4	1	5
United Nations	4	0	4
Pressure group	3	0	3
Sports figures	2	0	2
International governmental organizations	1	0	1
Non-legitimate opposition	1	0	1
Total	1424	201	1630

other experiences, activities, endeavours and struggles involving rural people go unreported.

A regional news agency: CANA News

CANA news was analysed to determine the character and definition of the agency's news bulletins in relation to the agitation over the New World Information and Communication Order. In doing so, use was made of randomly selected news stories from the agency's

Table 6.9   *Distribution of CANA's foreign news source by agency*

Agency	Number of stories	%
Reuters	63	90.0
Others	4	5.7
CANA	3	4.3
Total	70	100.0

general news bulletin between the months of March and November 1989.

News source and news focus
CANA appears as a unique case in terms of foreign news source. There are two main reasons for this: first, the monopoly of Reuters as a major foreign news source, accounting for 90 per cent of news stories, thus marginalizing both CANA and other agencies, which account for 4.3 per cent and 5.7 per cent respectively (see Table 6.9); second, and as a result of the Reuters dominance, the impact of CANA as a direct foreign news source is hardly felt in the Caribbean region, and there is very little activity by other international news agencies. The creation of CANA, therefore, has not necessarily meant, as Michael Manley envisaged, the provision of world news from a Caribbean news agency. This is not unexpected given the desire of CANA's owners to nurture an agency modelled on Reuters, with whose operations they were satisfied.

In determining the character of foreign news in CANA's bulletins, the data in Table 6.10 shows that Economics is the most prominent category. Here again, the major issues range from activities of the entrepreneur class such as import and export, to state involvement in loan negotiations. Economic performance as assessed by economic elite actors is also a major issue within this economic category. Sports as a category comes third with 11.5 per cent. Rather than an indication of the extent to which sport has become so prominent in the lives of the region's people, this reflects the time frame within which sample stories were selected. The period saw the involvement of the West Indies cricket team in overseas test matches, with widespread local media attention in its activities, and the preparatory matches of the Trinidad and Tobago football team for the 1990 World Cup also put sport high on the Caribbean agenda. Accidents/Disasters/Scandals came second in the classification, Aid fourth and Politics fifth. That Accidents/Disasters/Scandals came second is perhaps an indication of the image of the Caribbean in international

Table 6.10   *Distribution of story types in CANA's foreign news by subject*

Type	Number of stories	%
Economic	40	16.4
Accidents/disasters/scandals	31	12.7
Sports	28	11.5
Aid	26	10.6
Politics	25	10.2
Social services	15	6.1
Culture and the arts	13	5.3
Personalities	13	5.3
Crime	12	4.9
Development issues	11	4.5
Military	10	4.1
Science and technology	10	4.1
Religion	9	3.7
Total	243	99.4

media. The coverage of Aid is dominated by the activities of state representatives, while Politics is, as in the case of NAN, confined to the observable activities of political parties and political elite actors. An interesting observation is that Development issues takes a marginal tenth position, accounting for only 4.5 per cent of the total coverage. Even Crime (4.9 per cent) is placed higher in the classification than Development issues, but since a large proportion of CANA's foreign news originates from news agencies (especially Reuters), it is evident that the image of the Caribbean created by the international media is one that associates the region with crime rather than development.

Another interesting feature is that the Caribbean is the most prominently reported region in most categories, with the Advanced Industrialized Countries coming in second. The only areas where the Caribbean did not come first are Science and Technology, Religion, Personalities and Military. The Third World and Socialist countries as regions record very low distribution levels, showing that they are seen as minor news locations for CANA (see Table 6.11).

Actor focus
The distribution of actors and their nationality in CANA's foreign news (Table 6.12) reveals another imbalance: more Caribbean actors are reported than any other. Actors from the Advanced Industrialized Countries rank second, and from the United Nations/Inter-regional and Intra-regional Organizations as a single 'Supranational'

Table 6.11 *Regional distribution of story types in CANA's foreign news*

Type	Caribbean	Socialist	Third World	Advanced industrialized	Others	UN	All
Economic	20	3	3	9	2	3	40
Accidents/disasters/scandals	20	1	2	7	1	0	31
Sports	16	1	1	8	2	0	28
Aid	10	2	1	10	1	2	26
Politics	12	1	2	8	0	2	25
Social services	8	0	0	3	2	2	15
Culture and the arts	8	0	1	1	2	1	13
Personalities	4	1	1	5	0	2	13
Crime	7	0	1	3	1	0	12
Development issues	5	2	2	1	1	0	11
Military	1	1	1	3	3	1	10
Science and technology	2	2	0	5	1	0	10
Religion	2	0	1	2	3	1	9
Total	115	14	16	65	19	14	243

Table 6.12   *Regional distribution of actor nationality in CANA's foreign news*

Region	Number of stories	%
Caribbean	346	57.3
Advanced industrialized	161	26.6
Supranational	34	5.6
Third World	33	5.4
Others	26	4.3
Socialist countries	3	0.4
Total	603	99.6*

*Percentage is below 100 due to the rounding effect.

category third. The Third World and Socialist countries rank fourth and sixth respectively.

What emerges from this distribution is that CANA reports primarily actors from the Caribbean, exactly the kind of lopsided coverage the Western news agencies were criticized for by Third World countries. In addition, the regional cooperation among Third World countries advocated in the NWICO debate is not reflected in CANA news. Another feature of the distribution (Table 6.13) worth pointing to is that the top three categories of actors most reported in the news are Minister/Government Official, Industry/Corporate Official and Head of State, which account for 178, 96 and 86 stories respectively, while Ordinary Citizens are present in only 10 stories. The top three fall into the category commonly referred to as 'elite actors', and that these are given the greatest prominence shows the elitist character of CANA foreign news, as well as the reinforcement of the existing social structure in which ordinary citizens are marginalized.

The domestic news: CANA covers the Caribbean
In studying CANA's domestic news, as with NAN, the aim was to identify the dateline of stories in terms of their urban or rural origin (Table 6.14). In this regard, it is again interesting to note the massive imbalance that favours urban centres (94.1 per cent of all stories), the residence of society's bureaucratic, corporate, diplomatic and academic elites. If the existing international information order is one of imbalance favouring the powerful and stronger nations, the domestic information order is no less fair.

Story types
In terms of story focus (Table 6.15), this disparity is continued: Economics, Accidents/Disasters/Scandals, Sports and Politics are

Table 6.13 *Regional distribution of actor types in CANA's foreign news*

Actor type	Caribbean	Socialist	Third World	Advanced industrialized	Others	UN	All
Minister/govt official	93	4	19	47	4	11	178
Industry/corporate official	52	0	3	37	4	0	96
Head of State	61	2	6	14	2	1	86
Group of nations	15	0	4	7	2	6	34
Regular forces of state	13	0	5	9	3	0	30
Legislature	15	0	2	11	1	0	29
Sports figures	17	0	0	7	4	0	28
News media/journalists	11	0	2	7	1	0	21
Criminal	12	0	5	3	0	0	20
Trade union/workers	10	3	2	3	0	0	18
Academic/scientist	6	2	0	5	1	2	16
Ambassador/diplomat	2	1	3	5	2	3	16
International government organizations	4	0	2	3	2	3	14
Judiciary/judges	10	0	2	2	0	0	14
Others	4	2	2	4	1	1	14
Religious bodies	5	0	2	4	2	0	13
Legitimate opposition	5	0	1	7	0	0	13
Pressure groups	5	0	3	3	0	0	11
Ordinary citizens	9	0	1	0	0	0	10
Royalty	2	0	1	5	0	0	8
The United Nations	0	0	0	2	0	6	8
Celebrities	6	0	0	0	0	0	6
Military	0	0	2	4	0	0	6
Non-legt opposition	2	0	4	0	0	0	6
Regular army	0	0	2	3	1	0	6
Irregular dissident group	0	0	0	0	0	0	0
Other international bodies	0	0	0	0	0	0	0
Total	359	14	73	192	30	33	701

Table 6.14   *Setting of domestic news in CANA's news bulletins*

Story type	Number of stories	%
Urban	32	94.1
Rural	2	5.8
Total	34	99.9

Table 6.15   *Distribution of story types in CANA's domestic news by setting*

Story type	Urban	Rural	Both
Economics	12	0	12
Accidents/disasters/scandals	6	4	10
Sports	6	1	7
Politics	7	0	7
Aid	5	0	5
Crime	4	1	5
Personalities	4	0	4
Culture and the arts	3	0	3
Developing issues	3	0	3
Social services	3	0	3
Science and technology	2	0	2
Military	1	0	1
Religion	1	0	1
Total	57	6	63

covered more prominently in the urban centres, giving the impression that there exist only economics, politics and sport in these centres. That accidents, disasters and scandals are found in both urban and rural areas reflects the kind of fate that accompanies a marginalized people, whether in the rural areas or the urban slums. It is, however, interesting to note that the little heard about Development is reported in an urban setting, thus removing the rural populace once more from the processes of so-called development.

Actor types
The three most prominently reported types of actor (Table 6.16) in CANA's domestic news are Minister/Government Official, Head of state and Industry/Corporate Official, followed by Diplomat, Sports figures and Journalists. It is again interesting to note that Ordinary Citizens continue in their position of marginality, being reported on only four occasions.

Table 6.16 *Distribution of actor type by setting in CANA's domestic news*

Actor type	Urban	Rural	Both
Minister/government official	151	9	160
Head of State	79	3	82
Industry/corporate official	41	0	41
Ambassador/diplomat	34	0	34
Sports figures	31	3	34
News media/journalists	23	2	25
Criminals/prisoners	19	2	21
Judiciary	15	1	16
Academic/scientists	14	0	14
Entertainers	11	3	14
Ruling party	6	3	9
Group of nations	7	1	8
Regular forces of state	6	1	7
Other bodies	6	0	6
Religious body/clergy	5	1	6
Ordinary citizens	4	0	4
International governmental orgs	3	0	3
Trade union	3	0	3
Pressure group	2	0	2
Students	2	0	2
Traditional rulers	2	0	2
Non-legitimate opposition	0	0	0
Regular army	0	0	0
Total	464	29	493

Conclusion

The data collected in the course of this analysis indicate that far from fracturing the old information order, national and regional news agencies in the Third World actually consolidate that order in a number of ways.

They do this by relying on the same international news agencies for the greater part of their foreign news content and by relegating the general news service to the back seat in favour of the more viable economic or financial services that may help consolidate revenue bases and generate profit. The search for a viable revenue base, especially in an era of dwindling government subvention, has led to the commercialization of the News Agency of Nigeria, thus making access to the agency's services a highly monetary function. Several Third World news agencies want to follow in the footsteps of CANA, a 'successful' agency that started generating profit, thanks to the marketing of the Reuters financial data file to the corporate public of the Caribbean region (see Martin and Musa, 1987).

The old order is further consolidated as Third World news agencies select certain news types, locations and actors for inclusion in news bulletins, while eliminating others. Yet a demonstrable rise in the quantity of regional and national news flows in most Third World countries (in favour of various indigenous agencies) is not accompanied by a similar increase in quality.

Emphasis on balancing information flows and creating a new order at the international level has led to a neglect of the domestic dimension of the information order which suffers from another massive imbalance: all these limitations or shortcomings constrain Third World news agencies from providing alternative news. They are thus forced to disseminate a news product that reflects a skewed version of reality in so many ways that, in the final analysis, consolidate the prevailing order, both nationally and internationally.

Nevertheless, a lesson can be learned from the various attempts to create news self-reliance in the countries of the Third World: neither state structures as in NAN nor private enterprise as in CANA hold out any meaningful hope for realizing the New World Information and Communication Order.[3] Neither structure represents the expressions and desires of the majority of Third World citizens, but of their corporate and ruling classes. The right to self-determination and the NWICO can only be realized through the participation and involvement of the great majority of these citizens. In this context, democratization of the communication process and structures is fundamental for the realization of the New World Information and Communication Order.

Notes

1. The negotiating team was set up to discuss the findings and proposals of two different studies commissioned to establish a Caribbean regional news agency. The first was a UNESCO feasibility study which appeared in 1969 as a report entitled *Commonwealth Caribbean Regional Cooperation in News and Broadcasting Exchange*; the second was a 1972 UNDP-commissioned re-examination of the subject.

2. Among others, PANA aims to promote development journalism, so its news content always contains a heavy emphasis on development issues.

3. We need to understand the nature, composition and character of the post-colonial state in order to appreciate the behaviour of its dominant institutions (see, for example, Barnett in this volume, Alavi, 1972; Beckman, 1982; Leys, 1981).

7

Communication and Global Security:
The Challenge for the Next Millennium

Phil Harris

In November 1994, Inter Press Service (IPS) celebrated its thirtieth anniversary. From its creation in 1964 to today, IPS has made giant strides in creating a global information agency which ranks alongside other major international news agencies with more than a century of experience and consolidation.

IPS has rapidly developed as an international news agency, with staff and infrastructure in over 100 countries in all regions of the world. It has achieved in just three decades what many other news agencies have taken more than a century to put in place. But, just as the world scenario has changed dramatically in this same period, particularly in the last six or so years, so too has IPS.

The major new factor at the global level that has forced IPS to identify the best ways of taking the agency forward into the next century is the post-1989 change in the international system, with the collapse of the Soviet Union and communism, and the subsequent threat to the identity of the 'Third World' as an entity 'balanced' between two major superpowers.

The dismantling of the Berlin Wall, the prospect of a 'new world order' (however fragile the first steps may have been) and the dilemma these developments mean for the countries of the South have obliged IPS to reconsider its role as a Third World news agency and as an alternative to the major traditional news agencies.

While never a homogeneous bloc, the Third World is witnessing massive internal schisms that threaten to unravel the common thread that runs through all societies suffering more or less serious forms of underdevelopment. At the same time, the newly independent republics of the former Soviet Union are vying for the attention of the international donor community, threatening to divert the focus from the suffering of two-thirds of the world's population. Even worse, these new republics (not to mention an increasing number of major industrialized countries) are themselves afflicted with some of the more negative conditions that were once believed to be synonymous with the Third World alone: unemployment, poverty, homelessness, internal social conflict, refugee movements, migration, and so on.

Numerous experts are now saying the concept of the 'Third World' is dead; there are no longer the other two worlds, the industrialized and the communist. To a certain extent this is true, but it does not contain the whole truth.

What is happening at the planetary level in the few years that remain before the dawn of the twenty-first century is a mushrooming of threats to humankind at the individual and social levels. The menace of nuclear annihilation may appear to have disappeared with the end of the Cold War, but a whole series of new threats now hang over individuals as physical and social beings, and these threats know no geographical or cultural boundaries. They range from environmental pollution, through the collapse of welfare values, to denial of basic human rights.

It is within this context that IPS took the decision at the start of the 1990s to update its role as an international news agency, originally set up to give prominence to the voices of the developing world. Today, the challenge is to transform the agency into a truly global communication system dedicated to offering a differentiated 'market' – or, more accurately, 'constituency' – systematic, continuous and in-depth coverage of global issues.

Nowhere is this more important than when working with the international non-governmental organization (NGO) community. If the decade of the 1980s was one in which NGOs expanded rapidly, widening the scope of their activities and consolidating themselves within their respective societies, the 1990s represents a major turning point in terms of their intrinsic relevance to political activity at local, regional and international level.

In fact, the collapse of state communism in the countries of the former Soviet Union and Eastern Europe, and the disappearance of bipolar superpower rivalry, provided fertile ground for the transformation of NGOs into representatives of 'civil society', a concept that grew out of the ashes of the 'old world order' and the hopes for a 'new world order' that would be characterized by greater social participation in decision-making and policy implementation.

To a certain extent also, the 'triumph' of one type of political system over another (dramatically represented by the tearing down of the Berlin Wall), heralded a new era in which, in theory at least, the 'civil society' could begin to exert an increasingly important role as a counterbalance to an established system of power that suddenly found itself without an opposing power system. In a sense, what we see today are the first steps in replacing a decade-long relationship of political bipolarism with a new model of bipolarism at both political and societal levels. The new protagonist on the scene is 'civil society', which is steadily developing models and paradigms for injecting new life into old forms of relations between those who hold political power and those who do not.

One concrete manifestation of the extent to which NGOs, in the name of 'civil society', have come to acquire a role of major relevance was represented by the 1992 Earth Summit in Rio de Janeiro, where NGOs were recognized as 'legitimate' participants in the design of policies and plans to regulate action on the environmental front. Indeed, it was also largely thanks to concentrated NGO activity and pressure that the world's policy-makers actually came together in Rio to work out an action plan for the environment that subsequently saw the light of day as 'Agenda 21'.

The NGO Forum that ran alongside the official UN Conference on Environment and Development (UNCED) in Rio has since been followed by similar fora at the World Conference on Human Rights in Vienna (1993), the International Conference on Population and Development in Cairo (1994) and the World Summit for Social Development in Copenhagen and the Fourth World Conference on Women in Beijing (both in 1995), and Habitat II in Istanbul (1996).

Meanwhile, the events of 1989 and the new global political scenario in the making also represented a major new challenge for news organizations like IPS, which had originally been created to report on the political, social, economic and cultural development of the countries of the Third World, a geo-political construct that had been sustained by the rivalry between the two political superpower rivals of the Cold War era. Since its creation. IPS has also been working steadily to create new channels of communication South–South and South–North, with the aim of providing communication 'space' to those sectors traditionally neglected by or marginalized from the mainstream information circuits, and to involve new 'actors' in communication at national, regional and international levels.

With the major reshuffling of the international political cards represented by the end of that era, IPS has begun work on redesigning its objectives and activities in such a way as to be able to meet both its original mandate (since the development problems of the South did not disappear overnight with the collapse of the Berlin Wall) and a new objective: global human security.

The concept of global human security is based on the simple premise that the end of the Cold War may have been seen in many quarters as a major step towards the freedom of the planet's inhabitants from the threat of nuclear holocaust, but that peoples everywhere face more insidious threats to their well-being (such as poverty, unemployment, lack of social integration and denial of rights) – and these latter threats know no national or regional boundaries: they are global.

The information material provided by IPS has a special focus on issues that concern the underdeveloped, the poor, the marginalized, and the countries of the South in their unequal relationships with the North, and on common global issues that cut across South–North borders and areas of interest.

Communication, development and global human security

The Cold War may be over; the threats are not. The victors of the confrontation seem to be almost as troubled as the vanquished. The terrifying dimension of the global ecological drama, the lack of sustainable economic answers to the current crisis and the startling post-1989 collapse of models, concepts and ideological reference points has left the world on the edge of the abyss: survival offers no choice but a new political framework for international relations.

Important though the question of 'what went wrong?' is, the immediate task facing committed communicators is simply to put the issue firmly back on the international agenda, to start tracing the directions for crucial international political understanding. The world, the physical world, can no longer support the insane concepts of separate destinies, runaway consumerism, mushrooming military spending, thoughtless depletion of natural resources and the chronic blind eye towards underdevelopment. And the world, the thinking world, those in power, must react.

The possible scope of reactions varies. The idea of 'global interdependence' was agreed at the Rio Earth Summit. It sums up a number of basic, simple truths; for example, that the world's resources are limited, that gross inequalities and injustice bring not only suffering to millions of human beings, but catastrophe to the environment. It recognizes that environmental depletion in one part of the world will inevitably take its toll in other parts. In other words, it pictures the world as one.

The Earth Summit saw the largest ever participatory process in history, in terms of numbers of heads of state, of NGOs, of the private sector and of international organizations, and it was this new mix of official and 'unofficial' sectors that adopted the concept of global security as a new element in international cooperation. But the concept of 'global security' emerged during the Cold War as the point of balance to be reached among different military threats. That concept was very much related to the inter-governmental sphere, the natural outgrowth of a highly dubious idea of national security which gave the State the task of defining the individual's space for action and his or her duty to defend the state.

It is a crucial and new fact that Rio changed the sense of the concept away from that of a global agreement among states to avoid military threats into a wider and more sound concept: that threats are not only posed by military conflicts; that mismanagement of the environment and of the planet, for example, are also very much direct threats for peoples and societies everywhere.

It is a giant step in the direction of building the concept that we live today in a very interconnected planet, and that we are all globally responsible for its management. All states have an equal obligation which goes beyond their national sovereignty but, at the end of the day, it is still very much an inter-governmental concept. The limits of the concept of national sovereignty have been dramatically heightened by the realities of today: the massive flows of migrants from South to North and the daily dramatic scenes of famine in sub-Saharan Africa that have shaken the comfortable existence of many in the North and brought home a message many would have preferred not to hear – that acute poverty in one part of the world is inevitably reflected elsewhere and everywhere; that excessive richness is not possible without hurting others; that extreme suffering causes bitterness and holds the seeds of unrest.

Tribalism, xenophobia, racial and political intolerance, and economic protectionism are just a few of the hallmarks of the beginning of the post-Cold War era, both North and South. We just do not know what is going on. We cannot control the situation. We have lost our long-established enemies; many of us are looking for new ones; some have already found theirs. We cannot yet see what lies ahead, but it does not look very pleasant if we let the blind forces of 'basic instinct' take over.

The moment has come to recognize the key role to be played by the individual as the main actor in the socio-political process, through the explosion of 'civil society' in which ever-increasing groups of citizens begin organizing themselves for the good of their societies at a moment in which the very concept of *the state* is in serious difficulty.

There is no doubt that it is the participation of members of that social fabric, both South and North, that has added a radically different reality to political, cultural and economic development in recent years. It is this social participation that puts the human factor into global security. In this context, defining the issue in these terms leads to reflection on the famous opening phrase of the UN Charter: 'We, the people of the world'. Today, that has become translated, for all practical intents and purposes, into: 'We, the governments of the world'.

That brings us to the challenge of defining a new political framework for North–South relations, and therefore for international cooperation. It is in the interests of all the people of the planet that we solve the problems that are a threat to humanity of today. The development effort of the South is not a local problem, of interest just to the people of the South. It is equally in the interests of the people of the North to solve problems that could pose a threat to them.

Official Development Assistance (ODA) cannot therefore be seen as it was at the height of the Cold War, as a variable in the East–West struggle. It cannot be seen as a sentiment of solidarity with the poor, or as a question of social justice. It is in the very personal interests of the people of the North that a very small amount of money (we are talking of less than 1 per cent of GNP, much of which flows back to the North anyway), should go towards eradicating the causes of those negative phenomena that can affect their work, their health, their very existence. But to achieve this, positive thinking and positive action is required. No new models, no new projects, no new hegemonies, no new universal truths – just new thinking. But to be really new, the thinking has to be matched with facts. Today we are witnessing a serious crisis of development aid, which is being cut everywhere. Of course, it is easy to look at the new priorities of Eastern Europe, Russia and Central Asia as the immediate causes of this crisis. But this is misleading, because what is in fact happening is that with the end of the Cold War, the whole notion of 'Third World' is in crisis.

Part of the answer could be that the Third World is no longer of strategic importance. It is the old phenomenon of *realpolitik* versus ethics. Foster Dulles, talking about Nicaraguan dictator Anastasio Somoza, once eloquently said: 'He is a son of a bitch, but he is our son of a bitch.' The Cold War gave birth to and nurtured countless sons of bitches all over the globe.

In the 50 years since the end of the Second World War, we were all brought up with the idea that we had different destinies. The people who lived in the East had theirs, those in the West had theirs. Caught in the middle was the Third World, which did not invent the Cold War – it was its victim, even as it is now the victim of peace. So the Third World also tried to invent its own destiny, which was to be different from those of the East and the West (the Non-Aligned Movement) or that of the North (the Group of 77). Now there is no longer a First World or a Second World. There cannot be a Third World. Today the term 'Third World' has lost political force, and is becoming synonymous with poverty, hunger and disaster. It is seen mainly as a problem of emergency and humanitarian aid. Europe is in a serious phase of post-Maastricht economic adjustment; Japan's economic balloon is greatly deflated, and (like Europe) it will take two or three years to re-inflate; and the United States is in deep economic trouble.

The sum total is less money. There is even less charity for those perceived by many in the North as the 'beggars of the world'. Recent years have seen an increasing – today, rapidly increasing – tendency to cut ODA. This trend was already in the offing with the new pressing requests for assistance from Eastern Europe: it has now become an inevitable fact

At a further level of analysis, and one which requires greater space and depth, it has to be stressed that a number of tools of development policy have been discarded in this process of reducing funds. For example, the multilateral system has been suffering: not only has the provision of voluntary funds not kept pace with pledges, but very fundamental global commitments in aid sectors such as child welfare, population, environment, science and technology, industrial development and education, which were adopted just a few years ago, are now well below required levels.

Geographic areas are also being reconsidered: it is no mystery that in the industrialized North, Africa is seen more and more as a 'black hole'. A special case in point is the issue of information and communication which received 0.4 per cent of ODA in 1991, and now probably stands at no more than 0.2 per cent (figures from the Development Assistance Committee (DAC) of the OECD). But, while many agree that you cannot have development without participation, it is difficult to see how you can have participation without communication.

In this context, it may appear little more than an academic exercise to discuss and agree on communication codes. But such an exercise is extremely important for international understanding. In recent decades, we have seen codes of communications which have corresponded to the sentiments expressed by donor countries for the people of the South. In the 1960s, the term was 'aid', which was abandoned as a result of the increasing partnership with recipient countries. In the 1970s we moved on to the term 'solidarity', which was clearly a bridge between two different destinies. In the 1980s, the new code became 'interdependence', which was based on the perception that we were all in the same boat, and that trade was vital for everybody. But, in reality, the decade of the 1980s was widely recognized throughout Latin America as 'the lost decade' and, indeed, most of the developing world went backwards, becoming net capital exporters subsidizing the rich North.

We do not, therefore, have to look for a new code of communications on the basis of which to build up a new political framework for North–South relations. It is the other way around: we have to look for a new framework and then find the appropriate code of communications. Maybe the term 'Third World' is now obsolete. But the problems of the South – and the people of the South – are not, and neither are their relations with the North, in a world where we no longer have different destinies but only different stages of development or underdevelopment.

The common thread linking the countries of the South is the attempt to escape poverty and stunted development. The common challenge facing the countries of the South is how to create the conditions for sustainable people-centred development. But if the 1970s was a period of widespread optimism for the potential of South–South cooperation, the development crisis of the 1980s forced the countries of the South to turn inwards to deal with internal development issues, weakening the impetus behind South–South cooperation. The development crisis dramatically reduced the capacity for collective action, and expressions of joint action such as the Group of 77 found themselves less and less capable of avoiding the shifting of the debate on key development issues into institutions and mechanisms dominated by the North.

Key to the revival of the fundamental role to be played by the Group of 77, among others, is communication and information, the amalgam that can bring nations and people of the South together, that can put key issues back on the global agenda, and that is all the more necessary in view of the fact that the North is well equipped with a sophisticated media and information system that functions to support and promote the value system of interests that lie at the heart of the North's agenda.

The importance of communication and information has taken on a new meaning in recent years, in a post-Cold War era in which the existing paradigm of superpower bipolarity has crumbled and nations, societies and peoples are struggling to orient themselves to a new global reality. Communication lies at the heart of this process of reorientation. Communication is the means through which the voice of the people and nations can be expressed, through which awareness can be created about the importance of the issues and processes that interest the countries of the South, issues and processes which have not disappeared with the fall of the Berlin Wall but have taken on new meaning and new urgency.

As international attention is pulled this way and that, first to this new crisis then to the next, dictated to by an international information system geared to presentation of sporadic, one-off events that flare up and mysteriously disappear off the face of the news map as suddenly as they arrived (the Sudans, the Angolas, the Mozambiques, the Somalias, the Iraqs, the Rwandas of the moment), the risk is that the underlying issues remain buried, unexplained, unaddressed.

Many have hailed the 'brave new world' of high-tech information as the 'global village', a world in which peoples everywhere are bombarded with news from everywhere and thus know more about what is happening everywhere. The reality is somewhat different: the globalization of information is a process in which the 'lowest common denominator' triumphs, in which the complexity of issues and processes disappears.

Against this background there remains the simple – but serious – fact that although the Cold War may be over, ethnic wars are mushrooming. Superpower conflict has given way to pressure for a unipolar 'new world order'. The developing countries are fast disappearing from the map of public interest (if they ever occupied any form of prominence in the first place) as international attention is diverted towards the fragmentation of nation states in the former 'Socialist bloc'.

What does this mean for the communicator?
Traditionally, the value system underlying the operations of the media worldwide has led journalists and other operators in the information sector to highlight the negative and conflictual: *bad news* is 'good news', *good news* is a non-sell. Nowhere is this more evident than in reporting across the North–South divide, and above all in reporting the realities of the Third World for publics in the Northern industrialized (some would say 'developed') hemisphere of the planet.

But the media have a duty to help people understand the situation in Third World countries as it affects the North, because the only way to mobilize the political will necessary to deal with issues of interdependence is through public opinion – one of the most important challenges in North–South relations.

The focus of the media on the negative, on conflict, on the sensational, on disaster, on corruption, on the abnormal, renders traditional information media practically institutionally incapable of producing messages that are conducive to the peace process or to creating what might be termed a *culture of security*. This term refers to the framework of conditions and values that are prerequisites for rendering society (at all levels: local, national, regional, international) conflict-free and thus in a position to meet more effectively basic human needs and ensure basic human rights.

It has to be admitted that unfortunately for the peoples of the Third World, in many, many cases, the information media have been even more guilty than their counterparts in the North of actively promoting a culture that does not lend itself readily to the creation of a climate of peace because they have been, and still are, closely tied to ruling and economic elite interests. From the point of view of the South, therefore, what is needed first and foremost is the liberation of information media from the ties of those interests that have little to gain from peace, and to create the conditions for the full and free development of democratic forms of communication that permit the people to participate actively in dialogue and consultation.

However, it has to be noted that the destiny of the Third World is not only a question of the policies adopted by its political and economic elites; it is closely intertwined with the international strategies designed in the ruling chambers and boardrooms of the major powers of the North. In this context, it has to be noted that the Western media have not informed their publics about the gross inequities in the ever-present and never-reformed international economic system which divides the world into the 'haves' and the 'have-nots', into North and South.

Erskine Childers, an adviser to the United Nations, has argued that it was the establishment media that helped kill all proposals for a New International Economic Order 15 years ago, both by editorializing against it and by ignoring arguments from the Third World that a more equitable system was also in the interests of the North.[1] Today, a major concern is that the chances for future progress in North–South cooperation have deteriorated in the last ten years, in large part because the Third World has lost its geo-political significance, and has been losing it even more rapidly in the aftermath of the collapse of the Berlin Wall and the end of the Cold War.

According to US communication sociologist George Gerbner, the New World Information and Communication Order (NWICO) is being implemented in reverse: there is less balance than ever in the news flows between North and South, and there is now greater potential for hostilities between North and South.[2] Gerbner has referred to the 'historic change in the total cultural environment' that has taken place in recent years, in which events are made possible and propelled by a 'tidal wave called television' controlled by a 'shrinking conglomerate of companies that have something to sell'. At the centre of this change is an increasingly homogenized depiction of the world and the pervasive role of violence in it.

The challenge facing communications today is how to convey information to people who do not normally seek it, to make new efforts to gain control over the media, to put cultural policy-making on the political agenda, and to devise ways of ensuring participation that is freer, more democratic, and presents a wider range of alternatives. This should be what lies at the heart of the much-voiced 'New World Order' that we are told the world is about to usher in, but we have to be careful to place the debate on a new world order in the correct historical perspective.

As Kofi Awoonor, Ghana's Permanent Representative to the United Nations and then chair of the Group of 77, pointed out in mid-1991, throughout its history the West has not accorded the status of 'man' to everyone and has upheld exploitation and discrimination of all kinds.[3] In the last decade, he argued, there has been a widening of the gap between rich and poor, with many developing countries having been forced into adopting 'socially debilitating economic reforms' which, unaccompanied by reforms in the international order, are likely to come to nothing. As noted by Awoonor:

> The *only* obstacle toward peaceful changes in the illegitimate world order is the lack of will on the part of the current beneficiaries. That is why the decolonization of information and communication should command the highest priority attention in the North–South dialogue.

The end of the Cold War is not a victory if it is transformed into the basis for a world order that consigns the majority of its citizens to malnourishment, illiteracy, hunger, racial abuse and continued conflict.

What characterized the 'old order' was the dependence of the Third World on the two superpowers and other industrialized countries, the gaping divide between North and South in technological knowledge and its use, the cultural domination of the South by the North, and the generation of instability, rivalry and war arising from these factors.

With the end of the Cold War, many have argued that the threat of superpower military aggression is no longer a sword of Damocles hanging over the international community. As a consequence, it is argued, the world has become a more secure place to inhabit. This view is based on a myopic definition of 'security' which fails to recognize that global security is not just a question of freedom from military or armed aggression but more fundamentally a composite concept that depends on a series of 'freedoms', including freedom from hunger and want, freedom from environmental degradation, and freedom from stereotypes and prejudice. It is not just a question of reducing the threat of armed belligerence but of how we go about satisfying basic societal needs such as food, clothing, housing, education and health care.

What is called for in today's rapidly changing – and deteriorating

– world is a communication environment supportive of global human security, where the emphasis is placed on the well-being of society at all levels. Citizens need much more individualized information to understand the complex reality that surrounds them. The faster events unfold and change takes place, the greater the need for comprehensive and continuous information that provides the necessary context and reference points for interpreting the world. But this is something that goes far beyond the reach or even competence of the news media *per se*. The demand is for *communication* interchange and dialogue between and among persons and groups, in full respect of different social, political, economic or cultural status.

Communication is the amalgam that can help unite people of different cultural, political and socio-economic backgrounds, and nowhere has this become more necessary than in Europe where there has been a recent increase in xenophobic pressure and attempts to 'protect' group and/or ethnic interests from presumed external threats to well-being. Fear and distrust are the offspring of ignorance and prejudice which can only be combated with balanced information and democratic communications. Only better communications can help break down the stereotypes that create tension and conflict between peoples.

In this context, the Third World has traditionally been under-reported and misrepresented by the Western media, in large measure due to its geo-physical and 'psychological' distance, but in many European countries the Third World is now much closer at hand thanks to the immigrant community, and consequently the need for communicators to provide 'host' publics with fair and balanced information about Third World realities has become all the more urgent. Part of the challenge is to do away with 'information terrorism' and start explaining unfamiliar trends, processes and phenomena rather than rejecting or misrepresenting them.

This is where organizations like IPS come in. When it was created it was clearly identified by its founders as a new mechanism for the promotion of intercultural communication (between people of diverse cultural backgrounds within national societies, within geographical regions and at the international level, in both South–South and South–North directions). The need to establish an organization such as IPS responded directly to the recognition that much of the misunderstanding and ignorance pervading international relations was a by-product of inadequate or non-existent communication channels. To improve understanding between peoples, it was necessary to create an infrastructure that would help permit people to communicate more effectively.

Defined in this manner, IPS came into being as an organization markedly different in orientation and structure from the major world news agencies. In fact the constitution of IPS as an international cooperative (now formally an international association) of its journalists was a deliberate demonstration of one major difference – that IPS bore no allegiance to any one national market or political base.

More importantly, however, IPS took shape as a concrete demonstration that the communication process is about more than mere information. Traditional news agencies were never designed to improve communication or increase dialogue between and among peoples, social sectors, groups and nations – they were in business almost exclusively to collect and disseminate information for reproduction in media organs worldwide. This, in essence, is a top-down process in which there is little space for dialogue, exchange of opinion, and so on. Those who own or control the media instruments and channels 'inform' those who do not, and the latter become almost 'passive' recipients of 'pictures of the world' prepared for them by others with no possibility of helping construct those images.

Communication, on the other hand, is by definition a horizontal process – an interchange between persons and groups, irrespective of social, political, economic or cultural status and background. Information is news, a product of the vertical relations between the message-makers and the message-receivers. Communication is dialogue, horizontal interaction between individuals, groups and societies.

IPS and global communication

On the basis of this premise, IPS set out in 1964 to help promote a new global communication strategy in which the various forces actively involved in supporting and implementing the processes of development and cooperation could find their space. The principal aim was to put into practice a communication system that would help ever wider 'audiences' or 'constituencies' understand and begin to play an active role in the surrounding environment, to be able to act and not just react.

How did IPS conceive this 'challenge' and how is it actually being implemented today?
IPS operates on a number of different, but complementary, fronts that distinguish it from conventional news media and make it more than just another news agency, even if IPS recognizes the news component in any communication strategy and does place major,

but not exclusive, emphasis on its news-gathering and dissemination operations.

The organization's operations are divided into three major branches, which taken together are directed toward improving South–South and South–North communication capacities, and opening up space to those traditionally marginalized or excluded from communication systems:

1. *IPS Third World News Agency* – an independent, non-profit information service specializing in in-depth and contextualized coverage of processes and issues that affect the Third World and the development process.
2. *IPS Telecommunications* – a division created to help upgrade Third World communication and information structures through the transfer of technology and training programmes in which IPS know-how is adapted to specific Third World needs.
3. *IPS Projects* – a division established to execute a wide range of programmes in cooperation with international and multilateral donor agencies in the fields of training, information exchange and the setting up of alternative networks that give communication access to 'new actors' (such as rural populations, migrants, refugees, children and women).

The importance of the latter two operational divisions is an indication of the stress IPS puts on the promotion and opening up of communication links between Third World societies, between the Third World and the North, and between non-governmental and other non-elite sectors.

With the 1990s having opened with the tumultuous and historic changes in various corners of the globe, but with the vast majority of humankind still (and in many senses increasingly) cast to the fringes of international society, it is the task of news agencies concerned with development issues to find appropriate ways of approaching and covering the plethora of issues that make up the on-the-ground situation in the developing countries.

Take just the core issue of development, for example. Development is intrinsically about people – it is by and large a question of human development. The key concerns that merit attention are:

- the extent to which people's basic physical needs are being met;
- the extent to which people's socio-cultural, political and intellectual rights are safeguarded and promoted;
- the extent to which agricultural, industrial and other activities are carried out in such a way as to ensure a liveable environment for future generations.

The last aspect touches on the much-used (and oft-abused) idea of 'sustainable development', a concept which is central to current concern with development policy and its impact on the environment. 'Sustainable development' refers to forms, policies and programmes that are designed to meet the needs and aspirations of present generations without compromising those of future generations. The concept recognizes that development can only be sustained through the informed and active participation of the people whose improved welfare is the objective.

Unfortunately for those of us involved in the business of communicating to and with others on development issues, 'development journalism' has been done so sloppily for so long by so many people. That does not mean the concept of and need for development journalism is no longer valid, but it does mean taking care to provide information in a way that avoids hackneyed phraseology and says something interesting and intelligent. Above all, it means discarding the myth that development reporting accentuates the positive – but it doesn't accentuate the negative either.

Coverage of human-interest development reveals the reality of rural life, the grime, the injustice, the squalor, as well as the success stories: the kind-hearted, the brave, the ordinary . . . the everyday. Development writers have often been told: don't touch coups, earthquakes and disasters – they're told that's for the event-oriented Northern wire services. This is nonsense. Coups have to be touched – better still, predicted. The task of the journalist should be to report the processes, the common citizen's gripes which feed the collective national frustrations that periodically erupt in military mutinies.

Development reporting is also writing about earthquakes and floods and typhoons, kneeling down to the human level of the tragedies – the casualty patterns of floods in Bangladesh that wash away the landless who settled in danger zones because they had nowhere else to live, or the deadly landslides in Nepal caused by tree-cutting higher up the mountains. Development is about change. People, societies, value systems and even landscapes evolve. The small things have to be woven into a larger pattern. As snakes disappear, so do the charmers.[4]

Communication and dialogue: promoting the culture of peace

If a 'new world order' is to mean anything, it must give priority to the human being and people's welfare, since crisis in society or between societies is a crisis of collective security. Peace is a question of human security and, in an interdependent world, a question of global human security that does away with the glaring differences between North and South.

In the transition to a 'new world order', whatever shape that order may take, the developing countries stand to lose heavily if North–South economic imbalances are not adjusted. But progress in political détente has not seen its counterpart in economic entente, so that while the developing world is opening its doors to global integration, the developed countries are erecting ever greater protectionist barriers that penalize the already struggling economies of the South.

Communication is the key to promoting a vigorous dialogue between the Third World and the industrialized countries on global economic issues such as debt and the environment, to put an end to the crisis of development and to help narrow the rift that separates the two hemispheres of the planet. It is imperative to find forms of communication and information that actively serve to create a culture of peace and solidarity, of cooperation and dialogue. Only if this culture of peace exists can one begin to speak of the security of each and every individual inhabiting the planet, a security that derives not only from the lack of violence but from the guarantee that basic needs can be met.

Notes

1. Erskine Childers was speaking at a meeting of the IPS International Council on Information and Development in Rome in 1991, organized to discuss international media coverage of the Gulf War.

2. George Gerbner, speaking at the same meeting.

3. Kofi Awoonor, speaking at the same meeting.

4. The author thanks Kunda Dixit, Regional Director for IPS Asia-Pacific, for this description of 'development journalism'.

8

An Inclusive NWICO: Cultural Resilience and Popular Resistance

Pradip N. Thomas

Nearly two decades have passed since the publication of the MacBride Report. During the last 20 years, extraordinary changes have taken place at both international and national levels in the realms of politics and economics. The dismantling of the former Soviet Union and Eastern Europe, the continuing imbroglio in West Asia and the growth of ethno-religious conflict in various parts of the world are some of the more obvious discontinuities in a turbulent era. Ideologies and received ways of understanding have been interrogated and exposed for their lack of commitment to the democratic norm. This is as true of the former Soviet version of socialism as of the West's version of monetarist capitalism.

The Non-Aligned Movement (NAM) is a mere semblance of its former self. Its original role as a 'tribune' of the South, exemplified in its support for freedom movements in South Africa and Palestine, its independent stance in support of non-alignment as a course of action to be followed by the South in the face of the politics of the Cold War, as well as its role as a protector of the economic interests of the South, have been seriously undermined by internal contradictions and its inability to redress post-Cold War realities, including the issue of restructuring the United Nations.

UNESCO, like the UN system in general, is undergoing a major crisis. Its global agenda for 'communications' is notable for its singular lack of commitment to the democratization of communications structures, processes and environments.

The liberal economic climate and global flows in information and culture aided by the growth of the transnational empire have led to a homogenization of structures, processes, tastes and expectations. On the one hand, the policy-making power of the transnational corporations (TNCs) has increased in contrast to that of governments and international regulatory organizations. On the other hand, in spite of the peripheral location of the South, there have been significant attempts at redefining power relationships, particularly in the realm of technological innovation – the recent history of the satellite industry in India as well as the development of the PARAM super-computer are instances of indigenization, despite a US-led moratorium on transfers of technology in certain key areas.

The exercise of power and its direct or indirect manifestations in public life has been challenged by 'resistances' at various levels by environmental groups, women's organizations and labour unions, among other grassroots forms. The recent readings of subaltern history have demonstrated the resilience of popular resistance, its autonomy and strength. The volumes in the 'Subaltern' series edited by Ranajit Guha (1982–92) contain numerous illustrations of peasant rebellions in India that contributed to the making of an independent country. These struggles are, in each case, shown to be autonomous manifestations of nationalism, independent of the elite, their discourses and their ways of understanding reality. What these studies have established is the existence of 'resistances' that are based on categories of thought that have led to understanding and action at local-specific levels, independent of received, dominant discourses from both the Left and the Right. These studies are based on another reading and interpretation of the exercise of power. They also warn us against the tendency to reify the notion of power, its exercise or its denouement. The changeable status of power situations, motivations, objectives and processes, and the possibility of institutionalized 'resistances' signify a terrain that needs to be mapped prior to evolving a coherent policy on the democratization of the media. A pragmatic assessment of the politics of cultural change, as well as an understanding of needs and expectations, is a necessary premise for evolving coherent, realizable communication objectives.

In a sense, the present-day changes in the political economy of nations have been the recorded events of the more manifest stirrings of history in the making. What have not been recorded, registered, let alone understood, are the reasons animating these conflicts of interests. The resurgence and resistances embodied in shared local categories (i.e. caste, religion, sub-cultural affiliation, etc.), embodied in what one critic, Ashis Nandy (1987) terms the language of 'self', 'continuity' and 'spiritualism', are in a way the latent underpinnings of history as it is forming, a history that will for the first time also be shaped by a Southern agenda. It is within this conceptual context that an understanding of NWICO, an assessment of the limitations of the alternative media movement and mapping the basis for a revitalized NWICO are situated.

NWICO: impact and limitations

That the NWICO as encapsulated in the MacBride Report has had at best only a marginal impact on the restructuring of international communications relations is a well-attested fact. While the objectives of the NWICO included the democratization of communications, the curbing of the power of the transnational media lobby and the encouragement of autonomous media policies in the developing world, its energies were primarily directed toward achieving a balance in the flow of information between the North and the South. What the NWICO provided was a 'moral platform', a *raison d'être* for the restructuring of global communications systems in favour of a system whose control was proportionately distributed between the North and the South.

The elevation of concerns in communications to a global agenda remains the most significant achievement of the NWICO. However, with significant exceptions like the Pan-African News Agency (PANA) and the fledgling Namibian Press Agency in terms of news services, the direct impact of NWICO is difficult to assess. There have been indirect fall-outs, including the formation of a variety of associations and unions of concerned journalists and communication academics like, for example, the Union for Democratic Communications and the International Organisation of Journalists; the teaching of NWICO principles at communication schools in the South; as well as a heightened sense of the worth of national culture *vis-à-vis* global culture at the level of governments in the developing world. NWICO concerns have also percolated down to grassroots levels where they have been incorporated into local agendas for the democratization of communications, and networks like the Philippine-based 'People in Communication' have taken their working philosophy from the principles of the NWICO. But such examples are few and far between.

The case of PANA may be taken as a typical illustration of a more general set of problems affecting Southern news agencies. The history of PANA, its growth and development, have been well documented (see Ansah, 1986; Churchill, 1991; Musa, 1990). At one level, it is a success story – the establishment of a regional news service ostensibly directed toward breaking the monopoly of the 'Big Four' in Africa. However, while its establishment did help the cause of an 'indigenous' news-gathering and distribution system, its continuing inability to compete with the commercial strategy of Reuters, as well as its susceptibility to political 'pulls and pressures', has in effect guaranteed a crisis in perpetuity.

Musa (1990) has drawn our attention to PANA's survival

strategy, i.e. a blind imitation of Reuters' trade in financial information. Churchill (1991) has commented on both the lack of local-level new-gathering facilities in a number of African countries that has effectively stymied PANA's operation and the fact that, while PANA has only one exchange agreement with an African state, Reuters has 39 such agreements and Agence France Presse 33. While local exigencies have played their part in frustrating the potential of relatively autonomous regional news agencies, the continuing existence of neo-colonial lines of control, particularly in the area of media policy in Africa and elsewhere, points to an enduring reality – the continued existence of classical forms of media imperialism. As Churchill (1991: 24) has pertinently remarked:

> What remains to most direct media imperialism strategy is policy-making control. France is a forerunner in this domain. Since 1968, the country has instituted annual meetings of Francophone African Ministries of Information in Paris. Coordinated by the French Foreign Secretary, the Minister of Cooperation and Culture and the director of Institute France Presse (IPF), these meetings were aimed at harmonising media policies in Francophone Africa within a general framework of French global media strategy.

Theories of 'media imperialism' have had to account for new and changing realities, emerging contradictions and shifting complexities, i.e. the reality of Southern forms of 'media imperialism' – for example, the flow of Hindi films to South Asia, the Middle East and certain parts of Africa; the extent of the Hong Kong-based 'Whampoa' group's hold over satellite-based entertainment in Asia (Star TV); and the reach of Brazil's 'Globo'. But the fact remains that enduring asymmetries and international monopolies have blocked the growth of Southern challenges to the hegemony of Western media corporations. Sinclair's (1990) assessment of the growth of the Mexican television industry, particularly Televisa, is tempered by his comment that for all its successes as a Mexican media transnational, its status is ultimately conditioned by US capital, and Mexico's dependent status in the world economy. This is a stark reminder that a form of limited incorporation has been the only fall-out after a decade or two of unequal competition.

To an extent, the foregoing examples illustrate some of the weaknesses of NWICO. The emergence of private media monopolies in the South capable of competing with established Western transnational media interests is in reality of little consequence to the democratization of communications. Nurtured on the ethics of transnational industry, i.e. quick profits, the exploitation of markets of least resistance, and the de-unionization of labour, and often in league with their counterparts in the West, these Southern corporations have merely contributed to the growth of transnational capitalism. They have for the most part been manned by private and public elites. In fact, the agenda of the NWICO was set by national elites and this was oriented toward the transfer of power to regional and national media networks rather than to the democratization of media at local levels. This is not an indictment of the concerns of the NWICO but the reiteration of a historical fact that governments in the South have more often than not used the NWICO platform for redressing international media realities rather than intra-national realities.

The Janus-like role played by Indira Ghandhi, the former Prime Minister of India, ardent supporter of the NWICO, as well as the main architect of centralized media policies in India, is a telling example of the type of political leader who supported the NWICO. Mrs Gandhi, while addressing the Non-Aligned Movement summit in New Delhi in 1976, had by then already declared a state of emergency in India. While she berated the Western media in general for distorting political realities in the South (see Righter, 1978), she had already, under the draconian Maintenance of International Security Act, imprisoned a large number of journalists opposed to the state of emergency, closed down the oppositional press (the *Indian Express* in particular) and amalgamated the existing news services in India into one centrally-controlled enterprise, Samachar; she imposed strict censorship laws and expelled a host of foreign journalists opposed to her strain of politics (see Kharkanis, 1981; Rao and Rao, 1977). This ambivalent stance continued in the 1980s with the centralization of public broadcasting on the one hand and the championing of 'justice' and 'freedom' at international fora on the other. President Suharto of Indonesia and the former President of Zambia, Kenneth Kaunda, among many other leaders from the South, may quite legitimately be taken to task for using NWICO to achieve narrow, personal ends.

The problem with the NWICO has nothing to do with its concerns *per se*, but more to do with its philosophical premises. Freedom, justice, participation and access are laudable objectives. But who defines what these are and how they are to be realized? What does a 'reciprocal' flow of communication mean in a traditional society that lives according to its own set of categories? In a context that is seeing the rise of 'many worlds and many voices', what is the point of supporting the cause of national culture instead of national cultures? Colleen Roach (1990: 296), in an article on NWICO, has identified the need for a three-pronged analytical approach, focusing on, (1) class analysis and national elites, (2) women and the New World Information and Commication Order, and (3) the case for de-linkage – as a necessary basis for evolving a new framework for NWICO. But such prescriptions are problematic, for they not only fall back on a 'conspiratorial' thesis, but also presume the worth of a particular analytical approach: class over others, such as 'caste' in India, or 'ethnicity' in South Asia in general. De-linkage, in spite of its theoretical idealism, remains an impossibly romantic solution.

There are very few examples of countries that have – at various stages in their history – opted for an isolated, independent approach to national development. Myanmar (Burma), Tanzania, Guinea-Bissau, Cuba and China followed a policy of de-linkage that was successful to a certain degree. Today, in the context of the global spread of capitalism, de-linkage as a realistic option for developing countries has become an almost improbable choice. A complex era and complex histories, both past and present, demand a sophisticated and relevant theoretical framework – one that is in tune with lived reality.

Take, for instance, the continuing conflict in the Punjab, a state in India that has for a decade or more been embroiled in a struggle against the Indian state as a whole. This is not a simple case of class struggle. It is at one and the same time a struggle between the centralizing tendencies of regionalism; a struggle over defining identities – the Sikh identity as a separate, autonomous identity from the dominant Hindu one; and a struggle over language issues – the Gurmukhi (Sikh) script versus Devanagari (Hindi), among others. These struggles are overlaid, and attain complexity in their interaction with other discourses – state security, separatism, armed struggle, Sikh fundamentalism, the Sikh diaspora, and so on. The struggle over 'communications' at both global and local levels needs to be similarly grounded in a much more thorough and analytically relevant framework.

The limitation of NWICO, as well as the alternative media scenario in general, is that they have both been supported by philosophical premises and universals that have been narrowly defined in terms of Western liberal morality and ethics. While universals are absolutely necessary, it is imperative at this stage of history that other universals from non-Western societies be allowed to contribute substantially to the overall process of defining moral and ethical universals. In other words, unless particular versions of these universals are allowed to develop in an autonomous manner, what we will be left with are restricted codes for understanding reality. Karl Otto Apels (1992: 15) has commented on this tradition of European universals and its manifestation in Western liberal thought:

It is a historical fact that ever since the start of the conquest of the world by Europe, the repeated and constant condemnations of such tragic manifestations of this imperialism as the extermination of the Indians or the African slave trade have themselves proceeded from the universalist thinking of European philosophers. This is as true of Latin American liberation theology and philosophy as it is of 'dependence theory'. It holds true to the point that in the fields of morality or legal theory, it is hard to imagine any philosophy with universalist pretensions that could attract consensus support around the world starting from premises other than those of the tradition of European thought.

If the NWICO is to remain relevant to the democratization of communications at local levels, it must be open to local-specific ways of understanding and culture-specific ways of dealing with communication problems as well as their solutions. The relevance of NWICO at an international level is of the utmost importance to democratization; however, this concern needs to be situated within a more substantive understanding of intra-national communication realities, problems and their solutions.

NWICO and communication alternatives in the South

The history of alternative communication strategies in the South predates the agenda of the NWICO. Examples of the use of the media, particularly folk forms for anti-Establishment purposes, abound from time immemorial. Periods of acute crisis caused by famine, oppression by local and national despots, and failure of 'the system' to live up to expectations, as well as the curtailment of the right to self-expression, have indirectly led communities to find alternative sources for expression, understanding and sense-making. This is as true of the role played by the Indian People's Theatre Association during the colonial area, as of, for example, popular media initiatives in Chile during the Allende era, in South Africa during the anti-apartheid struggle and the transition to democracy, during the Zimbabwean independence movement, and the EDSA revolution in the Philippines. But, unlike in former times when sustained alternatives were not the norm, the present era has witnessed the emergence of popular cultural movements, networks and a variety of groups involved in using media for alternative purposes. Popular theatre initiatives in Palestine, Kenya, Jamaica and Brazil, to name a few; women's video collectives in India; women's newsletter groups in Mexico; critical approaches to media education for local communities in South Africa; media documentation centres around the world, and networking initiatives are some of the different alternative approaches in existence today.

That these efforts to create sources of popular expression for exploring the politics of the possible stem from the NWICO is one way of understanding this relationship. Another plausible approach would be to take the position that the alternative media sector has been nurtured by an autonomous agenda and that its existence predates the concerns of the NWICO. Whatever the position taken, it can be argued that because of its location in a discourse conducted in the womb of Cold War apologetics by national elites, the NWICO has not been able to translate its rhetoric into reality, particularly at local levels.

While alternative media initiatives and movements have contributed to the democratization of communications, this movement is itself undergoing a severe crisis of credibility. The institutionalization of alternatives has been a less well-attested fact. And self-criticism has been a premium reserve, whether this be from popular cultural movements in Latin America, Asia or Africa. The reasons are manifold – co-option of such initiatives by the state, the real limits to 'conscientization' as a sustained activity, the lack of sustained theoretical development in this area, the politics of cultural praxis, the institutionalization of the non-governmental sector, the mushrooming of popular cultural initiatives that are based on an inadequate understanding of local cultural realities, a crisis of form, and the inability of popular cultural initiatives to encounter and make sense of emerging complexities at local, national and international levels. The politics of funding, the emergence of right-wing resistance, and the inability to translate the rhetoric of participation into actual performance have been some of the other reasons for this state of affairs.

To take an example, the praxis of popular theatre has definite roots in experiments carried out in Latin America by Augusto Boal, among other theatre activists. This was exported via the cultural action theories of the Brazilian pedagogue Paulo Freire to various parts of the world, India included. The wholesale importation of techniques of theatre and their limited adaptation to local cultural forms has had a negative impact on the credibility of popular theatre in India. Very few groups have made serious attempts to evolve popular theatre out of an encounter with the richness of local cultural traditions. While many groups with a smattering of knowledge of local folk forms have attempted to use folk theatre ostensibly for liberation purposes, the net effect has been rather counter-productive. More often than not, there has been popular resistance to such attempts, followed inevitably by a lack of credibility for such initiatives. Such examples abound not only in India but in other parts of the world, where the strength of tradition and the status quo have been able to withstand current popular cultural initiatives.

The promise of liberation through popular cultural struggles has not occurred, in spite of a heightened increase in popular consciousness. While crisis situations have frequently led to a consolidation of popular cultural initiatives (as in Zimbabwe during the late 1970s, in the Philippines in the mid-1980s, in South Africa in the late 1980s, and in different parts of Latin America, most notably Chile, during the last three decades), it has invariably been the case that the sustainability of these movements has been compromised in the course of time. There are effective networks of popular cultural organizations in various parts of the world, but their inability to translate their vision into a significant political alternative has been a visible limitation. On the basis of this reality, it could be argued that, given the complex nature of lived contexts and the non-correspondence of often complexly interrelated interests, identities and expectations within regions, any hope for a convergence of interests across identities, classes or castes will remain a characteristic that surfaces primarily at times of grave national crisis. Even at such times, as has been recorded in the 'Subaltern' studies series mentioned earlier, there is space for a variety of responses.

The lack of theoretical sophistication in our understanding of popular cultural struggles at local levels has been challenged by writers such as Jesus Martin-Barbero (1989, 1993), who puts forward the case for a multi-dimensional approach to the study of popular culture that is rooted in local-specific understanding of mediated reality, the transactions, negotiations and 'receptions' that are tied to context and identity, and that are changeable over time. In a real sense, his approach complements other significant attempts to understand popular perspectives – for example the victims' perspective in the case of communal riots in India (Das, 1990), localized variants of popular resistance expressed in subaltern movements (Guha, 1982), and tradition-based resistances to modernization (Nandy, 1988; Alvares, 1979). In each of these cases, the multifaceted nature of resistances, of an understanding of reality based on local categories, has been celebrated at the expense of dominant discourses and approaches to understanding reality. The following assessment illustrates some of the dimensions of this emerging understanding of popular culture:

> To ask what role the mass media play in everyday life means asking questions that would tell us what people actually do, what they listen to or look at, what they read or believe. It means finding out about that other side of communication which would reveal the *uses* people make of the media, uses by means of which communications without political

power or social representation assimilate the offers within their grasp, sexualise melodrama, derive satire from a poor sense of humour, laugh and cry without ideological change, revitalise in their own way their everyday life and traditions by converting the deficiencies into a technique with which they express their own identity. (Martin-Barbero, 1989: 23)

In part, the relative failure of popular cultural struggle can be put down to the strength of traditional structures, processes and practices, as well as the resilience of traditional culture. Popular culture in many parts of the world has not been able to provide a complete alternative to existing cultural modes. In very many instances, folk forms are a part of a seamless web of cultural continuities. They are not forms of communication outside the community, but media that are an integral part of both the ideology and consciousness of a given community.

Take, for example, the folk theatre form from Tamil Nadu, 'Terrakoothu'. Basically a form of street theatre, performances are directed toward reinforcing the logic of village Hinduism and re-integrating the community into the larger Hindu ethos. It plays an important role in consensus formation – it congeals a sense of community, reinforces the community's link to its faith, provides a sense of shared identity and maintains a continuity with tradition, presents a contextualized interpretation of the Hindu scriptures in order to cater to changing societal norms, and allows the community to participate in its rituals as well as entertainment (leisure) functions. Its reinforcement of caste divisions, legitimation of status hierarchies, and sustenance of the order of the community were by-products of this process of consensus formation. But it also has a positive role to play – preventing, accommodating, calming feelings of rootlessness/anomie and binding fissures in the community. This range of roles is the strength of traditional media, and it is the lack of it that has affected the sustainability of popular cultural struggles in various parts of the world.

NWICO towards the twenty-first century

Over the last few years, a number of media researchers has brought our attention to the fact that changing media realities at a global level makes it imperative that the NWICO restructure its global agenda. Breman (1990), for example, has analysed a key site for struggle today – the moves led by the United States to include trade in information within the general purview of the General Agreement on Tariffs and Trade (GATT); Hills (1992) has focused on the increased structural power of the United States and its role in pressurizing international organizations such as INTELSAT, the

International Telecommunications Union, GATT and the World Bank to formulate friendly telecommunication policies *vis-à-vis* the rest of the world. Negrine and Papathanasspoulos (1991) have assessed factors that have led to the 'internationalization' of television, including changes on organizational, content, funding, regulation and reception levels; and Sreberny-Mohammadi (1991) has argued the case for a much more sophisticated analysis of cultural imperialism, one that is anchored in an assessment of the culture of imperialism and its continuation in the modern era.

These new developments, and many more besides, have changed the landscape of global communications. The complex nature of changing communication realities at an international level, characterized by the concentration and diversification of transnational media monopolies, the increasing use of information technology for 'surveillance' purposes by the United States and other nations in the West, the assaults being made on the 'public' role of broadcasting and other media, make it all the more imperative that the NWICO reinforce its commitment to the democratization of communications between nations. It is absolutely necessary that a mapping of this terrain be carried out by concerned proponents of the NWICO.

NWICO has a dual role to play – at international level, and at national, regional and local levels. If the NWICO is to fulfil its mandate to the peoples of the South, it must be conversant with and receptive to voices from the South – local-specific categories, identities, structures and processes, and local ways of dealing with the democratization of communications, defining access and participation. We need to take seriously Cushman and Kincaid's (1987: 7) reading of the Eastern approaches to communication that enable 'the reflective transformation of individual subjective interpretation into sacred institutional interpretation of experience'. This 'reflective process' as the authors point out, 'is internal to the individual although it may be assisted by external messages'. We need to recognize that this is an approach to communication ethics that goes beyond the objectives of morality and inter-subjectivity to a consideration of the self in its pursuit of transcendent goals. Whereas in Buddhist ethos, *Dhukka* (sorrow) is the crux of life; *Anicca* (impermanence) is the basis for all life; *Anatta* (the absence of true self) is the only non-illusion; and *Dhamma* (the way), consisting of morality, meditation and wisdom, is the only means to the larger end of Enlightenment, we are presented with a discourse that is based on an intuitive, spontaneous knowledge of reality rather than a rational, logical one.

The issue at stake is one of recognizing the diversity of communication realities, problems and their solutions, and the corresponding need for NWICO to be open to other universals. The growing incidence of conflict around the world today, based on the politics of ethnicity, nationalism and religion, may be seen as an attempt by various 'publics' to reinstitute particular memories that had been forced into oblivion through the 'imposition of hegemonic temporalities' (Baxi, 1991: 25). The limitations of a globally applicable, patently Western version of secularism, social change and growth, couched in an Occidental framework and rooted in its 'inevitabilities', has been the stimulus for another development. In this connection, Rowe and Schelling's (1991: 228) observations on the narrowness of homogenizing tendencies worldwide, especially their denial of 'other particulars' and 'other universals', is a pointer to a new approach to understanding cultural and media realities:

> Part of the violence produced by global homogenization is the illusion that there is only one history, an illusion which suppresses the differences between the different histories lived by different groups of human beings. There is a further point: historical memory is a vital cultural action in the making, and preservation of those differences and the destruction of memory a prime means of domination. Nor is it appropriate to speak of a single popular memory: there are a variety of differentiated memories.

The challenge for NWICO in the twenty-first century includes its ability to incorporate and understand the global in the local and the local in the global (Sreberny-Mohammadi, 1991). This understanding must flow from the recognition that there are communications root-metaphors other than those from a Western origin, and must create the space for local-specific solutions to local-specific communication problems. At the same time, there is a need to re-centre people as the subject of change. In order to reconnect people to the objective of communication for social change, it is necessary that institutionalized alternatives, in theory and practice, be exorcized, and that attempts are made to evolve new alternatives based on recognition of the plurality of local cultural identities, discourses, practices and situations. Unless NWICO as a movement seriously considers the implications of these new developments, both at global and local levels, its relevance to the South may turn out to be, at best, marginal.

Note

* In preparing this chapter, the author recognizes insights shared by Philip Lee.

The Future of the Debate: Setting an Agenda for a New World Information and Communication Order, Ten Proposals*

Richard C. Vincent

The end of the Cold War has not offered a solution to many of the world's conflicts. Current world conditions have not led to a reduction in political tensions, internationally or within countries. Fundamental to these political strains are communication flows, rights and access. These were among the major issues addressed in the 1970s when the UNESCO-appointed MacBride Commission (UNESCO, 1980a) studied world communication conditions, and they appear to be just as relevant today.

The New World Information and Communication Order (NWICO) debate of the 1970s and 1980s was criticized for its inability to sharply delineate the problem, for its failure effectively to merge the NWICO with a major examination of economic concerns, and its inability to find an equitable solution to the perceived imbalance of information flow and exchange. 'So far as the [new world] information order is concerned,' observes Eli Abel, 'the plain fact is that nobody knows what it would mean. . . . The new world order obviously means different things to different people. It is more slogan than plan of action' (Abel, 1982). Obviously, this situation of uncertainty leads to some confusion.

The NWICO debates proved quite destructive for UNESCO and the World Administrative Radio Conference (WARC) dialogue on the topic. Yet UNESCO and other inter-governmental organizations (IGOs) may never have been ideal fora for the debate. It was too political an issue for bodies which are heavily controlled by Western powers and rely on them for a large share of their financial support. When the United States became uneasy with criticisms of itself and its political position, the NWICO debate in particular offered a convenient outlet for venting frustrations. The United States withdrew its membership and cited the NWICO debates as a central reason for the move. In support of the United States, both the UK and Singapore eventually withdrew their membership too, leaving UNESCO with one-third less annual funding. The United States alone had been contributing roughly a quarter of the total budget. While it is becoming increasingly clear that the Reagan administration had other motives for the withdrawal, the irony is that one reason still cited is UNESCO's support of the state licensing of journalists. While this was once advocated by Sean MacBride, it was never included in the final MacBride Commission report. The United States was lamenting its loss of control in the international decision-making body much the same as some Non-Aligned nations are today concerned with the size of the voting bloc held by the oil-rich, but relatively sparsely populated Middle East.

We are now at the point where the United States is considering re-entry into UNESCO. Yet even this is being done with caution and scepticism. In April 1993 the *Washington Post* called for re-entry in an editorial which noted that the grossly mismanaged and politicized body has changed, and 'now promotes press freedom, not government control of media' (1993: A22). In May 1993 a United Nations Association panel, headed by former Senator Robert T. Stafford, recommended re-entry (Meisler, 1993: A3). In August that year, a task force headed by Assistant Secretary of State Douglas Bennett recommended a return by October 1995 (Meisler, 1993: A3). Even with these endorsements, however, the *New York Times* (23 February 1994) urged the country not to 'rush back into UNESCO', though Secretary-General Frederico Mayor has 'cut the payroll and generally returned UNESCO to its original mission as a promoter of literacy, a protector of cultural movements and a champion of a freer flow of information'. According to the *New York Times* (1994), one of the primary roles of UNESCO should be 'to represent the world's cultural conscience by speaking out against the deliberate targeting of cherished monuments – and then to restore as best it can what wars tear apart'. With the continuing move toward political conservatism and isolationism in the US government, the eventual effect on UNESCO, as well as the United States' willingness to work in cooperation with bodies such as the United Nations, is still very much in doubt (Harris, 1995: 3).[1]

Whether the United States, United Kingdom and Singapore ultimately rejoin is not really the prime issue. How effective a forum UNESCO can ever hope to be, for the dialogue on communication equity, is. Projected UNESCO ventures seem to be directed toward emphasizing concerns which are commonly undebatable (UNESCO, 1990). Programmes for the education of East European journalists have been established, for example, but nothing similar to the controversial debates of the 1970s remains.

Fortunately, other parties have been providing leadership, and serving as effective hosts for continued discussions on these extremely important issues. Note the June 1989 Los Angeles meeting of the Union for Democratic Communications and the National Lawyers Guild that addressed the nature of cultural human rights (Union for Democratic Communications and the National Lawyers Guild, 1989), the October 1989 World Association for Christian Communication (WACC) international congress in Manila, concentrating on communication rights within a depoliticized milieu, and the first MacBride Round Table convened in Harare, Zimbabwe, in late October. The Round Table, a communications rights advocacy group, was organized to help evaluate world communication ten years after the MacBride Report was published (UNESCO, 1980a). Aside from reviewing original concerns of the MacBride Commission, the rapid expansion of communication technologies was also raised as a compounding issue. Investment was encouraged to help enhance communication infrastructures in developing countries. The gathering argued that media operation standards should be set by media professionals, and underlined the idea of a free and responsible press, without excessive government or commercial control.

In its Sixth Annual Statement (Honolulu, 1994), the MacBride Round Table urged the United States, United Kingdom and Singapore governments to take immediate steps to rejoin UNESCO. 'We believe it is time that UNESCO should reactivate its resources, and renew its commitment, towards democratization of global communication structures,' the statement says.

During the Honolulu meeting, Mustapha Masmoudi, one of the original members of the MacBride Commission, argued that the world must 'make communication technologies the symbol of modernity and democracy,' and that media should be reinforced in their role as consolidator 'of human rights in communication'. The Round Table also recognized the marginalization of indigenous peoples from communicative links and appealed for dedication of communication resources funds for their cause. It was further declared that in order to meet the needs for cultural and socio-political emancipation, women, grassroots and citizen organizations must be ready to seize their own communication power and develop alternative media (*Editor and Publisher*, 1994: 23). The Round Table held in Tunisia in 1995 showed that this body is becoming an important international voice in world communication rights advocacy.

Other meetings and organizations have spoken out for communication equality and related concepts. Among these are the International Symposium on New Technologies and the Democratization of Audiovisual Communications (Videazimut and CENDIT), the Agencia Latinoamericana de Información (ALAI), and the World Association of Community Radios (AMARC). A new coalition, the Telecommunications Policy Roundtable based in Washington, DC, organized itself in October 1993 with the purpose of working toward the implementation of public interest principles in the design and construction of the so-called information superhighway. Other interesting movements to affirm communication as basic to life and crucial to all members of the world community are the 'People's Communication Chapter', at present being coordinated by Cees J. Hamelink of Amsterdam, and the Cultural Environment Movement led by George Gerbner of the University of Pennsylvania (Hamelink, 1994).

Looking ahead: the growing imbalance in communication resources

In spite of some improvements in the past 20 years we still see a tendency toward limited and biased world news flow patterns. A major concern continues to be that newspaper content often appears to have a US and/or Western bias. US news agencies are said to manage 80 per cent of the international news in Latin America, for example, and in many countries a significant percentage of both national and regional news is thus controlled (Beltrán and de Cardona, 1979: 39; Masmoudi, 1979: 172).

Many studies report such imbalances (Marham, 1961; Gonzalez-Manet, 1988).[2] While the exact level of dominance has been challenged, questions centre around the degree of negativity, not its presence or absence. Others point out that the United States is not the only culprit; other Western press/media institutions are also to blame (Atwood and Bullion, 1982: 104, 126).

The MacBride Commission (UNESCO, 1980a) was concerned with more than news media, of course. Equity in the availability and use of other communication technologies was just as important a concept as the criticism of traditional media. In this vein, 24 countries of the Organization for Economic Cooperation and Development (OECD) account for 70 per cent of the world's telephone mainlines and 90 per cent of mobile phone subscribers, yet have only 16 per cent of the globe's population. In addition, the developing world has access to only some 10 per cent of the electromagnetic spectrum. Today over half the world's population has not yet made a telephone call, and this is a century-old communication technology. What is missing is the recognition of communication as a basic social opportunity or primary good.

The principle of justice has long been a tenet of political theory. Mill reasons, for example, that the absence of property can be just as oppressive as a lack of constitutional rights:

> No longer enslaved or made dependent by force of law, the great majority are so by force of poverty; they are still chained to a place, to an occupation, and to conformity with the will of an employer, and debarred by the accident of birth both from the enjoyments, and from the mental and moral advantages, which others inherit without exertion and independently of desert. That this is an evil equal to almost any of those against which mankind have hitherto struggled, the poor are not wrong in believing. (Mill, 1967: 710)

Rawls (1971: 11) argues for equal opportunities and a social contract conceptually more general than that found in Locke, Rousseau and Kant. Communitarian theorists take this notion further and argue for a 'politics of the common good' (Sandel, 1984: 16–17; Taylor, 1986). Tehranian (1990), writing on communication technologies, holds that modernization undermines traditional communities and he examines the roles of libertarian, étatarian, and communitarian strategies. He ultimately argues for a communitarian perspective and its ability to foster a rediscovery of community. The key is to provide an environment wherein all are empowered to define their own social aims (Herzog, 1986: 484). Hence social equity is a prerequisite of a modern society. Golding (1994: 9), however, warns that there are unequal opportunities in the communication revolution, and existing gaps are likely to worsen. Communication equity is possible through the *provision of opportunities* for all people to access and use the various channels of public interaction.

Just as the flow of carcinogens resulting from the Chernobyl nuclear accident could not be fully tracked for the first 10, maybe 20, and possibly 30 or more years, so too will the fallout of populations living in a communicatively deprived environment be grossly impaired. Yet many members of the developed world and the Western governments themselves are often impassive to these woes. It is just as important for farmers to discuss better methods of rice production, for rural doctors to be able to dialogue with their large city counterparts, and for students to have access to the best educational resources as for stockbrokers to access current market data, for the military to use sophisticated surveillance systems, and for merchants to be linked to their suppliers via computers. What good are the technology and systems of modern communication if they fail to help the least advantaged of our society? It is a moral imperative to share these resources.

With 70 per cent of the Third World's children suffering from malnutrition, 82,000 children starving to death each day, and one billion illiterate in the population these are no longer matters global citizens can afford to ignore (Davidian, 1994). The consequence of the inequities in the distribution of basic goods is a moral dilemma we must confront. These plights will ultimately affect us all, even if we live thousands of miles away from the afflicted.

Consider the plight of the people of Kikwit, Zaire, a city of half a million, where they have no radio or television, and electricity operates a mere two hours a day. When the deadly Ebola virus broke out there was no way to dispense simple hygienic advice to the people of the city and surrounding countryside. Medical students had to use battery powered megaphones. The next time such a life-threatening virus surfaces it may not be possible for modern science to readily identify it and enact a programme for its containment. If next time the virus spread beyond Third World villages and cities the consequences could be disastrous for all. And all of this might have been more easily avoided if basic communication systems were available for the sharing of health and nutritional information.

Many portions of the world, of course, are still without modern telephone systems, basic broadcasting, accessible newspapers, sufficient libraries and post offices. When we look at computers we find that just 4 per cent of the global supply is owned by people in the Third World. Often communication resources have not been introduced because Western businesses do not realize pre-set profit margins for their efforts, or existing organizations such as the International Monetary Fund (IMF), the United Nations Conference on Trade and Development (UNCTAD), the General Agreement on Tariffs and Trade/World Trade Organization (GATT/WTO), and the International Bank for Reconstruction and Development (World Bank) fail to provide adequate resources for such development. This is a time when many developing countries are actually becoming poorer as they have increasing debt burdens largely as a result of steep interest rates and the collapse of commodity prices. Thanks to this unserviceable debt, in the 1980s many countries lost all the gains realized during the previous two 'Development Decades' (Adams, 1994: 35–40).

Ten proposals for a New World Information and Communication Order

Considering the lack-lustre performance of world news flow over the last 20 years, the increasing presence of transnational corporations in the developing world communications sector, the proliferation and complexity of the new communication technologies, ten proposals are offered here in the hope of framing a productive and meaningful debate on the future of the NWICO. Each point is seen as providing an avenue for commitment to action. The term 'communication' is used to refer to all communication and information channels, and applies to traditional as well as mass media. Emphasis is placed on, but not limited to, mediated communication as this was the focus of the original MacBride Commission inquiry. The guiding principle in all of the proposals is the notion of achieving social equity through communication.

1. Communication equity goes hand in hand with a fairer distribution of wealth/resources and power.
2. Developing countries cannot achieve equity through capital assistance alone.
3. Adequate communication flow monitoring is a task that both academic and professional communicators must assume.
4. Communication equity must apply to the use, access and distribution of all communication technologies.
5. The liberal arts and sciences are keystones of a humanitarian-based communication education.
6. Communication must be cultivated as a global exigence.
7. Commercial interests cannot be dominant over cultural concerns.
8. Communication could help in the restoration of the world's different cultures.
9. New alternatives and diverse forms of international awareness and consciousness-raising must be explored.
10. Communication should be considered a basic human right.

1. Communication equity goes hand in hand with a fairer distribution of wealth/resources and power
When UNESCO introduced the New International Economic Order (see Glossary) debate, some 75 per cent of the world's population was earning about 30 per cent of the world's income. Where the average per capita income for industrialized nations was $2,400 annually, it was a mere $180 in developing countries (Galtung and Vincent, 1992: 75). Conditions have not changed markedly since that time.

It is impossible to divorce the world economic order from its communication order. One is an integral part of the other. There is strong evidence to suggest it is unlikely that an increase in communication capabilities alone can ensure the development of a country. The development of communication and the economy appear to be inseparable. According to recent research, the expansion of communication technology seems to be directly tied to the status of consumable income (Vincent, 1994). While some may interpret this as an indication that nations should be encouraged to develop their own economic dependencies, this author takes a different approach and argues that such findings support the notion that the industrialized world has not done enough to promote communication equity, and that communication equity can be sought only when programmes for general long-term economic aid are also being implemented (Vincent, 1994). The notion that a proliferation of communication technology can 'free' an economically destitute population from tyrannic rule as promoted by Pool and others, must be challenged (Pool, 1979a; Schiller, 1980).[3] The adoption of all media technologies, old and new, appears to be closely tied to basic social conditions such as illiteracy, education levels and health care (Vincent, 1994). The assumption made here is simply that economic resources *and* communication distribution methods and policies are concurrent processes in development.

Communication equity can begin with an equity in news flow. The direction and volume of news flow is our concern at the moment. The movement of news can be between distant nations as well as immediate neighbours. While one might believe that news flow between neighbouring nations should be high, this is not always borne out by the literature (Stevenson and Cole, 1984: 37; Vincent and Riaz, 1990; Sreberny-Mohammadi et al., 1984). The perceived political importance of larger world powers and former colonial patterns often affects the balance of news flow.

But the issue does not end with news flow. Transnational firms dominate much of the manufacturing of communication hardware, software, programming and data transmission markets. Even when radio and video equipment is manufactured locally, it usually is through affiliates of transnational firms such as Sony, Sanyo, Philips, ITT, GTE, Hitachi, Toshiba, Panasonic, Sharp, Cable and Wireless, Thomson-CSF, CIT-ALCATEL, and Ericsson. Most countries in Latin America, Africa and Eastern Europe are heavily dependent on imported computers and computer parts. During the mid-1980s, for example, some 70 per cent of the computer market in Chile was in the hands of five transnationals, IBM, Digital, NCR, Burroughs and Wang. Today, 46 of the top 100 worldwide information and communication business groups are from the United States. United States, West European and Japanese firms comprise almost all of the list of the 100 firms most active in information and communication sales, with only two Australian (Telecomm Australia and News Corp.), one New Zealand (Telecoms New Zealand), one Canadian (Bell Canada Enterprises), one Korean (Lucky Gold Star), and one Brazilian (Telebras) firms represented

(UNESCO, 1989). Of the top 25 companies, ten are American (IBM, ATT, Xerox, GTE, General Motors, General Electric, Bell South, Nynex, Eastman Kodak and Bell Atlantic), seven are Japanese (NTT, Matsushita, NEC, Toshiba, Fujitsu, Hitachi and Sony), two are French (France Telecom, and Cie Générale d'Electricité), two are German (Deutsche Bundespost, and Siemens), and one each from Netherlands (Philips), UK (British Telecom), Italy (STET), and Canada (Bell Canada) (UNESCO, 1989).

Even though most of the above are Western-based corporations, we should not conclude that the West has *carte blanche* on intelligence that may help foster the growth of such development. Factors such as political or business climate may have had a moulding influence. Note that since 1979 only 75,000 of the 220,000 Chinese students who went abroad have actually returned to China (Plafker, 1995: 23). The United States and other Western countries have been major benefactors of this brain drain.

International decision-making bodies such as the UN, UNESCO, International Telecommunications Union, the International Monetary Fund, the United Nations Conference on Trade and Development, the General Agreement on Tariffs and Trade, and the International Bank for Reconstruction and Development are largely creations of the developed world and are often structured to help maximize agendas put forth by Western nations.[4] Such a scenario creates the dilemma observed by Werner Levi where 'the deciding state . . . has to use power to have its goals accepted while the antagonized states have to use power to frustrate these goals. Unless some political decision is based upon complete consensus, its binding force rests upon the power backing it' (Levi, 1974). Levi goes on to conclude that 'characteristics of power are more conducive to making the international political system inadequate in its task'.

The issue of skewed power structures found in international organizations is addressed further below, but at this point we note that alternative mechanisms do exist in the private sector. I call attention to alternative trade organizations such as Christian Aid (London), the World Development Movement (London), Alter Trade Japan (Tokyo), Co-op America (Washington), the International Federation for Alternative Trade (Demeern, the Netherlands), North & South Exchange AB (Göteborg, Sweden), Traideireann (Athlone, Ireland), and Women's World Banking (New York) from the industrialized world, plus Alter Trade Corporation (the Philippines), Coordinación Nacional de Organizaciones (Mexico), Community Development Society (India), Last Hope International (Nigeria), New World Trading (Chile), and Nyumba Ya Sanaa

(Trade not Aid) (Tanzania) in the developing world (Brown, 1993). These and many other existing organizations represent the alternative structural possibilities which can help balance flows in international trade. In the meantime it is imperative that Western business people, government officials, educators, etc. also become attuned to and respect what other people in the world have to say. Westerners too need to learn how to be good world citizens.

The concentration of power specifically in the communication industries will be discussed later. Communication is not based on a natural resource held by any one country or group of countries. It is technologically possible for all who have the capital and the necessary institutions to develop the appropriate infrastructure. The problem of inequity occurs when information distribution technology and services have been developed during a short period of time when the wealthiest countries continued to hold a sizeable advantage in the market-place. But communication is too vital a resource to be controlled like other consumable commodities. Future development may hinge on the availability of and access to contemporary communication channels. Devices must be found to allow the greater sharing of these resources with the wider world community (this notion is further developed in proposal 6). Profit alone must not be the sole factor guiding the access to availability of communication technologies and systems. To restrict access to communication solely on the basis of inability to pay would be a grave oversight. There must be alternatives which would help better serve all.

If we hope to establish a more equitable world communication system that includes equity in news and information flows, then we must also attend to economic and political inequities worldwide. One does not seem possible without the other. To do this we must explore cooperative national arrangements for the co-development of communication technologies and services. The concern of decades earlier over the concentration of communication power of North over South, and the control of manufacturing by Western trans-national corporations is possibly even greater today.

*2. Developing countries cannot achieve equity through
capital assistance alone*
For many years, the question of Western dominance of information flow, largely through news agencies, was at the heart of the NWICO discussions. While about 120 countries and territories had news agencies, some 40 countries had none, and this included 24 countries with populations greater than one million (International Commission for the Study of Communication Problems, no date). Of great concern were the so-called transnational news agencies (TNNAs) –

Agence France-Presse (France), Associated Press (USA), Reuters (UK), and United Press International (USA) – which dominated in both size and technological strength. These organizations wielded much control over global news flow, with bureaux or offices in more than 100 countries.

Some welcomed the Non-Aligned News Agency Pool (NANAP), housed in the Yugoslav agency Tanjug, for its potential to provide a more competitive spirit in international news distribution. It never became the strong international news force that was hoped, though. It was a news exchange for agencies, with some 90 members, but not a genuine news agency. NANAP stories tended to offer a wider variety than the TNNAs, and were mostly event rather than crisis-oriented (Kirat and Weaver, 1985). The weakening of the non-aligned movement in this post-Cold War period, however, hindered its further development. This news pool with regional redistribution centres proved less effective than alternative news agencies might be (Kirat and Weaver, 1985: 46). Often NANAP stories appeared to be just as, or even more, biased than Western reports they were supposed to counter, with heavy reliance being placed on government information sources. Stories tended to be extremely short and were criticized for lacking 'interpretative background, investigative reporting, and contextual material'.

Another alternative has been the Inter Press Service, with management headquarters in Rome (see Chapter 7). IPS has proven to be a fairly effective organ overall. It is organized as an international cooperative of journalists. It is non-profit making. All stories originate in, or relate directly to, the Third World (Ogan and Fair, 1984). IPS is *process* rather than *event*-oriented in its reporting. It has earned a reputation as the 'alternative' news agency on Third World affairs. While Giffard has observed that it works extremely well as a news source for developing countries, more recently he acknowledged that IPS was still at a comparative disadvantage because it had not made enough inroads with the Western press (Giffard, 1983, 1992).[5]

The IPS network covers some 100 countries. Service is in eleven languages, including Hungarian, Arabic and Swahili. Special features focus on issues concerning women, development, the environment, agriculture, energy and religion. Yet even the IPS is experiencing problems in the post-Cold War period. There appears to be less interest in news of developing countries in the West today. Traditional Western powers such as the United States and United Kingdom are proposing deep cuts in development spending, and there are many more nations now in the quest for aid, partly as a result of the collapse of the Soviet Union. Even the European Union is approaching expansion with caution as many Eastern European nations now seek membership.

One more agency worth mentioning is the Pan-African News Agency (PANA; see Chapter 6). It was established by the Organization of African Unity (OAU) in 1979 and became operational in 1983–85. Headquartered in Abidjan, Ivory Coast, PANA was started as a pool for news exchange between African government agencies with the staff producing its own features, which were independent of the various nation governments they reported on. PANA also chose to retransmit news from other African news agencies through five redistribution agencies (Jakubowicz, 1985). PANA received praise as an alternative news agency concept (Haule, 1984). The challenge seems to be to create alternative news agencies in the developing world that can stand free of government control, and continue to be financially sound. So far PANA seems to have had difficulty with both. Concerning government control, many formal and informal controls potentially exist in any system, democratically based or otherwise (Galtung and Vincent, 1996). Even in the 'free press' environment of the United States, both direct and indirect censorship exists.

In Asia, there are the national news agencies – Kyodo of Japan; Yonhap of South Korea; the New China News Agency (Xinhua); the Press Trust of India; APP of Pakistan; PNA of the Philippines; KCNA in North Korea; Anatar of Indonesia; and Bernama of Malaysia – and there is even the ambitious ASEAN regional effort, the Asia-Pacific News Network (although this lacks central organizational controls). But a high-profile region-wide agency has yet to emerge. As John English has observed, Asian news agency stories tend toward provincialism, and this gives them 'negligible news value in the originating country, much less in neighbouring nations' (English, 1982). In Asia there is no powerful, alternative news agency that can compete directly with the TNNAs.

Asia is a continent from which a good regional news agency could emerge, and the north-east Asian nations may represent the strongest potential for guiding such a venture. To date, however, no one country has shown the necessary leadership nor has found a way to break the language barrier necessary to organize such a cooperative news agency.

When UPI was in trouble, it was a Middle Eastern organization, Middle East Broadcasting Centre Ltd, that came to the rescue. Japan has made some financial inroads to 'buy into' Western media – the Japanese electronics giant Matsushita Inc.'s purchase of MCA (Music Corporation of America); the demise of the American company AMPEX as the video technology leader, etc. – but these have been single-nation efforts. A news agency controlled only by Japan would not best serve the regional interest referred to here. Tremendous potential exists for multinational media arrangements in North-East Asia, and a region-wide news agency would have phenomenal potential. Larger regional interests might also be well served through such a venture. Sapru does hint at a potential problem with cooperative news agencies when he writes on the Reuters–Associated Press of India (API) arrangement, noting how favourable political situations are vital for news agency arrangements to be credible and viable (Sapru, 1982). The problem that arises is: just how does one sponsor government-independent news agencies when governments are often the best sources for capital? This and other issues must still be addressed before a viable system can be created. Perhaps a system that incorporates the freedom and responsibility found in portions of the NANAP, IPS and PANA plans may be the answer. More discussion is necessary.

The need for diversity spreads to the use and operation of information networks as well. Related to this is the so-called 'information superhighway' which has been proposed by US President, Bill Clinton, and Vice-President Al Gore. Yet criticism can be directed toward this superhighway notion, for its failure to include the world's disadvantaged groups in the telecommunications superstructure proposal. The 'information superhighway' is often compared with the Internet system which has recently risen to international prominence. The Internet is a group of worldwide information resources available on-line by computer. Access to the Internet, however, is still largely in the West and in the industrialized parts of Asia.

When we speak of an information superhighway of the future, we run the very real risk that such a communication thoroughfare will be an exclusive highway of the developed world, which will drive the 'haves' and 'have-nots' even further apart than they are today. Even if wide access to the information highway is ultimately possible, certain tolls and tariffs will still prove effective barriers to use and entry in many portions of the world. Note the prohibitively high cost of telephone use in China and sub-Saharan Africa. Until quite recently the transfer of a few kilobytes of data cost as much as one US dollar. Hence the market-place can be easily used to control access to the information superhighway. The greater the expense of access, the higher the likelihood that larger portions of the world's population – both developed as well as developing – will remain 'information poor'. Given their record, it is not likely that commercial interests will overwhelmingly support free and low-cost services for the poor without wide-scale public pressure.

UNESCO, for example, has recognized the perils of poor access to information networks. Just as the physical library has been a tool to progress and growth, so too does access to information resources help foster development and intellectual independence today. One campaign that recognizes the importance of newer electronic modes of communication is the UN's development of women's information networks which began during the United Nations Decade for Women (1976–85). Other cases are the media and nutrition projects of the World Health Organization, family planning programmes in the UN Population Fund, and social development activities of the UN Children's Fund (UNICEF), but more of these information and resource development plans are needed (Hamelink, 1994).

3. Adequate communication flow monitoring is a task that
both academic and professional communicators must assume
News flow research has been dominated largely by North Americans (Lent, 1976: 170). This literature still lacks solid theoretical insights and tends to be methodologically crude, with little hypothesis testing.

News flow has not been studied with the vigour that it should have been. One answer is simply to carry out more research on world news flow. Both micro- and macro-studies can be performed on individual country experiences and on region-wide news flows. Another approach is to find new perspectives, to allow not only politically determined agendas to guide our inquiries, and to experiment with other theoretical paradigms (Nordenstreng, 1994a, 1994b).

Recent efforts have attempted to correct some of these shortcomings. The latest project is the result of the changing global political environment and the many recent technological developments that have affected the way in which news and television flows have developed. Through this effort, Nordenstreng (Tampere, Finland), Sreberny-Mohammadi (Leicester, England), Stevenson (Chapel Hill, North Carolina) and others continue to carry on international news monitoring which began with the support of UNESCO in the 1980s. One objective is to find more applicable research methodologies. Qualitative research generally, and specifically the cultural studies approach which stresses the media milieu's intricacies and diversities, are being explored, by some, as an alternative to what they see as the more restrictive simple content analyses of earlier days. As Sreberny-Mohammadi puts it, 'there are questions to be asked about the global maps that national news media provide and whether these reflect an emerging global, shared news agenda, or whether regionalism remains a key factor in news selection' (Sreberny-Mohammadi, 1994). The ultimate purpose of this group is to explore policy-making implications of the current trends in news flow.

But research must not be limited to news media. Many other information channels bear watching. Very little reliable information is currently available on specific telephone uses, mobile telephone ownership, the availability of video-conferencing facilities, the number and extent of teletext services, the true availability of personal computers, or the number of Internet users in developing countries versus the West. So far, the research on many of the new communication technologies has been limited to the industry's marketing needs, and little is known about the social consequences of these technology uses. For example, what do the mobile telephone and the digital pager mean for women? Are these and other new communication technologies vehicles for fostering equality and independence, or are they a control mechanism by means of which men can continue to monitor the activities of women even if the latter now have careers outside the home (Davis, 1994)?[6] And when researchers examine the communication industries, the neo-liberal tendency is to argue for free competition and a competitive market model (Preston, 1994). In such a view, the activities of trade unions and government controls for collective social benefits are commonly chastised. Take, for example, the situation in Ireland. Here is a culture with a wonderful oral communication tradition, and the telephone became a natural vehicle for the proliferation of such a communication activity. But almost overnight this changed when new pricing policies placed timed line usage charges on consumers for all 'local' as well as 'long distance' telephone calls. The result is that Irish use of the telephone has since changed radically. While Ireland is a place where people also have strong face-to-face communication traditions, one must still wonder about the long-term implications of this pricing policy.

These and other issues of the world telecommunications industry have hardly been studied by the academic community, which has shown little support for a meaningful research agenda, in part by placing a high preference on simple marketing studies which usually lack theoretical and methodological sophistication.

4. Communication equity must apply to the use, access and distribution of all communication technologies
Some have argued that any inequities in international communication can be largely remedied through the proliferation of new communication technology. It was thirty-five years ago that the United Nations Economic and Social Council called for developed nations

to aid less developed countries with their communication and information needs, and it has been some twenty years since the Non-Aligned countries asked for reorganization and resource-sharing of information technologies.

Yet communication inequity continues throughout the world. This imbalance involves radios, television, telephones and other newer technologies. Use of many voice and data transmission devices also requires higher levels of literacy. Efforts are under way worldwide to explore new uses of both traditional and more recent communication technology, and how they might enhance the perception of marginalized groups and societies. Alternative communication is a concept that is increasingly taking hold; it refers to alternatives that exist to the mainstream media. Of these, perhaps the liveliest are those which are referred to as 'community media'.

Community media are communicative operations which encourage a broad base of participants. These participants often cut across social, economic, cultural and organizational boundaries, as they unite for a common goal. Activities range from Radio Rurale that offers agricultural training, health campaigns and talks for women in the Congo, community video centres in Zimbabwe, community television in India, small radio stations in Latin America, and public access cable television channels in the United States, to travelling theatre productions in Nigeria, Botswana, Kenya, Tanzania, Zambia, and throughout the Caribbean.

Others seek to provide complementary voices for their communities. This may take the form of so-called alternative newspapers, radio stations or electronic network data bases. The latter are multiplying rapidly because of the phenomenal growth of the Internet, a computer accessible network of data bases and topical fora. The United States, Europe and Brazil have developed many alternative data bases, while alternative newspapers have been particularly significant in popular movements in Zimbabwe and South Africa, and even mainstream Philippine radio such as the Labour-Party-supported station in Cebu, the University of the Philippines' DZUP, and the Manila Archdiocese Radio Veritas have provided alternative voices during times of martial law and military rule. While these media provide an alternative voice to organs that support the status quo, they are presented here as complementary media, offering additional outlets to the mainstream.

In this section we must also discuss the role of women in communication: as part of the communication workforce, or the media portrayals of women's roles. Even in the industrialized world the number of women employed as journalists, film directors, in broadcast management, etc. tends to be embarrassingly low. In Finland,

47 per cent of the print media workforce is women, while in the United States it is 41 per cent. Only 37 per cent of Australia's journalists are women, and in Spain it is a mere 17 per cent (UNESCO, 1989). In many Asian, African and Middle Eastern countries, you can count the number of women in leadership positions on one hand. As for media content, stereotypical images of women still abound. Imagery is sexist and demeaning and ranges from the unflattering use of sex objects in US rock videos and international advertising to the submissive, subordinate and subservient portrayals of women in the melodramas produced by many nations (Vincent et al., 1987; Vincent, 1989; Greenberg, 1980; Greenberg and D'Alessio, 1985; Greenberg et al., 1980). While this negative imagery may have improved slightly as academic and social criticism has been directed toward such stereotyping over the last few decades, the problem persists.

Throughout the Third World the status of women is even more discouraging. Almost all business and media leaders are male. From the ownership of property to the threat of slavery, and from restrictions on basic social opportunities to subservience in domestic and relational situations, women are still treated in disparaging ways. Freer communication can open lines of dialogue on these vital human rights issues, and communication media can be utilized in helping to encourage such dialogue and introduce new social and political perspectives into community rhetoric.

Choices of empowerment do exist for women and other minorities through alternative media and networks. Hamelink (1994: 143) relays one example of Moroccan women publishing a newspaper, *Tamania Mars*, in addition to their domestic duties. The newspaper helped bring women's issues to the forefront of public discussion.

As a communication society we need to help promote the continued development of community, alternative and complementary media. This can be done in nations where alternative media already exist, as well as other places where such opportunities would be presented for the very first time.

We now have new communal voices that were never allowed to speak heretofore. Throughout Eastern Europe many public interests are now gaining access to the airwaves, and the multitude of political parties makes for a very active debate forum. In Poland, for example, so-called private television only started in 1994. Much confusion still exists. The intelligentsia who previously catered to the government and found themselves with *carte blanche* access to media no longer command such unilateral acceptance; now they must put forth new efforts to convince the populace of the validity of their ideas.

In South Africa a handful of non-governmental radio stations were established in 1994–95, and it is these voices which are being given air space before the commercial system is developed and expanded. Previously, the use of alternative newspapers helped provide a liberating voice for South Africa, but now groups who never before sought to communicate messages publicly are finding that radio is an entirely new dimension for promoting relevant community discussions.

What is further needed is mediation among marginalized communities, academics, professional communicators, policy-makers and NGOs to help identify resources, create an operational plan, and set both short- and long-term objectives.

5. The liberal arts and sciences are keystones of a humanitarian-based communication education

There are reasons to be concerned about journalism both within and outside the West. In the United States many media editors perpetuate a US-as-centre paradigm. The reasons for this are nationalism and the paradigms of Western journalism education. Journalists of developing countries, on the other hand, are faulted for helping to perpetuate a Western point of view, when their training often came from the West (Golding and Elliot, 1979: 8–9).

Adefemi Sonaike argues that many 'media practitioners in developing countries must reorient themselves away from the established definition of "news" which they have imbibed through their training in the West' (Sonaike, 1988). It is common in the United States and elsewhere for journalism education to emphasize trade practices of application-oriented courses over a stronger liberal arts perspective which would help cultivate intellectual growth. In many curricula tributes to the glorification of communication's technological wonders takes precedence over theory and research-based instruction. On US college campuses today political apathy is now at an all-time high, according to the UCLA Higher Education Research Institute that has been conducting annual surveys since the mid-1960s (Sanchez, 1995: 3). If this is a problem with college students generally, then how can media and communication students escape? Communications and media educators may have to work even harder now to provide an appropriate environment for professional training.

Perhaps the question which should be addressed is: what is it that the junior communicator will be able to 'communicate' after s/he graduates from such a programme? Many communication education programmes appear more interested in creating job opportunities than an environment for the intellectual growth of communication practitioners and consumers. We see many examples of this in the Eastern European UNESCO-journalism training programmes, the US programmes for Asian and Latin American journalists, and other similar programmes worldwide. While some successful journalists advocate a training programme that emphasizes more than the practical, the profession is still divided on whether or not this is the best approach.

UNESCO documents and resolutions over the last 15 or so years have been calling for a plan whereby developing nations would strive 'to achieve improvement of their own situations, notably by providing their own equipment, by training their personnel, by improving their infrastructures and by making their information and communication media suitable to their needs and aspirations' (UNESCO, 1980b). The question remains unresolved, however, of how exactly such programmes should be implemented.

To help improve journalism generally the following are recommended: (1) strengthened journalist training programmes including a stronger 'grassroots' emphasis; (2) the creation of a journalist exchange programme within regions; and (3) an examination of curricula in journalism education programmes with the purpose not necessarily being to replicate programmes found in the West.

It is the grassroots arena that holds perhaps the most optimistic hope for a continuation of NWICO-inspired goals and philosophies. Both journalist exchange and the modification of journalism curricula could lead to an increased public awareness of these important communication issues and the implications such concerns have at the individual, national and global levels. It is here that specialized periodicals can be developed to help promote a regular international flow of news, alternative radio can offer programming quite distinct from that of the mainstream media, and networks and databases can be established to provide channels of discourse outside of those within the mainstream media. Equally, media literacy programmes can be developed which encourage education through critical thinking and knowledge of media image production (Bailey, 1994). Special interest groups, development groups, non-governmental organizations and labour organizations can all be connected through these alternative communication channels.

6. Communication must be cultivated as a global exigence
As noted earlier, much dialogue has focused on the US-proposed 'information superhighway'. Criticism has been directed at the plan's failure to include the world's disadvantaged groups in the telecommunications superstructure proposal. The essence of a democracy is the ability for all to communicate. How will the

Table 9.1 *Global distribution of radio receivers*

Continents, major areas and groups of countries	Number of radio broadcast receivers per 1000 inhabitants		
	1970	1980	1989
Africa	55	109	177
America	689	920	989
Asia	40	99	182
Europe and former USSR	448	560	701
Oceania	544	900	1020
Developed countries	619	867	1023
Developing countries	48	96	176
Africa (excluding Arab states)	35	94	154
Asia (excluding Arab states)	38	97	180
Arab states	130	172	263
Northern America	1348	1870	2016
Latin America and the Caribbean	183	252	342

Source: UNESCO, *Statistical Yearbook 1991*, Paris: UNESCO, 1991a: 6.8

information imbalances found in earlier communication systems be eliminated this time? The so-called information superhighway threatens to widen the gap between the information rich and the information poor. Even the extremely conservative US Congressional Leader, Newt Gingrich, acknowledges the problem in what may have been a half-hearted proposal that poorer Americans should perhaps be given tax credits to enable them to purchase personal computers (*International Herald Tribune*, 1995: 30).

When examining UN and UNESCO listings of communication devices per capita, a study by the author found increases in most of the categories examined (Vincent, 1992). While in recent years the percentage of increase has been greater among developing countries than developed ones, the existing inequities are still readily apparent. There was an 18 per cent increase in radio receivers for developed countries between 1980 and 1989 versus the 83 per cent increase in developing countries. Nonetheless, the total number of radio receivers per thousand is still 581 per cent greater in nations with developed economies (see Table 9.1). Although this is obviously better than the 903 per cent difference in 1980, it should still be a matter of some embarrassment for the West. And radios are perhaps the most widely affordable of the present communication technologies, given their low cost and ability to circumvent literacy and energy-shortage problems. Similar trends can be seen with other

Table 9.2   *Global distribution of television receivers*

Continents, major areas and groups of countries	Number of television receivers per 1000 inhabitants		
	1970	1980	1989
Africa	4.7	18	36
America	212	331	404
Asia	20	38	62
Europe and former USSR	205	325	373
Oceania	193	308	379
Developed countries	259	418	489
Developing countries	10	24	52
Africa (excluding Arab states)	1.5	11	22
Asia (excluding Arab states)	19	36	60
Arab states	23	60	102
Northern America	405	661	796
Latin America and the Caribbean	57	99	158

Source: UNESCO, *Statistical Yearbook 1991*, Paris: UNESCO, 1991a: 6.9

communication media. At present there are 940 per cent more television receivers in developed countries, and there is 1,883 per cent greater newspaper consumption (see Tables 9.2 and 9.3). In addition there is a 1,783 per cent difference in non-newspaper and book consumption (UNESCO, 1991a).

The 1980–89 increases for sub-Saharan Africa (64 per cent), non-Arab State Asia (46 per cent), and Latin America and the Caribbean (36 per cent), using radio receivers as a case in point, are all markedly low. Northern America still has 589 per cent more radios than Latin America and the Caribbean (UNESCO, 1991a).

There is a markedly low telephone penetration in many developing countries of the world. Growth levels are exceptionally low in many countries, including the zero- and near-zero growth levels of the Central African Republic, Ethiopia, Madagascar, Malawi, Niger, Sudan, and Tanzania, among others. In examining world data, even where some growth can be observed, it seems to be at very low levels – often less than ten per hundred inhabitants throughout the Third World, and in many cases less than one per hundred on the African continent. Ironically, the Tokyo area today has more telephones than all of Africa with its 500 million population, and in all of the developing countries of Asia, Africa and South America together there are fewer phones than the number found in all of Japan (Richter, 1991: 6).

Table 9.3   *Global variation in newsprint consumption*

Continents, major areas and groups of countries	Newsprint consumption per inhabitant (Kg)		
	1970	1980	1989
Africa	0.9	0.7	0.7
America	18.1	21.1	22.5
Asia	1.4	1.8	2.2
Europe and former USSR	9.0	9.8	10.7
Oceania	31.2	29.0	31.7
Developed countries	18.2	19.6	22.6
Developing countries	0.9	1.0	1.2
Africa (excluding Arab states)	1.0	0.7	0.7
Asia (excluding Arab states)	1.5	1.8	2.2
Arab states	0.5	1.0	1.1
Northern America	42.8	46.0	52.5
Latin America and the Caribbean	3.6	3.5	3.6

Source: UNESCO, *Statistical Yearbook 1991*, Paris: UNESCO, 1991a: 6.3

As noted above, it was hoped that new, emerging technology would help place Third World countries on a more 'equal' footing with the rest of the globe, based on the assumption that technology will be affordable and widely accessible. Given the earlier cited imbalances, such an argument can be strongly criticized. The new technology is expensive and frequently requires higher literacy levels than many of the traditional media. Gonzalez-Manet (1988: 83) argues that this further increases developing world dependency on the developed world, noting that the complex technology requires major changes in development strategies, and this leads directly to 'not only asymmetry in communication flows, but also a qualitative leap in the mechanisms of dependency'. He further argues that this could lead to new patterns of 'cultural imperialism' built on a 'monopoly of communications know-how and techniques'. Clearly much must be done before communication equity becomes a worldwide reality. It is not only many in the developing world who are being excluded, but members of the First World as well. Too often communication availability is one of the factors that tend to separate the 'haves' from the 'have-nots' in the world community. These are difficult questions which must be addressed by policy-making such as the World Trade Agreements and GATT, and the ITU. In addition, how may we ensure that information technologies are more evenly distributed?

Women and other 'minorities' (which in some places are, in fact, majorities), and grassroots and citizens' organizations of all kinds, must seize their own communication power and access the media or develop alternative media. Comparatively inexpensive technology, like video, on-line computer links and desktop publishing, can facilitate development. An increasingly 'smaller' world demands that we use these vehicles to communicate with one another effectively.

7. Commercial interests cannot be dominant over cultural concerns

Too often commercial interests alone dictate the manner in which communication systems develop in a capitalist world. Perhaps no system is a better example of the pitfalls one can encounter than that which we have in the communication industries of the United States. Although many of the media have been regulated, the use of regulatory commissions in the United States has more often led to a protected market-place for business interests than helped to ensure the maintenance of communication rights for consumers. One need look no further than the United States' history in the regulation of broadcasting, telephone, cable, etc. Gallant efforts were made to protect consumers during the days of the Judge Warren Burger District of Columbia Appellate Court, and in recent legislative attempts to re-establish the Fairness Doctrine, and revise the Communications Act, but these have been short-term efforts and tend to be exceptions rather than the rule. There is no reason to believe that US communication will change markedly soon.

While all national experiences are different, the problems experienced are often similar. This is not meant to be an attack on capitalism, but rather an appeal to place greater concern on the human dimension. To do so we may have to shift the emphasis found in many of the leading Master in Business Administration (MBA) programmes today. Business ethics and social implication theories cannot be ignored any longer. Without a recognition that the societal component must be considered in business, we run the risk of sacrificing many of our basic human rights.

In the United States the pragmatic constraint of limited natural resources gave way to more general philosophies as the basis for regulation of broadcasting and common carrier communication for most of the twentieth century. Arguing that communication resources were limited and expensive to establish and operate, these communication media were tightly controlled to promote the 'free flow of ideas' in a community. While present thinking (Compaine, 1979) appears to favour a counter-argument that new technologies provide a diversity of communication channels, the gross inequities between the developed and developing world in the modern communication spectrum help make the diversity argument null and void. The wide-scale unavailability of communication technology, as well as the lack of say by the Third World in determining its communication future, paint a grim picture. There seems to be little hope for major improvement without marked political change. Thus we turn to contentions by Dworkin (1981), who argues that we must examine 'which aspects of any person's economic position flow from his choices and which from advantages and disadvantages that were not matters of choice' (Dworkin, 1985: 208). The formulation of international policies for the construction of a new communication technology environment may be the only solution. In other words, human rights interests may not now be best served by communication policies that are largely guided by market forces.[7]

Quite different possibilities would be the sharing of industry expertise without even the expectation of a minority capital interest or resale before the technology is fully outdated. Still another would be the subsidy of economic development training and implementation programmes specifically geared to the communication industry with the promotion of Third World communication industry independence as its primary goal.

Some may question the suggestions made here, asking if these proposals support a return to regulation when many are talking about a more limited role for government in industry and services. This rhetoric has led to so-called 'privatization' and 'deregulation' moves in Europe, the United States and elsewhere. But it is my contention that these trends, at least as they are being currently enacted, are grossly unfair to minorities and the underprivileged. In many cases these nations never really abandoned regulation, but simply disguised it. In demonstration I turn to recent activity in US communications.

Since the early days of the Reagan administration, there has been a large-scale effort to lessen government regulation of the industry. This began with the relaxation of statutory duties and changes in ownership qualifications. In broadcasting (although we can look at telephone and other technologies as well), where the system has been in place more or less in its current form for over seventy years, previous ownership of a station means an *a priori* right to continue if one wished.[8] Even during the days of tighter regulation a broadcast licence was rarely lost, even when there were fairly major infractions of rules. New ('drop-ins') or available frequencies were usually in smaller communities, and low power channels had a mere fraction of the power that regular stations were allocated. Consequently a prospective new licensee could only be allocated one of these newer but weaker stations, or had to raise capital and wait for an existing station to enter the market. The more attractive a station in terms of audience reach and allocated power, the more expensive it would be, possibly millions of dollars. Expense alone would prohibit many, if not most, minority and women's groups from making such purchases.

True deregulation would remove governmental control *and* redistribute all frequencies fairly, possibly through an open lottery. This would jeopardize existing licence holders, however, and in their minds be prejudiced against them, given the risks they had to endure while they were operating the station. So deregulation has often meant the abolition of many nuisance regulations while failing to open the system in a truly equitable fashion. Hence, as observed above, the United States never really dropped regulation, but simply opted to camouflage it. My call for specific regulations to protect public interests therefore does not appear to contradict any existing trends.

8. Communication could help in the restoration of the world's different cultures
It has been argued that many attributes of national cultures have been victims of dominating Western (particularly American) generated imagery, influenced by television, film and advertising. But communication media can also help reverse these trends through a campaign of awareness and consciousness-raising, and local image production.[9]

Of major concern here is the ease by which 'culture' can be imported, and the cultural producers tend to be a handful of countries with heavily developed television and motion picture industries. In recent years films, videotapes and newspaper copy do not always have to be hand-carried across national borders. Electronic transmission and satellite technology have led to a phenomenon known as trans-border data flow. The internationalization of CNN (the Cable News Network) and MTV (Music Television) are prime examples. Not only are unique cultures being threatened by the importation of foreign visual media programming, but stereotypes are being formed and perpetuated about people and lifestyles in the countries where this programming is produced. Throughout the world there are many people who believe that all Americans must be as cold and calculating as J.R. Ewing of *Dallas*, or that US cities are filled with violence and crime.

In the late 1980s, countries such as the United Arab Emirates, Ecuador, Iceland, Brunei, Peru, Zaire and New Zealand received more than two-thirds of their television programming from other countries. Senegal, Algeria, Singapore, Tunisia, Ireland, Mauritius, Cyprus and Zimbabwe all received more than one-half (Berwanger, 1987). It has been estimated that between 80 and 90 per cent of all films are imported from the United States, France, Germany, Italy and the United Kingdom. Even in Europe, 91 per cent of the television fiction in Denmark is imported, while 51 per cent of the United Kingdom's programming is. The proliferation of video cassette recorders is also leading to the importation of films worldwide. Head (1985) and De Sola Pool (1979b) originally argued that, once produced, local programming would prove more popular than imported programming, given its more locally relevant nature. Yet this does not seem to be what has happened (Svendsen, 1994: 16). Foreign programming is still more popular in many countries throughout the world.[10] A major reason is exemplified by a Norwegian Broadcast Corporation estimate that foreign films cost fifteen times less than domestic films for comparable length and subject matter (Lund, 1988). One way to measure a programme's audience is to divide its total cost by the number of viewers (or each 1,000 or 100,000 viewers), yielding a total cost per viewer. From a production standpoint, a programme costing fifteen times more than another might also have to attract a fifteen times larger audience to be thought of as financially comparable.

During the United Nations Decade devoted to indigenous people, it was interesting to see what happened to one particular cultural group and its worldwide image – the Hawaiian people. The modern image of Hawaiians has probably been largely moulded by episode upon episode of *Hawaii Five-0*, *Magnum* and other American television series. In Finland, a favourite dinner is Hawaiian pork, and the local Pizza Hut restaurants sell a 'Hawaiian' pizza. The only common ingredient that apparently lends itself to the Hawaiian name-calling is pineapple. But what does this tell us about Hawaiian culture? Would the people of Hawaii distinguish these dishes as being related to their islands?

Can an entire culture be reduced to attractive, scantily clad Polynesian women dancing the hula for tourists dressed in loud coloured shirts and dresses while eating pineapple? Is this preservation of a culture? If you watch television, you might think so.[11] How much, on the other hand, do we know about the Hawaiian people and their sovereignty movement? Do we realize that Hawaiian people are at the bottom end of the island's socio-economic ladder? This does not attract much press, and certainly does not seem to fit into a Hollywood producer's image of this vacation mecca. The point is that *most* of us have an image of a majestic Pacific island chain, yet this is built largely on media imagery, and tells only a portion of the story. The needs and struggles of Hawaii's people somehow fail to make it into the Hollywood scripts that stress homogeneity and stereotypes over cultural preservation. In recent years there has been a renewed pride in being Hawaiian, in speaking the language, and in celebrating the culture. The question that remains is: when will movies and television realize there is more to Hawaii than the beaches, hotels and condominiums of Waikiki? Similar criticisms can also be made of numerous other world cultures.

9. New alternatives and diverse forms of international awareness and consciousness-raising must be explored
A basis of all democratic societies is the ability to express opinion as well as access information. NWICO was not an attempt to specifically promote the interests of any one nation, but an effort to recognize the universal importance of communication in building and maintaining a democratic society. While few would object to the principles in general, many do fault the process by which such goals of equity would be achieved.

The NWICO dialogue has shifted from government and inter-governmental organizations (IGOs)[12] to non-governmental organizations (NGOs) and grassroots groups.[13] Issues such as NWICO may simply be too political when necessarily combined with other variables such as political, economic and social matters. Too much may be perceived to be at stake by various governments for the existing inter-governmental organizations to sponsor effective channels for such discussions.

While NWICO issues are no longer debated in UNESCO, they are still being expressed in the activities of various professional and grassroots organizations. A number of meetings have been convened with NWICO as either its exclusive, or at least major discussion topic. Among these were a World Association for Christian Communication (WACC) sponsored colloquium in London in September 1990; a WACC and Institute for Latin America seminar in Lima in November 1990; the Intercontinental Journalists' Conference in New Delhi in November 1990; a Gannett Foundation Media Centre conference on 'News and the New World Order' held in New York City in January 1991; and an Inter Press Service Council on Information and Communications June 1991 meeting in Rome that centred on press treatment of the Gulf War (Mowlana and Roach, 1991). Another demonstration of interest can be found in the production of a thirty-seven-page bibliography on the NWICO by the Prague-based International Journalism Institute in June 1991. This is the first of a series of resources intended to 'serve journalists' in light of the continuing importance of world news flow (International Journalism Institute, 1991).

Another organization that has recently emerged to promote the principles contained in the original NWICO philosophy is the MacBride Round Table on Communication cited earlier. The Round Table was created in 1989 to stimulate discussion of issues embodied in the 1980 MacBride Report (UNESCO, 1980a). The group was named after the chair of the UNESCO committee that prepared the report. The MacBride Round Table is an international media advocacy group of scholars, journalists and other communication experts devoted to the monitoring of world communication rights and balances, and reporting findings to community groups, UN agencies, NGOs and the news media. The MacBride Round Table reports on communication equity problems worldwide. Of particular concern to the group is the perception of marginalized groups and societies.

Other groups and organizations noted above – such as the Union for Democratic Communications, WACC, the Agencia Latinoamericana de Informacíon, the World Association of Community Radios, Videazimut (Montreal), the Telecommunications Policy Roundtable, and the 'People's Communication Charter' have sponsored dialogues which embody many of the principles of the MacBride Report.

One advantage of NGOs and related groups is that they provide the mechanism whereby international decision-making is being expanded. Special interests are now finding that they have better representation and lobbying power when dealing with governments and IGOs. In such an environment new programmes of assistance and development might be negotiated. This provides an option when older institutions such as the World Bank might be perceived as having ulterior and potentially contradictory motives.

An example of the power of such negotiations can be found in recent environmental agreements between the developed and developing world. When told they must balance their own economic development with protection of the environment, members of the developing world responded: why? It was by exploiting the environment that you, the North, helped build your national wealth. Now, when it is our turn, you tell us we must instead protect the environment? Things are as they are because of your actions! One solution has been in proposals to excuse portions of national debt, which many of these nations will have difficulty repaying anyway, in exchange for the permanent protection of a portion of the rain forests. Hence we have a so-called 'win-win' situation. The likelihood that such agreements will be produced with the aid of NGO involvement is much greater than if they were negotiated by governments alone.

It can easily be argued that many of the existing institutions designed to promote economic and social development internationally inherently protect existing First World national agendas. Recall the observations on power structures by Levi (1974) cited earlier. New mechanisms must be explored to promote alternative channels for international negotiations and regulations. NGOs and other grassroots efforts represent one possible alternative for the processing and equitable distribution of our communication resources.

It is within the activities of the MacBride Round Table and similar groups that the principles of NWICO may thus have the greatest chance for wide-scale implementation. By working toward the status of an independent international commission, the Round Table will strengthen its influence even further. It is through such methods that communication may be implemented as a tool in the formulation of a democratic society.

10. Communication is a basic human right
A major feature of the NWICO debate has been the 'right to communicate', and the concept is being referenced again today. The right to communicate is based on Article 19 of the Universal Declaration of Human Rights which states that 'everyone has the right to freedom of opinion and expression . . . and this includes the freedom to hold opinions without interference' (United Nations, 1948). The UN Charter (1945) deals with human rights generally, with some believing that they are now part of customary international law (Sieghart, 1991: 29). The Declaration of Human Rights has been interpreted as an affirmation that all should be able to communicate as well as have access to communication channels. Recently this has evolved to include the right to self-determination and development in peace (Frederick, 1992: 257–60).

As technology has proliferated the reasoning can be expanded to mean the right to use more individualized technology that offers fewer filters to the communication process. With these newer technologies users can access information and data bases directly, and have less costly access to long-distance electronic mail services, information resources, and dialogue hotlines that are normally topic-specific. Although these new channels of communication offer wider public access than ever before, the equity of access is still questionable at best. Electronic computer network access is quite common in the United States and Europe, and is spreading in Asia and Eastern Europe, but is much less widely available in South America, Africa, Central and South Asia.

Progressive efforts are under way to help provide alternative communication voices in communities across the globe. These include networks originating in the scientific and academic communities, corporations, governments, institutions, and on an individual user basis. On a more traditional level we have data bases that expand public access to documents on public policy issues. One of these is the Minnesota E-Democracy project that offered a nonpartisan arena for circulating election position papers by candidates running for hotly contested Governors' and US Senate offices in that state in 1994. Minnesota E-Democracy used the Internet to provide these resources and hoped to build an interactive medium for citizens to dialogue on the election and other public policy concerns. In California, on the other hand, law makers recently passed legislation to create a master plan for providing any identifiable public record available in an electronic format to individuals (State of California, 1994). Cases involving alternative public media were cited earlier in this chapter. These are all encouraging developments and others are likely to follow.

One example of a grassroots effort to promote communication is a recent move by the Brazil Popular Video Association which is installing two dozen or more television screen exhibition poles in open spaces in Brazil's cities. The hope is eventually to place these video screens nationwide. It is described as a national network of popular television, based on the democratization of communication media. This alternative media movement offers a choice other than commercial programming and provides an outlet for videos produced by social movements which might otherwise have limited circulation. The public exhibition is viewed as an experimental laboratory for testing the concept of a future, and more widely available, popular television network. Alternative media are being used more and more to help provide a diversity of voices in a community, and to offer the public a true option to status quo points of view.

We must also work toward adoption of communication as a human rights component through appropriate national and international bodies. If governments are reluctant to commit themselves to such principles, then other channels must be used to help promote this goal. Communication advocacy groups, NGOs and other vehicles can be used to help realize such an objective. If public pressure mounts government officials will find it more difficult to ignore the issues, and it might even become politically embarrassing not to support such a campaign. It is through such activities that the notion of communication as a basic human right will be advanced.

Conclusions

Former US President George Bush often referred to a concept he labelled a 'new world order'. Yet there was never great clarity on the specific details of such an order. John Steinbruner likened the Bush-inspired new world order to Voltaire's sarcastic remarks on the 'Holy Roman Empire': 'neither holy, nor Roman, nor an empire' (Steinbruner, 1991: 20). In recent years the new world order appears to place certain nations and people at the top, while perpetuating a system of second-class societies and economies.

The so-called 'new world order' advocated by Bush and promoted by current United States, Western and United Nations policies has not provided many of the answers one might expect of a *'new* order'. While political supremacy *has* been addressed in much of the dialogue on the topic, issues of democracy and human rights are largely ignored (Chomsky, 1994).

Some believe that any inequities present in international communication can largely be remedied through the proliferation of new communication technology. To reiterate, the belief is that such technology will be extremely affordable and will hence be accessible to a larger population than older technology (e.g. the mass media). The gist of this argument is that technology will help place Third World countries on a more 'equal' footing with the rest of the globe, and people in general on a more equitable plane with elites. Yet even if this is a possibility, and this might be strongly debated, as recently as 1992 at the World Administrative Radio Conference, where global negotiations take place under the authority of the ITU, the agenda was almost entirely oriented to needs of the developed countries. Little, if any, earnest coalition-construction was discussed with countries in the South (Hudson, 1991; O'Siochru, 1993).

Before a truly equitable situation can evolve, international policy decisions must first be addressed. GATT/WTO, ITU, the World Bank and other bodies should join together and dialogue on communication access. Current inequities like the international satellite orbit allocations favour developed countries and work against those who have developed the technology more recently. These policies need to be rethought, even if commercial interests of the industrialized world have to make some sacrifices. Future inequities are possible in radio frequency allocations and high definition television standards, as well as in the ultimate design of the previously mentioned information superhighway. International regulatory bodies must reconsider current allocation strategies, and balance their own short-term commercial interests with the longer-term social interests that a communication-literate world population would ultimately offer.

Mill argues that 'the principles of individual freedom and political and social equity' are preconditions of an open civilization (Mill, 1962: 122–3). I believe that a free society goes hand-in-hand with open communication. Yet communication is becoming more complex as each day passes. The proliferation of new technologies and the convergence of existing technologies help create a system where societal communicating is no longer very simple. Effective communication is necessary, however, if we all hope to be active members of the world community. It is imperative that we master the channels of speech and information access. Without such command, political and social inequities are likely to persist.

The political effect of the New World Information and Communication Order concept has been something less than conclusive on this point. Yet a more equitable communication flow and greater accessibility should still be our goal. Whether UNESCO can succumb to political pressures and still provide leadership and an effective setting for resolving these issues remains to be seen. But changes are both appropriate and necessary. We must all work for greater communication opportunities and equality. Collectively it can be done. The principles of the New World Information and Communication Order were basically good ones, and we should not allow them to be lost in the quest for greater industrial development and self-serving national politics.

Notes

* The author wishes to thank the faculty and students in the Department of Communication, University of Helsinki and the Centre for Communication and Information Studies, University of Westminster (London) as well as colleagues at Dublin City University for their helpful comments and criticisms on earlier drafts of this chapter.

1. The United States currently spends a mere 1 per cent of its annual budget on foreign aid.

2. See Marham (1961), where all foreign stories in seven Latin American dailies were found to come from AP, UPI and Agence France-Presse; also see Gonzalez-Manet (1988) for an interesting discussion on development and communication technology.

3. Pool (1979a) and others have proposed that new communication technologies may help resolve problems in the Third World. Jussawalla (1979: ID–7) believes that 'telecommunication provides two way links that enable people in backward regions of a country to participate and share in the process of economic development'. Sussman and Lent (1991: 15) refer to this as neo-conservatism that is 'inclined toward reifying a technological-determinist model where "systems" govern, seeking quantifiable rather than real social costs and benefits of communication instrumentalities'. Schiller (1980),

on the other hand, cautions against such technologies, noting that their use could result in increased dependency by Third World countries on the industrialized world.

4. Note the division that occurred in the Group of 7 (G-7) recently when alarm was expressed at the United States' unwillingness to intervene as the dollar plunged against most international currencies. The Group of Seven is a group of finance ministers from the world's seven most industrialized nations, charged with offering a 'united front as they attempt to shape policies for the world economy' (Friedman, 1995: 1).

5. Use of IPS has been largely by the developing world press.

6. For an example of research questions which may be applied to new communication technology and gender, see Davis (1994).

7. Observe that the 'Report of the Independent Commission for World-Wide Telecommunication Development' (Maitland, 1984) recommended to the ITU that TNCs should participate in telecommunication transfers to developing countries, yet this has never happend and Sir Donald Maitland is still critical of the industry's failure to respond positively (see Glossary).

8. In principle you never could own a broadcast licence in the US because the airways have always been considered public. One only owns the station along with its equipment (transmitter, etc.). Yet stations have frequently been bought and sold, often for extremely high profits, and the transfer of licence has generally been pro forma.

9. The establishment of a television channel exclusively devoted to Gaelic language programming in the Irish Republic is an excellent example of the possibilities for local cultural image production. A similar television operation serves the people of Wales in the UK.

10. Although some programme genres such as locally produced soap operas, news and sports still retain their wide appeal.

11. Television, of course, is not the *only* way by which cultural stereotypes are formulated and/or perpetuated.

12. This includes UN bodies.

13. Over 2,300 NGOs participated in the 1993 meeting, the second World Conference on Human Rights, in Vienna.

Glossary

Phil Harris

In this Glossary we have provided brief definitions and explanations of many of the key terms used in debates about international communications. We have concentrated on those institutions, events, organizations and concepts which are most commonly found in such discussions, especially those alluded to by contributurs to this volume. The Glossary does not attempt to offer explanations of technological terms. Writing on 'cultural imperialism' and international communications can often be obscured by a miscellany of acronyms, and by frequent use of summary phrases about development which are deployed only loosely, and often inaccurately. This Glossary which should assist in the interpretation of such discussions, as well as providing additional information for readers of this volume, is a revised version of a Glossary originally compiled by the authors in 1991 as a ready-to-use editorial support for journalists writing on the Third World and development issues. The Glossary was the central component of a multi-reference package for journalists prepared within the framework of a joint IPS/UNITAR training programme.

Aid

The term is often used loosely to cover all forms of development finance, but it refers to net flows of Official Development Assistance (ODA), which the Organization for Economic Cooperation and Development (OECD) defines as official sector grants or loans on concessional financial terms aimed at promoting economic welfare and development.

Technical cooperation grants are included in aid, but grants and loans for military purposes are excluded. Aid is 'tied' when the recipient is obliged to make purchases with it from the donor country. But, even if aid is not 'tied', it often finds its way back to donors through, for example, the payment of disproportionately high salaries for Western experts, or private investments by Third World elites in Northern economic activities or deposits in Northern banks.

The Brandt Commission Report noted that there has been a major change since the 1960s in the composition of total flows of development finance to the South – from largely ODA to commercial, mainly from private bank loans, direct investment and export credits. One important consequence of this change has been the heavy and increasing debt service burden on the countries of the South.

Algiers Action Programme

The 1973 Conference of Non-Aligned Nations in Algiers adopted an action programme introducing for the first time the concept of the New International Economic Order (NIEO).

Appropriate technology

Technology specifically designed for the needs of the South – where the greatest needs are in the traditional agricultural and informal sectors – and not just second-hand outdated techniques from the industrialized North.

Appropriate technologies can take the form of cheaper energy sources, simpler farm equipment, capital-saving building, services and manufacturing processes, smaller factories and scales of operation, and consumption technology which meets local incomes and product requirements.

According to the Brandt Commission Report, only the countries of the South themselves can decide which machines and systems suit their own local needs, since transnational corporations (TNCs) and other commercial firms that control most technological developments are unlikely to direct research into non-profitable areas.

The report adds that 'appropriate technology is relevant to both rich and poor countries. Industrialised countries too need more appropriate technologies which conserve energy and exhaustible resources, which avoid rapid job displacement and which do not damage the ecology. . . . It is quite possible that rising energy costs, afflicting both North and South, will eventually compel corporations in the North to concentrate more on new kinds of techniques which may be appropriate to many parts of both North and South.'

Article 19

An international human rights organization set up in 1986 to promote the right to freedom of opinion and expression, and the right to seek, receive and impart information and ideas through any media regardless of frontiers. The organization, which takes its name from 'Article 19' of the Universal Declaration of Human Rights, has established an international research and information centre in London to document and combat censorship on a global basis.

Baker Plan

The strategy first proposed in 1985 by then US Treasury Secretary James Baker for easing the Third World debt crisis. The plan called for US$29 million in extra loans from commercial banks and international finance bodies over three years. Loans would be provided on condition that developing nation borrowers committed themselves to market-oriented growth policies.

The strategy focused on adjustment programmes in borrowing countries, debt rescheduling to buy time, and new lending by private banks to finance basic investment. The plan never got off the ground. It was followed by another US initiative – the Brady Plan.

Brady Plan

Put forward by US Treasury Secretary Nicholas Brady in March 1989, the plan was drawn up to 'revitalize the current debt strategy' by having banks accept a reduction in debt or debt servicing and provide new loans to debtors.

Specifically, the plan included steps to permit negotiated debt or debt reduction schemes, financing specific debt reduction programmes by international financial institutions, more timely disbursement of financial support, rescheduling and restructuring of debt through the Paris Club (see Glossary entry), additional financial flows, reduction of administrative barriers to debt reduction, measures to stop capital flight and improvement of the economic environment in debtor countries.

A key component of the plan was its call for the World Bank and the International

Monetary Fund to use their own resources to support debt reduction arrangements. The Brady formula, which replaced the earlier Baker Plan, was criticized by private creditor banks, who said it made little sense to provide new loans to heavily indebted countries at the same time as writing off or reducing older loans to the same countries. As a result, banks agreed to reduce existing debt but showed themselves increasingly reluctant to lend new money.

Brandt Commission
Officially the 'Independent Commission on International Development Issues', the 18-member commission was set up in 1977 in an attempt to revive the North–South dialogue under the chairmanship of then Federal German Chancellor Willy Brandt. In February 1980, the commission published *North–South: A Programme for Survival*, a report containing recommendations on relations between Third World and industrialized nations.

The report also called for the convening of a summit meeting of some 25 leaders from industrialized and developing nations. Such a summit was subsequently held in Cancun, Mexico, in October 1981. A subsequent report was published by the commission in February 1983 with the title: *Common Crisis, North–South: Cooperation for World Recovery*.

Brundtland Commission
The commission (officially the World Commission on Environment and Development – WCED) comprised 22 leading personalities from all regions of the world under then Norwegian Prime Minister Gro Harlem Brundtland. It released its report – *Our Common Future* – in 1987.

The commission argued that the future is based on sustainable development – 'meeting the needs of the present without compromising the ability of future generations to meet their own needs'. The decision of the UN General Assembly to hold the UN Conference on Environment and Development (UNCED) in Rio de Janeiro in June 1992 was a direct response to the WCED Report.

Cancun
A conference on cooperation and development was organized in October 1981 in Cancun, Mexico, bringing together heads of state, prime ministers or other top officials of 22 countries – 14 from Third World countries and eight from the industrialized world.

> *Third World*: Algeria, Bangladesh, Brazil, China, Côte d'Ivoire, Guyana, India, Mexico, Nigeria, Philippines, Saudi Arabia, Tanzania, Venezuela and Yugoslavia.
> *Industrialized world*: Austria, Britain, Canada, Federal Republic of Germany, France, Japan, Sweden, and United States.

The conference, an attempt to revive the North–South dialogue, followed a call for such a meeting in the first report of the Brandt Commission.

Centrally planned economies
The dominant characteristic of the former socialist system (which collapsed in the late 1980s) in the Soviet Union and other Eastern European nations, centrally planned economies were based on public (state) ownership in a strictly controlled internal and external market. All economic sectors were under the centralized control of political elites, with a heavy emphasis on industrial production.

Charter of Economic Rights and Duties of States
Adopted by the UN General Assembly in 1974, the Charter develops themes in the Declaration on a New International Economic Order (NIEO) agreed earlier the same year. The Charter stresses, among others, national sovereignty over natural resources and economic activities, non-intervention by transnational corporations (TNCS) in host countries' internal affairs, and free and non-discriminatory development of international trade.

It also stresses generalized preferential economic treatment for Third World countries, South–South economic cooperation, just and equitable terms of trade for developing countries, and international cooperation to preserve the environment.

Civil society
Refers to that dimension of public life which is neither government nor private sector, but goes well beyond the immense world of NGOs: it includes all the socio-cultural structures of societies, in which ever-increasing groups of citizens begin organizing themselves for the good of their societies at a moment in which the very concept of the *state* is in serious difficulty.

Conventionally, 'civil society' is used to describe groups of people who come together voluntarily and who neither exercise formal power nor make profit. These include social movements, non-governmental organizations (NGOs), foundations, religious groups, grassroots and community groups, trade unions, clubs and associations of all types.

The participation of 'civil society', both South and North, has added a radically different reality to political, cultural and economic development in recent years.

Cold War
The post-Second World War period (1945–89) in which the rivalry between the two superpowers – the United States and the then-Soviet Union – took the form of a 'war of words' – a conflict carried out at the level of propaganda and disinformation. To avoid international military combat between states armed with nuclear weapons, confrontation moved into the arena of information and intelligence. The Cold War is generally said to have ended with the dissolution of the Soviet empire and the collapse of the Berlin Wall in 1989.

Common Fund
Created in 1989 within the framework of the UN Conference on Trade and Development (UNCTAD), the fund is aimed at helping the international commodity trade, particularly developing country exporters, and was incorporated in the Integrated Programme for Commodities (IPC) adopted by UNCTAD-IV in Nairobi in 1976. The fund is structured along two main lines of activity, financed through two separate accounts:

- The *First Account* serves as a source of finance for International Commodity Organizations (ICOs) set up under International Commodity Agreements (ICAs) that contain buffer stock provisions. There are currently two ICOs that rely on buffer stocks (those relating to cocoa and natural rubber).
- The *Second Account* helps to finance commodity measures other than stocking, such as research and development, quality and productivity improvement, and market development, as well as efforts to promote local processing and find new uses for commodities.

Conditionality
The policy of multilateral and other lender's (such as the International Monetary Fund: IMF) requiring that the use of the lenders resources be closely linked to moves by the borrowing country to implement economic adjustment policies geared to restoring a viable balance of payments position and sustainable growth.

Conference on International Economic Cooperation (see North–South Dialogue)

Conference on Security and Cooperation in Europe (CSCE)
A series of international meetings (1973–75) culminating in the signing of a non-binding Final Act (see Helsinki Accords) recognizing the inviolability of post-Second World War frontiers in Europe and committing signatories to respect human rights and fundamental freedoms, and to cooperate in scientific, cultural and other fields. Participants included all European countries except Albania, plus Canada and the United States.

Council of Europe
Created in 1949, the council accepts as members European states which 'accept the principle of the rule of law and of the enjoyment by all persons within [their] jurisdiction of human rights and fundamental freedoms'. The 40 member states are Albania, Andorra, Austria, Belgium, Bulgaria, Croatia, Cyprus, Czech Republic, Denmark, Estonia, Federal Republic of Germany, Finland, France, 'the former Yugoslav Republic of Macedonia', Greece, Hungary, Iceland, Ireland, Italy, Latvia, Liechtenstein, Lithuania, Luxembourg, Malta, Moldova, Netherlands, Norway, Poland, Portugal, Romania, Russia, San Marino, Slovak Republic, Slovenia, Spain, Sweden, Switzerland, Turkey, United Kingdom and Ukraine. The council has two statutory organs:

- a Committee of (Foreign) Ministers, which has powers of decision and recommendation to governments;
- a Consultative (Parliamentary) Assembly, a deliberative body.

Debt
The current combined Third World debt burden stands at over US$1.3 trillion, and is largely the result of the expansion in the 1970s of international commercial bank loans to developing countries. This expansion occurred because surplus liquidity created by expanding Euro-currency markets, recycling of the financial surpluses of oil-producing countries through international banks and economic recession in the industrialized countries spurred banks into lending to developing countries.

The South Commission Report notes that while the surge in foreign borrowing by Third World countries may have been unwise and excessive, 'the net transfer of resources to the South at that time was on balance very favourable for the world economy' because it maintained a 'respectable level of growth and investment in developing countries' and in turn helped offset recession in the industrialized countries.

In the 1980s, however, the industrialized countries started introducing recessionary macro-economic monetarist policies to control growing inflation leading to a slowing-down of economic activity at home, depressing prices for commodities by reducing demand. At the same time, international interest rates rose to unprecedented levels, pushing up the cost of debt servicing. Thus, points out the South Commission, it was the South that bore much of the cost of controlling inflation in the North, by having to pay out more to service their debts while receiving ever less for their exports.

Public debt: the current outstanding debt for which the central government and its organs are responsible;

External debt: public debt owed to non-nationals of a country and repayable in foreign currency, goods or services. Such debt may be owed by governments, government agencies, sub-national government bodies or autonomous public bodies.

Developing countries

The non-industrialized countries of the world, also known as the countries of the South or of the Third World.

Development

A process of self-reliant growth achieved through the participation of the people acting in their own interests as they see them, and under their own control. The primary objective is to satisfy the basic needs of all the people through a democratic structure of government that supports individual freedoms of speech and organization, and respects all human rights. (This description is based on the definition provided in *The Challenge to the South*, the Report of the South Commission.)

Development assistance/finance (see Aid)

Development Assistance Committee (DAC)

A committee of the Organization for Economic Cooperation and Development (OECD) set up in 1960 as a forum for consultation between the OECD's main donors and the European Commission, the DAC's declared aim is to increase the resources channelled to the developing countries. The DAC does not act directly as an aid agency but rather as an instrument to improve, harmonize and coordinate the aid policies and programmes of its members.

Members are Australia, Austria, Belgium, Britain, Canada, Denmark, Finland, France, Federal Republic of Germany, Ireland, Italy, Japan, Netherlands, New Zealand, Norway, Sweden, Switzerland, United States and the European Commission.

Development cooperation

Commonly used to refer to the Official Development Assistance (ODA) policies and programmes of the Northern industrialized countries. When used in the North, the term rarely implies mutuality but rather top-down flows of finance (from North to South), often within the framework of a development strategy 'imposed' by the donor country.

To reflect the interdependence that marks North–South relations in particular and international relations in general, 'development cooperation' can be defined as the joint search by Northern and Southern partners for commonly acceptable solutions to identifiable problems affecting the development of Third World societies, bearing in mind the socio-economic and cultural diversity of the societies in question.

Development Decade

The United Nations designated Development Decades to focus attention on developing countries and accelerate the development of their 'human and natural resources' through effective international action. The first Development Decade was from 1961 to 1970, the second from 1971 to 1980, and the third from 1981 to 1990.

Economic Cooperation among Developing Countries (ECDC)

A ministerial meeting in 1977 of the Group of 77 in Arusha (Tanzania) agreed a short-term action plan for global priorities in Economic Cooperation among Developing Countries, primarily in the form of more regional cooperation and integration. The plan put the emphasis on mutual cooperation to increase self-reliance and economic independence, and to decrease dependence on the North without complete dissociation.

Officially backed by the UN Development Programme (UNDP), ECDC envisages South–South economic cooperation in fields such as trade, joint ventures, know-how and expertise, and monetary and credit issues. An important component of ECDC is Technical Cooperation among Developing Countries (TCDC).

Economic growth

An increase in a country's total output, which may be measured by the annual rate of increase in Gross National Product (GNP) or Gross Domestic Product (GDP) as adjusted for price changes.

Fair labour standards

There has been widespread criticism, even from trade unions in the North, that wages in Third World countries are often kept low by what the Brandt Commission Report identified as the 'exploitation of a weak and unorganized labour force, by excessive working hours or by the use of child labour'. The 1976 World Employment Conference warned against the use of unfair labour standards in Third World countries to make their exports more competitive. In 1978, the International Confederation of Free Trade Unions (ICFTU) called for a 'social clause' in trade agreements to control labour standards in exporting countries.

Food aid

Often sent to Third World countries as part of emergency relief programmes, food aid has been criticized for the political conditions which have often been attached and because it acts as a disincentive to agricultural production in the recipient countries.

The Brandt Commission Report argued that food aid need not work against local agriculture in Third World countries provided it is related to programmes for increasing investment in agriculture and 'effective demand for food is raised to clear the market at a price which rewards domestic producers'. The report also called for the phasing out of food aid as a direct input to investment once that investment has resulted in increased food production.

Fundamentalism

Originally referred to the conservative movement in North American Protestantism arising out of the millenarian movement of the nineteenth century (and represented by a wide variety of evangelical churches). Today, fundamentalism has come to be commonly associated with a protest movement in most contemporary Islamic societies, in which the cultural system of Islam has become politicized and its symbols used to articulate political and economic demands.

General Agreement on Tariffs and Trade (GATT)

Established in 1948, the Geneva-based GATT is a multilateral body that lays down a common code of conduct in international trading and acts as a forum for negotiations to overcome trade problems and reduce trade barriers. The organization came into being as a result of the proliferation of high protective tariffs around the world.

GATT regulations stipulate that only a government, or an authority acting on behalf of a separate customs territory, may be admitted. Approval by a two-thirds majority of members is required. Key GATT provisions guarantee most-favoured nation status (exceptions being granted to customs unions and free trade areas, and for certain preferences in favour of developing countries), require that protection be given to industry only through tariffs, provide for negotiations to reduce tariffs and lay down principles to help the trade of Third World countries. Third World countries, centred on the Group of 77, have been promoting within the UN Conference on Trade and Development (UNCTAD) joint negotiations and the adoption of general principles for world trade that take into account the unfavourable positions and deteriorated terms of trade of Third World nations. These efforts have been consistently boycotted by the industrialized nations which have resorted to bilateral or multilateral negotiations under GATT and in which the bargaining power of Third World countries is very limited on an individual basis.

In 1964, GATT set up the International Trade Centre to provide information and training on export markets and marketing techniques. The centre has been operated jointly since 1968 with UNCTAD. GATT established a Committee on Trade and Development in 1965 to keep under review the application of special provisions to help the trade and development of the less developed countries and other work on the trade problems of developing countries. An arrangement regarding international trade in textiles – commonly known as the Multifibre Arrangement (MFA) – was reached under GATT auspices in 1973, effective 1974.

GATT's major activity has been the holding of successive 'rounds' of multilateral trade negotiations for tariff-cutting and other trade liberalization measures. To date, there have been eight such rounds.

GATT membership now includes more that 110 countries.

Glasnost
The policy of 'openness' in Soviet affairs introduced by Mikhail Gorbachev, then head of the Communist Party of the Soviet Union and President of the Supreme Soviet.

Global human security
The framework of conditions and values that are essential prerequisites for rendering society conflict-free and thus in a position to more effectively meet basic human needs and ensure basic human rights. Global human security places the person at the centre of the concept of global security by putting the focus on the human dimension, on people, and not on the concept of the state or inter-governmental relations. It refers to the security of each and every individual inhabiting the planet, a security that derives from the guarantee that basic needs can be met.

Global human security is not just a question of freedom from military or armed aggression but more fundamentally a composite concept that depends on a series of 'freedoms', including freedom from hunger and want, freedom from environmental degradation, and freedom from stereotypes and prejudice. Today's challenge is to find ways of satisfying basic societal needs such as food, clothing, housing, education, health care, employment, respect and human rights.

Group of 5
A sub-grouping of the Group of 10, the Group of 5 (G5) consisted of the finance ministers and central bank governors of Britain, Federal Republic of Germany,

France, Japan and United States. The G5, a forum for influencing exchange rates and discussing International Monetary Fund/World Bank policy, has been superseded by the Group of 7.

Group of 7
The world's seven most industrialized nations: Britain, Canada, Federal Republic of Germany, France, Italy, Japan and United States.

Group of 8
The industrialized countries represented at the Conferences on International Economic Cooperation in 1975 and 1977 (part of what became known as the North–South dialogue): Australia, Canada, European Economic Community, Japan, Spain, Sweden, Switzerland and United States.

Group of 10
Brings together Belgium, Britain, Canada, Germany, France, Italy, Japan, Netherlands, Sweden and United States – with Switzerland as an honorary member – to discuss international monetary arrangements. The G10 also meets through its central bank, the Bank for International Settlements (BIS).

Group of 15
An association of 15 core member countries of the Non-Aligned Movement (see Non-Alignment) set up to maintain Third World pressure in the international arena on issues such as economics, finance and trade, given the growing disuse of the Non-Aligned Movement following the end of the Cold War. Members are Algeria, Argentina, Brazil, Egypt, India, Indonesia, Jamaica, Malaysia, Mexico, Nigeria, Peru, Senegal, Venezuela, Yugoslavia and Zimbabwe.

Group of 19
Refers to the 19 Third World countries represented at the Conferences on International Economic Cooperation in 1975 and 1977 (part of what became known as the North–South dialogue). Those countries were Algeria, Argentina, Brazil, Cameroon, Egypt, India, Indonesia, Iran, Iraq, Jamaica, Mexico, Nigeria, Pakistan, Peru, Saudi Arabia, Venezuela, Yugoslavia, Zaire and Zambia.

Group of 24
The Third World grouping within the International Monetary Fund (IMF) set up to gain access to IMF and World Bank credits under more favourable conditions. The G24 takes its name from its composition when it was established in 1971 – representatives from eight African countries, eight American countries and eight Asian countries.

Group of 77
The 132-member country Third World group within the United Nations system, originally established at the first UN Conference on Trade and Development (UNCTAD) in 1964 as a common bargaining front against the North.

Helsinki Accords
The Final Act of the Conference on Security and Cooperation in Europe (CSCE) signed 1 August 1975 in Helsinki by all European countries except Albania, plus

Canada and the United States, recognizing the inviolability of post-Second World War frontiers in Europe. The Final Act also pledged the 35 signatory nations to respect human rights and fundamental freedoms, and to cooperate in economic, scientific, humanitarian and other sectors. The Helsinki Accords are non-binding and do not have the status of a treaty. The agenda for the negotiations leading up to the Final Act consisted of four general topics or 'baskets':

- questions of European security;
- cooperation in economics, science and technology, and the environment;
- humanitarian and cultural cooperation;
- follow-up to the conference.

Independent Commission for Worldwide Telecommunications Development
(see Maitland Commission)

Independent Commission on International Development Issues (see Brandt Commission)

Intellectual property rights
The rights of original producers, creators, inventors or breeders to provide prior authorization for the subsequent reproduction or propagation of their property for the purpose of sale, and for the offering for sale and selling of such material. Intellectual property comprises industrial property (inventions, trade marks and design) and copyright.

Interdependence
Refers to recognition that in all spheres (economic, social, political, cultural, environmental, etc.) the well-being and future development of any one people, society or nation is inextricably linked to those of all other peoples, societies and nations.

In terms of relations between South and North, interdependence means that a joint effort is needed to overcome poverty and underdevelopment. While the South needs the North as an export market, supplier of necessary imports for production and consumption and source of technological and financial inputs, it also needs more cooperation with the North to achieve self-reliance.

At the same time, the North also needs the South since, as the South Commission Report puts it, 'the well-being of the North and the stability of the world as a whole cannot be consolidated without ending poverty in the South'.

International Bank for Reconstruction and Development (see World Bank)

International Commission for the Study of Communication Problems (see MacBride Commission)

International Development Association (IDA)
Set up in 1960, the IDA is known as the soft loan arm of the World Bank because it provides assistance for the poorer developing countries on terms designed to weigh less heavily on balance of payments than World Bank loans. IDA funds are known as credits – to distinguish them from the World Bank's loans – and come mostly from subscriptions, general replenishments from its industrialized nation members and transfers from the net earnings of the World Bank. Resources are replenished at three-year intervals. Credits from the IDA – currently with 137 members – are made only

to governments, carry ten-year grace periods, and have 40- to 50-year maturities at zero interest.

The stated aim of IDA is to promote economic development, increase productivity and raise the standards of living in the less developed areas of the world that are IDA members, by providing finance to meet their developmental requirements on flexible terms.

International Finance Corporation (IFC)

The private sector affiliate of the World Bank, IFC was set up in 1956 to assist the economic development of the less-developed countries by promoting private sector growth and helping mobilize domestic and foreign capital for this purpose. IFC investments and loans are usually directed toward productive private enterprises and financial enterprises such as investment and development banks, where sufficient capital is not otherwise available on reasonable terms.

Normally, IFC makes investments in the form of subscriptions to the share capital of privately owned companies, or long-term loans, or both. IFC members – currently more than 170 countries – must also be members of the World Bank. Legally and financially the IFC and the Bank are autonomous, though the IFC draws on the Bank for administrative and other services.

International Monetary Fund (IMF)

Established in 1945, the IMF's official aims include promotion of international monetary cooperation, expansion of international trade, promotion of the stability of foreign exchange systems, and alleviation of serious disequilibrium in the balance of payments of member countries.

A quasi-world central bank, the Washington-based IMF holds funds subscribed as quotas by members, partly in gold and partly in their own currencies. The fund makes medium-term loans (usually for a period of no more than five years) to member countries with balance of payments deficits, providing they agree to IMF conditions on economic adjustment.

The Brandt Commission Report noted that the IMF has been criticized because of the conditions it imposes for loans, which emphasize the cutting of domestic demand in debtor countries. According to the report, 'the Fund's insistence on drastic measures, often within the time framework of only one year, has tended to impose unnecessary and unacceptable political burdens on the poorest'. In particular, the Brandt Commission Report stressed that 'the deficits for which a government can be held responsible should be distinguished from those that are due to short-term factors beyond its control'.

In addition to its general loan facility, the IMF also operates a number of other facilities to deal with particular problems:

- The *Compensatory Financing Facility* makes loans to compensate for unexpected falls in export earnings from commodities.
- *Buffer Stock Facility* finances stock set up under International Commodity Agreements (ICAs).
- *Extended Loan Facility* offers loans for longer than normal terms (up to ten years) when solving a balance of payments problem requires structural changes in an economy.
- A *Trust Fund*, which is the repository for the profits made from the sale of IMF gold in the 1970s and to be used to give the poorer nations specially favourable terms in the use of the Fund's various facilities.

Together with the World Bank, the IMF is widely known as a Bretton Woods institution, after the name of the US town in which the 1944 UN monetary and financial conference that led to the creation of both institutions took place.

International monetary system
The world monetary system refers to the international framework of financial relations between countries, in particular exchange rate regimes, reserve systems (the distribution of the international means of payment or liquidity) and adjustment mechanisms. Instability in the international monetary system since the early 1970s has particularly hit the countries of the Third World, where the management of their own exchange rates, foreign reserves and debt has been negatively affected by fluctuating currency values.

International Organization of Journalists (IOJ)
The Prague-based IOJ was created in 1946 'to defend the freedom of the press and of journalists and to promote their material welfare'. The oldest and largest world organization of professional journalists, the IOJ has over 250,000 members in 120 countries and has consultative status with the UN Economic and Social Council (ECOSOC) and the UN Educational, Scientific and Cultural Organization (UNESCO). At its eleventh Congress in Harare, Zimbabwe, in January 1991, the IOJ declared itself 'politically independent and ideologically pluralistic' in line with changes taking place worldwide.

International Programme for the Development of Communications (IPDC)
Created in 1980 by the UN Educational, Scientific and Cultural Organization (UNESCO), the programme was a concrete outcome of the debate in the 1970s on the creation of a New World Information and Communication Order (NWICO). A major objective of the programme is to provide financial assistance to Third World countries to enable them to develop their own communication and information infrastructures and systems without having to rely on the technology, expertise and media of the industrialized countries.

International Telecommunication Union (ITU)
Officially set up in 1934 to encourage international cooperation in all forms of telecommunication, the Geneva-based ITU became a specialized UN agency in 1947. Its activities include the maintenance of order in the use of radio frequencies and their allocation, studying and making recommendations on technical and operational matters, and helping countries develop telecommunication systems. The ITU consists of a Plenipotentiary Conference, administrative conferences, an Administrative Council, General Secretariat, the International Frequency Registration Board and two international consultative committees (one for radio, the other for telephone and telegraph).

International Telecommunications Satellite Consortium (INTELSAT)
Set up in 1964 by the telecommunication agencies of 18 Western nations, INTELSAT owns communications satellites and the ground stations from which they are controlled. The consortium has a contract with the US National Aeronautics and Space Administration (NASA) to launch its satellites.

Latin American Federation of Journalists (FELAP)
The Mexico City-based federation was founded in 1976 to bring together the continent's journalists and media workers' organizations in defence of the national liberation struggles of Latin American peoples and their fight against transnational corporations.

Least developed countries (LLDCs)
A classification drawn up by the United Nations on the basis of three criteria: per person Gross Domestic Product (GDP) of US$ 100 or less at 1970 prices, share of industrial production of 10 per cent or less of GDP, and 20 per cent or less of literate persons aged 15 or over. The following countries are recognized as LLDCs:
Africa: Angola, Benin, Botswana, Burkina Faso, Burundi, Cape Verde, Central African Republic, Chad, Comoros, Djibouti, Equatorial Guinea, Eritrea, Ethiopia, Gambia, Guinea, Guinea-Bissau, Lesotho, Liberia, Madagascar, Malawi, Mali, Mauritania, Mozambique, Niger, Rwanda, Sao Tome and Principe, Sierra Leone, Somalia, Sudan, Tanzania, Togo, Uganda, Zaire and Zambia.
Asia and Pacific: Afghanistan, Bangladesh, Bhutan, Burma, Cambodia, Kiribati, Lao People's Democratic Republic, Maldives, Myanmar, Nepal, Tuvalu, Vanuatu, Samoa, Solomon Islands and Yemen.
Latin America and Caribbean: Haiti.

Less developed countries (LDCs)
The Development Assistance Committee (DAC) of the Organization for Economic Cooperation and Development (OECD) defines developing countries as LDCs, which it considers to be all Latin American and Caribbean countries, all African countries except South Africa, all Asian countries except Japan, all Oceanian countries except Australia and New Zealand, and in Europe, Cyprus, Malta, Poland, Turkey and Yugoslavia.

MacBride Commission
Set up by the 19th session of the UNESCO General Conference in Nairobi in 1976, the commission was officially known as the International Commission for the Study of Communication Problems, but came to be known as the MacBride Commission after the name of its president, Sean MacBride. The 16-member commission officially began work in December 1977 to 'undertake a review of all the problems of communication in contemporary society' and published a final report – *Many Voices, One World* – in 1980. The commission was widely held to have been created to put an end to Western criticism of UNESCO as an apologist for press control and censorship under the guise of the New World Information and Communication Order (NWICO).

Maitland Commission
Officially named the Independent Commission for Worldwide Telecommunications Development, but commonly named after its chair, Sir Donald Maitland, the commission met in 1984 to look at the problems of unequal distribution of worldwide telecommunications, aiming to bridge the gap between the telecommunications requirements of developing countries and the market interests of suppliers.
It called on industrialized and developing country governments, together with the International Telecommunications Union (ITU), to help improve and expand telecommunications in order fully to exploit the benefits of new technology.

Market economies
Characteristic of the industrialized Western nations, this refers to the capitalist economic system based on private ownership in a free market. The typical economy is based on the development of corporate wealth and a strong tendency toward monopolistic control of large private power blocs, with little centralized planning. Market economies place the emphasis on consumer goods production and services.

Market socialism
Also known as 'liberal socialism', market socialism is an economic system representing a compromise between socialist planning and free enterprise, in which enterprises are publicly owned but production and consumption are guided by market forces rather than by government planning. A form of market socialism was introduced in the former Yugoslavia in the 1960s in distinction to the centrally planned socialism of the then Soviet Union. A similar development occurred in Hungary in the late 1960s and early 1970s.

Marshall Plan
Formally called the 'European Recovery Program' (1948–52), this was a US-sponsored programme to rehabilitate the economies of post-Second World War Europe. The programme, first proposed by US Secretary of State George C. Marshall (hence its name), was motivated by the US fear that the poverty, unemployment and dislocation of the post-war period could render communism attractive to European voters.

The programme disbursed some US $12 billion in economic aid (mostly as direct grants, with the remainder in various forms of loans), and helped restore industrial and agricultural production, establish financial stability and expand trade. The Marshall Plan concept was extended by US President Harry S. Truman to underdeveloped countries under the Point Four Program initiated in 1949.

Middle East
The term has come to refer to the countries around the southern and eastern shores of the Mediterranean Sea, extending from Morocco to the Arabian Peninsula and Iran, and sometimes beyond. The central part of this general area was formerly called the Near East, a name given by Western geographers who divided the so-called 'Orient' into three regions:

Near East: the region nearest Europe, extending from the Mediterranean Sea to the Arab Gulf;
Middle East: from the Arab Gulf to South-East Asia;
Far East: those regions facing the Pacific Ocean.

The change in usage evolved during the Second World War when the term 'Middle East' was coined by the British military command in Egypt. The unifying element running through the vast area now known as the 'Middle East' is its inner core – the Muslim Arab world. In recent years, many international organizations, including the United Nations, have begun to refer to the region as 'West Asia'.

Multilateral agencies/organizations
International bodies to which the governments of individual countries contribute funds for subsequent disbursement by those bodies. The principal multilateral agencies are the United Nations and its specialized agencies.

Multilateral aid
Such aid is provided in two major forms:

- contributions (as part of Official Development Assistance – ODA) made to an international organization to be used in or on behalf of a developing country, and including an agreed percentage laid down by the Development Assistance Committee (DAC) of national contributions to the regular budgets of certain multilateral bodies which are only partly active in development;
- financial assistance and technical cooperation provided by an international organization to developing countries.

New International Economic Order (NIEO)
Refers to a fundamental restructuring of the international economic system governing flows of trade, capital and technology in order to weaken the domination of this system by the countries of the North and reduce the dependence of the countries of the South on the industrialized economies.

The concept originated as a term used in the action programme adopted by the 1973 Conference of Non-Aligned Countries in Algiers. A Declaration on NIEO was agreed by the UN General Assembly in May 1974. It contained 20 principles dealing with global economic interdependence, especially in the relationships between North and South, and reformulating these and all other international economic relations on the basis of equality and cooperation.

New International Information Order (NIIO) (See New World Information and Communication Order – NWICO)

Newly industrialized countries (NICs)
This refers primarily to the four Asian countries of Hong Kong, Republic of Korea (South), Singapore and Taiwan which have witnessed a rapid boom in manufacturing capacity and output. The four are often referred to as Asia's 'tigers'. The Development Assistance Committee (DAC) includes as newly industrializing countries the Latin American nations of Argentina, Brazil and Mexico.

New World Information and Communication Order (NWICO)
Based on recognition of the fundamental global imbalances in communication and information infrastructures, as well as in international flows of news and information (mainly in a North–South direction), the concept refers to a restructuring of the existing worldwide communication and information system to the benefit of the South. Originally coined as the 'New International Information Order' at the 1973 conference of Non-Aligned Countries in Algiers, the concept was seen as complementary to Third World calls for a New International Economic Order (NIEO).

The debate on restructuring the international information and communication system was taken up by the UN Educational, Scientific and Cultural Organization (UNESCO), and became the subject of bitter contention between the Western industrialized nations (and their media institutions) and the Third World, with UNESCO depicted as an active promoter of press restrictions and governmental control of the media. Proponents of NWICO view communication and information as serving social rather than commercial functions.

Non-alignment
This is the policy of avoiding political or ideological affiliations with major power blocs, officially pursued by most independent Third World countries. The construction

of the Non-Aligned Movement started in the 1950s, largely thanks to the work of three major leaders of the day – Gamal Abdel Nasser of Egypt, Jawaharlal Nehru of India and Josip Broz Tito of Yugoslavia.

The movement received a major impetus from the 1955 meeting of African and Asian leaders in Bandung, Indonesia, which was sponsored by Burma, Ceylon (Sri Lanka), India, Indonesia and Pakistan. Other countries represented were Afghanistan, Cambodia, China (People's Republic), Egypt, Ethiopia, Gold Coast (Ghana), Iran, Iraq, Japan, Jordan, Laos, Lebanon, Liberia, Libya, Nepal, Philippines, Siam (Thailand), Sudan, Syria, Turkey, Vietnam (Democratic Republic), Vietnam (South) and Yemen (Arab Republic). This meeting issued the *10 Bandung Principles*:

- respect for fundamental rights according to the principles of the UN Charter;
- respect for the sovereignty and territorial integrity of all nations;
- recognition of the equality of all races and all nations, large and small;
- non-intervention and non-interference in the internal affairs of other countries;
- respect for the right of each nation to individual and collective defence according to the UN Charter;
- rejection of participation in collective defence preparations destined to serve the particular interests of the great powers;
- abstention from all acts or threats of aggression or the use of force against the territorial integrity or political independence of another country;
- settlement of all international conflicts by peaceful means, such as negotiation and conciliation, arbitration or agreement before tribunals, as well as any other pacific means the interested parties may adopt along the lines of the UN Charter;
- encouragement of mutual interests and cooperation;
- respect for justice and international responsibilities.

The movement held its first summit (bringing together the leaders of 25 nations) in Belgrade in 1961, where the emphasis was on bringing peace to a world dominated and threatened by the United States and the then Soviet Union, and supporting the struggle of people under colonization.

Non-governmental orgnaizations (NGOs)

While there is little common agreement on exactly what constitutes a non-governmental organization, general consensus accepts that NGOs are normally non-profit-making, often voluntary, organizations whose policies and programmes are not influenced by the governments of the countries in which they are based. The Organization for Economic Cooperation and Development (OECD) defines as NGOs national and international voluntary agencies (secular and religious, including missions), foundations, trade unions, cooperatives, professional associations, certain institutes for training or practical research and university centres of a private nature and having some aid element in their operation. For the OECD, non-profit means not being engaged in commerce or industry.

In terms of development, NGOs are commonly characterized as organizations engaged in the 'informal' implementation of small-scale projects entailing a large degree of local participation. The NGO sector is acquiring growing recognition as an effective channel for Official Development Assistance (ODA) within the context of bilateral and multilateral cooperation.

North

Commonly used to refer to the industrialized countries, most of which are in the northern hemisphere, as opposed to the developing countries of the South or the Third World.

North Atlantic Treaty Organization (NATO)

Set up to implement the North Atlantic Treaty of April 1949, the objective of NATO was to establish a military counter-weight to Soviet military presence in Europe. Member countries are Belgium, Britain, Canada, Denmark, Federal Republic of Germany, France, Greece, Iceland, Italy, Luxembourg, Netherlands, Norway, Portugal, Spain, Turkey and United States. The primary purpose of NATO is summarized in Article V of the Treaty:

> The Parties agree that an armed attack against one or more of them in Europe shall be considered an attack against them all and consequently they agree that, if such an armed attack occurs, each of them . . . will assist the Party or Parties so attacked . . . to restore and maintain the security of the North Atlantic area.

The geographical scope of NATO covers Europe and North America, the North Atlantic area north of the Tropic of Cancer and the Mediterranean.

North–South dialogue

Started in the mid-1970s with the aim of negotiating changes in the global economic system to make it more equitable and supportive of development, the North–South dialogue has collapsed. The South Commission Report notes that any multilateral negotiations that do take place, such as the Uruguay Round, 'have been called by the North, with an agenda devised to further its global interests. They have been imposed by the North on the South.'

The first concrete initiative in the North–South dialogue was the first ministerial-level Conference on International Economic Cooperation (CIEC), held in Paris in 1975 and co-chaired by Canada and Venezuela, to discuss energy, raw materials, development and finance. The conference set up four commissions to study these issues.

The North–South dialogue maintained a reasonably high profile in the period 1974 to 1979, undoubtedly, argues the South Commission, because of Northern fears that the South's new-found assertiveness after the oil price rises of 1973 could lead to a damaging confrontation. 'For as long as that threat was perceived as possible, the North kept the dialogue going; when it subsided, the North withdrew.'

North–South negotiations basically ended at UNCTAD-V in Manila in 1979, where the North rejected a Third World attempt to recognize that all different aspects of the New International Economic Order (NIEO) were interrelated. The Cancun Summit was an effort to find political support for continuing the North–South dialogue, but it failed.

Official Development Assistance (ODA)

The Development Assistance Committee (DAC) of the Organization for Economic Cooperation and Development (OECD) defines ODA as official sector grants or loans on concessional financial terms ('soft' loans that contain a grant element of at least 25 per cent) aimed at promoting economic welfare and development. UN General Assembly Resolution 2626 of 24 October 1970, fixed the net ODA target for donor countries at 0.7 per cent of Gross National Product (GNP).

In 1988 the World Bank identified only five of the OECD's then 21 industrialized member countries with ODA levels over the UN target in 1988 – Norway (1.12 per cent), Netherlands (0.98 per cent), Denmark (0.89 per cent), Sweden (0.87 per cent) and France (0.73 per cent).

OPEC Fund for International Development
Set up in 1976 by the Organization of the Petroleum Exporting Countries (OPEC), the Vienna-based fund is a collective financial facility created to consolidate OPEC member countries' development assistance to Third World countries. Assistance from the fund is over and above existing bilateral and multilateral channels between OPEC countries and Third World beneficiaries. The fund's major operations are:

- to provide concessional loans for balance of payments support;
- to provide concessional loans for the implementation of development projects and programmes;
- to make contributions and/or provide loans to eligible international agencies;
- to finance technical assistance activities.

Organization for Economic Cooperation and Development (OECD)
Founded in 1961 to stimulate the economic progress of the Western industrialized nations and further the expansion of world trade, the Paris-based organization brings together 27 industrialized countries – Australia, Austria, Belgium, Britain, Canada, Czech Republic, Denmark, Eire (Ireland), Federal Republic of Germany, Finland, France, Hungary, Iceland, Italy, Japan, Luxembourg, Mexico, Netherlands, New Zealand, Norway, Spain, Sweden, Switzerland and United States – plus Greece, Portugal and Turkey (classified as middle-income developing countries).

A major objective of the OECD is to achieve the highest possible economic growth, employment and rising standard of living in member countries. At the same time, it emphasizes the maintenance of financial stability. The organization has attempted to reach this goal by liberalizing international trade and the movement of capital between countries. Another goal is the coordination of economic aid to developing countries through the Development Assistance Committee (DAC).

Organization of African Unity (OAU)
Formed in 1963 by the continent's then independent states to support the struggle for its total liberation and to defend their sovereignty, the Addis-Ababa-based OAU has since been concerned to promote a collective view for strengthening Africa's new nations (only relatively recently freed from colonialism) and improving their position in the global economy. The organization took the decision shortly after its creation to recognize boundaries inherited from the colonial period in a bid to avoid border conflicts. All African states are members.

Organization of American States (OAS)
Established in 1948, the organization was set up to work for social and economic development and to act as a peace-keeping organization for all American states, from the United States to the Caribbean and Latin America. The OAS replaced the Pan-American Union, created in 1910 as a follow-on to the International Union of American Republics set up in 1890. The organization, which has its Secretariat in Washington, has been strongly influenced by the United States, which managed to have Cuba expelled in 1962 on charges of 'exporting subversion'.

Organization of the Islamic Conference (OIC)
Set up in Jeddah (Saudi Arabia) in 1971, the organization aims to promote Islamic solidarity by coordinating social, economic, scientific and cultural activities. In particular, the conference has pledged to eliminate racial segregation and discrimination, especially as regards the Palestine Liberation Organization (PLO). The organization's

members cover more than 40 states including Afghanistan, Algeria, Bahrain, Bangladesh, Burkina Faso, Cameroon, Chad, Comoros, Djibouti, Egypt, Gabon, Gambia, Guinea, Guinea-Bissau, Indonesia, Iran, Iraq, Jordan, Kuwait, Lebanon, Libya, Malaysia, Maldives, Mali, Mauritania, Morocco, Niger, Oman, Qatar, Saudi Arabia, Senegal, Somalia, Sudan, Syria, Tunisia, Turkey, Uganda, United Arab Emirates and Yemen, plus the PLO.

Organization of the Petroleum Exporting Countries (OPEC)
The Vienna-based Organization of the Petroleum Exporting Countries (OPEC) is a permanent inter-governmental body created in Baghdad in 1960. OPEC member countries (all from the Third World) are the five founders – Iran, Iraq, Kuwait, Saudi Arabia and Venezuela – plus Algeria, Ecuador, Gabon, Indonesia, Libya, Nigeria, Qatar and United Arab Emirates. The objective of the organization is to coordinate and unify petroleum policies among member countries in order to secure fair and stable prices for petroleum producers, efficient, economic and regular supply of petroleum to consuming nations, and a fair return on capital to those investing in the industry.

During the 1960s, notes the Brandt Commission Report, OPEC had little effect on the low-price policies of the oil companies. But in 1973–74 it was able to quadruple prices, and double them again in 1978–79. The organization has suffered from internal disputes, with countries like Kuwait exceeding crude oil output quotas agreed by OPEC conferences.

Palestine Liberation Organization (PLO)
In 1964, the Palestine National Council (comprising representatives of Palestinians in territories occupied by Israel and those in exile) met for the first time and founded the Palestine Liberation Organization (PLO). The main political organization represented in the PLO is the Al-Fatah National Liberation Movement, founded in 1965 by Yasser Arafat, who has chaired the PLO since 1969. The second largest group is the Popular Front for the Liberation of Palestine, founded in 1967 by George Habbash. Other groups include the Palestine Communist Party and the Democratic Front for the Liberation of Palestine.

On 15 November 1988, a meeting in Tunis of the Palestine National Council – the Palestinian parliament-in-exile – proclaimed the independent state of Palestine.

Paris Club
The 'Paris Club' negotiates arrangements to defer payment obligations on credits extended or guaranteed by creditor country government agencies.

Perestroika
The policy of 'restructuring' in the Soviet system introduced by Mikhail Gorbachev, then head of the Communist Party of the Soviet Union and President of the Supreme Soviet.

Point Four Program
US policy of technical assistance and economic aid to underdeveloped countries – so named because it was the fourth point of President Harry S. Truman's inaugural address. Based on the success of the Marshall Plan, the programme was originally administered by a special agency of the US State Department, but was merged with other foreign aid programmes in 1953. The programme was designed to promote US

influence by making modern technological and scientific knowledge available to underdeveloped areas in Africa, Asia and Latin America.

Protectionism
The policy of protecting domestic industries against foreign competition through tariffs, subsidies or import quotas. The proliferation of high protective tariffs around the world led 23 nations to sign reciprocal trade agreements in the form of the General Agreement on Tariffs and Trade (GATT) in 1948. Third World countries in particular have been hit hard by various forms of protectionist barriers erected by the countries of the North to exclude Third World goods from Northern markets.

Ratification
Final approval of a treaty, convention or similar agreement with a signature. International agreements cannot be implemented until they have been ratified by a certain number of countries (which varies from agreement to agreement and is stipulated in the text of the agreement).

Regional cooperation and integration
Recognized by the Third World Group of 77 countries as fundamental for the realization of Economic Cooperation among Developing Countries (ECDC) and a decrease in economic dependence on the industrialized countries of the North. One key sector for such cooperation and integration is trade, where increased South–South exchange could help offset the negative consequences of protectionism in the North. However, South–South trade is hindered by the structure of the international economic system, in which physical and financial facilities for trade favour North–South patterns.

Regional development banks
Such banks are smaller but independent regional versions of the World Bank, in which capital is subscribed by member countries in the same way and loans are provided for the same purposes and on the same lines. The regional development banks include the African Development Bank, the Asian Development Bank, the Arab Bank for Economic Development in Africa and the Inter-American Development Bank.

Restructuring
The process whereby economies are modified to adapt to the changes brought about as old industries or other economic activities contract and new ones develop.

Rio Group
Brings together Argentina, Brazil, Chile, Colombia, Ecuador, Mexico, Peru, Uruguay and Venezuela in an effort to promote regional integration. Panama was also a member, but was suspended in 1988 in view of the political turmoil in that country.

Sahel
The sub-region of sub-Saharan Africa comprising the seven countries of Burkina Faso, Chad, Gambia, Mali, Mauritania, Niger and Senegal.

Self-determination
The process by which a group of people possessing a degree of national consciousness form their own state and select their own government. In the post-Second World War

period, self-determination became one of the primary goals of the United Nations. The UN Charter (under Article 1, Paragraph 2 and Article 55, Paragraph 1) clarifies two meanings of self-determination:

1. A state has the right of self-determination in the sense of having the right to freely choose its political, economic, social and cultural systems.
2. The right to self-determination is the right of a people to constitute itself in a state or otherwise freely determine the form of its association with an existing state.

Self-reliance

A concept that encompasses recognition by many Third World countries that escape from the current crisis in which they find themselves means moving away from obligatory dependence on the dictates of the industrialized economies and international financial institutions. Self-reliance is the objective of Third World societies searching for the path toward equitable and sustainable development, where the development of Third World societies is fuelled by their own resources, both individually and collectively. A major key to self-reliance is the adoption of a people-centred approach to development in which priority is given to meeting the basic needs of the people in sectors such as food security, health, education and employment.

Services

Non-tangible artefacts created by an economic system and including banking, communications, retail and wholesale trade, professional services (such as engineering and medicine), non-profit economic activities, consumer services and government services (including defence and administration of justice). Service industries are one of two major categories of economic activity – the other being goods industries (such as agriculture, mining, manufacturing and construction) which produce tangible artefacts.

Society for International Development (SID)

Founded in 1957 as a forum for the exchange of ideas between and among people interested in international, economic, political and social development, the association is today the world's largest membership organization devoted to international development. A non-governmental organization, SID has more than 9,000 members in 132 countries, and much of its work is carried out through approximately 90 SID chapters. The Rome-based SID has three primary objectives:

1. to promote international dialogue, understanding and cooperation for social and economic development that furthers the well-being of all peoples and a truly interdependent world of self-reliant nations;
2. to encourage, support and facilitate the creation of a sense of community among individuals and organizations committed to development at local, regional and international levels;
3. to advance the science, processes and art of social and economic development through educational means, including research, publications and discussion.

Solidarity

In the context of relations between North and South, the term refers to mutual action to find an answer to problems afflicting the socio-economic development of Third

World peoples. Solidarity is based on recognition of the interdependence that characterizes international relations at all levels.

South

Commonly used to refer to the developing countries of the Third World, most of which are located in the southern hemisphere of the world, as opposed to the industrialized countries of the North.

South Commission

A group of 28 individuals brought together in 1987 from all continents of the South, acting in their personal capacities to analyse the problems faced by the countries of the South, the strategies they have adopted to deal with them, and the lessons to be drawn in the context of current and future international conditions. The Commission was chaired by then Tanzanian president Julius Nyerere.

The main objective of the commission, which issued its report, *The Challenge to the South*, in August 1990, was defined as helping the peoples and governments of the South to be more effective in overcoming their many problems, in developing their countries in freedom, and in improving the lives and living conditions of their peoples.

Underlying the recommendations contained in the commission's report regarding appropriate strategies for and conducive to development of the South is recognition that responsibility for this development lies in the hands of the peoples of the South, and in this context the report stresses the need to expand South–South cooperation.

The commission urged the governments and peoples of the South to implement a Programme of Priority Action for South–South Cooperation, including the following suggestions:

- The success of South–South cooperation depends on supportive national policies. Each Third World country's development plans and national policies should reflect an explicit commitment to such cooperation.
- To develop the South's human resources, fuller use should be made of the South's educational institutions in meeting the needs of countries with inadequate facilities.
- In the area of financial cooperation, priority attention should be given to strengthening regional and sub-regional clearing and payments arrangements, as well as export credit facilities.
- A debtors' forum and a South Bank should be established.
- There should be effective use of the framework for easing all forms of South–South trade created by the Global System of Trade Preferences (GSTP) among developing countries which became effective in April 1989.
- Cooperation among business enterprises of the South should be promoted at bilateral, sub-regional, regional and inter-regional levels, with preferential treatment being given to investment and technology flows from other developing countries.
- A process should be started to review food security and set up coordinated national food-stocks and jointly-managed emergency food reserves within regions or sub-regions.
- A strategy for South–South scientific cooperation should be developed.

At the same time, the commission recognized that development of the South is closely tied to an improvement in relations with the North – 'the issue for the South is not whether to cut its links with the North, but how to transform them. The relationship must be changed from exploitation to shared benefit, from subordination to partnership.'

The South Commission called for immediate negotiations to revive the North–South Dialogue through a six-point Global Programme of Immediate Action:

- Action to stop the net transfer of resources from South to North, to remove the overhang of the Third World's external debt, and to scale down debt servicing.
- Establishment of multilateral arrangements for protecting the global environment and ensuring sustainable development, while respecting the freedom of governments to set their own national priorities.
- Doubling of the volume of concessional transfers of resources to Third World countries by 1995, primarily through multilateral agencies, with the additional resources being devoted to food production, provision of other basic needs, population control, energy security and other environmentally sensitive areas.
- Setting up independent international mechanisms to evaluate the requirements of developing countries, as a step toward depoliticizing negotiations between international financial institutions and developing countries.
- A timetable for lifting protectionist barriers that damage the growth of Third World exports to the North, provision for the stabilization and support of the international prices of primary commodities of special export interest to developing countries, and a commitment to negotiate international agreements for these commodities.
- The incorporation of contingency provisions in international arrangements to protect developing countries against excessive fluctuations in international interest rates, exchange rates and terms of trade.

Special Drawing Rights (SDRs)

Standard units of account of the International Monetary Fund (IMF), SDRs form an international reserve currency, originally introduced by the Group of 10 in 1969. They are issued to IMF members from time to time in proportion to their fund quotas, comprise part of any loan made by the fund, and are only traded between central banks (and the Bank for International Settlements – BIS). They are not used in commercial transactions. SDRs are known as 'special' because they are additional to the credit facilities already existing for IMF member countries and are not repayable.

The Brandt Commission Report argued for an increase in the use of SDRs within the international monetary system only if they became 'the principal means of increasing global liquidity'. The report called for an 'SDR link' in increasing world liquidity, based on the argument that 'new reserves should be allocated to those countries which are most likely to experience balance-of-payments deficits and high domestic adjustments', a category which comprises many Third World countries. The Brandt Commission wanted to see developing countries receive a larger share of new unconditional reserves than they normally receive through allocations proportional to the IMF quota system.

Specialized agencies of the United Nations

The Charter of the United Nations defines such bodies as 'agencies established by inter-governmental agreement and having wide international responsibilities, as defined in their basic instrument, in economic, social, cultural, educational, health' and connected fields, which are related to the United Nations. The specialized agencies are the following:

Food and Agriculture Organization
Inter-Governmental Maritime Consultative Organization
International Civil Aviation Organization
International Development Association (World Bank affiliate)
International Finance Corporation (World Bank affiliate)
International Fund for Agricultural Development
International Labour Organization
International Monetary Fund
International Telecommunication Union
UN Educational, Scientific and Cultural Organization
UN Industrial Development Organization
Universal Postal Union
World Bank
World Health Organization
World Intellectual Property Organization
World Meteorological Organization

Strategic Arms Limitation Talks (SALT)

Negotiations between the then Soviet Union and the United States aimed at curtailing the production of strategic (long-range or inter-continental) nuclear weapons. The first agreements (SALT-I in 1972 and SALT-II in 1979) were intended to hold back the arms race in strategic nuclear weapons. SALT negotiations stalled under US President Ronald Reagan, who was eventually forced by the North Atlantic Treaty Organization (NATO) and the peace movement to resume talks under the name of Strategic Arms Reduction Talks (START).

Strategic Arms Reduction Talks (START)

Begun under US President Ronald Reagan, START was a follow-on to the Strategic Arms Limitation Talks (SALT) and opened in Geneva in 1982. The then Soviet Union withdrew in 1983 in reaction to NATO deployment of Cruise and Pershing missiles in Europe. With the end of the so-called 'Cold War' in the late 1980s and détente between the two superpowers – the Soviet Union and the United States – talks resumed and agreement was reached on reducing strategic arms stockpiles in Europe.

Structural adjustment

The process of making policy changes in a country's economy to adjust it to a changing environment, usually external. Countries implementing structural adjustment programmes have had to cut public expenditure to reduce budget deficits and meet debt repayment obligations. This has resulted in hardships for the people, mainly declining income per person and real wages, rising unemployment and under-employment, deteriorating social services such as education and health, and worsening nutritional standards. Third World attempts to minimize the negative effects of adjustment programmes have led to a search for alternative approaches and three major concepts have emerged:

- 'adjustment with growth and equity' (IMF/World Bank)
- 'adjustment with a human face' (IMF)
- 'adjustment with transformation' (UN Economic Commission for Africa – ECA)

All three approaches call for a return to the true meaning of socio-economic development, which covers economic growth, adjustment to a changing international and national economic environment, equity and social justice.

Sub-Saharan Africa
All countries south of the Sahara, excluding South Africa – that is, all African countries other than Algeria, Egypt, Libya, Morocco and Tunisia. The heavy dependence of sub-Saharan African economies on a single commodity or narrow range of commodities is more precarious than in any other group of countries, and they are more vulnerable to commodity price fluctuations and deteriorations in commodity terms of trade. While 70 per cent of the population is dependent on the land for a living, land erosion is widespread and increasing at the rate of 8 million hectares per year. Average Gross National Product (GNP) per person is declining and population growth is continuing to outpace economic and social advances.

Sustainable development
Development which meets the needs and aspirations of present generations without compromising those of future generations. The concept recognizes that development can only be sustained through the informed and active participation of the people whose improved welfare is the objective. The term became popularized largely through *Our Common Future*, the final report of the World Commission on Environment and Development (WCED), also known as the Brundtland Commission. 'Sustainable development' is often incorrectly equated with purely environmental concerns, omitting the importance of the social, political, economic and human resources dimensions of the concept, although a key concern of 'sustainable development' is to protect the productive capacity of the environment.

Tariffs
Taxes levied on commodities traded across the border of a country, or the borders of a group of countries that have formed a customs union. Tariffs are sometimes called customs or duties. In relation to international trade patterns, tariffs applied by industrialized countries have served to protect domestic industry against Third World imports by allowing domestic producers to charge a higher price for their goods than competitors.

Technical assistance
A form of aid given to less developed countries by international organizations such as the United Nations and associated agencies, governments and foundations, and comprising the provision of expertise to promote development. Also known as technical cooperation, technical assistance can involve sending experts to teach skills in specialized areas (such as irrigation, agriculture, forestry, fisheries, public health or education). It can also take the form of scholarships, study tours or seminars in the industrialized countries of the North.

Technical Cooperation among Developing Countries (TCDC)
Within the framework of Economic Cooperation among Developing Countries (ECDC), Third World countries have supported proposals to try to upgrade their indigenous technological capacity through collective efforts. Officially backed by the UN Development Programme (UNDP), TCDC calls for the countries of the South to

share skills and establish where necessary regional and sub-regional centres to adapt and develop technology, in a bid to decrease dependence on Northern technology. The Brandt Commission Report saw the possibility of more industrially advanced developing countries such as India, Brazil and Yugoslavia taking a lead in TCDC. Through TCDC, greater attention is given to the use of the most relevant skills and technical knowledge available in Third World countries for the solution of problems in other Third World countries.

Technology transfer
Technology can be transmitted in a variety of ways, from sales of machinery and know-how, through training and technical assistance, to participation in the construction and operation of an overseas firm.

The Brandt Commission Report argues that 'the sharing of technology is a worldwide concern . . . But clearly it is most important to the developing countries; and it can even be argued that their principal weakness is the lack of access to technology, or of command of it.' However, the report warns, while the 'economic and social objectives of a developing country will both determine the choice of technology, and be determined by it', the countries of the Third World can only benefit from acquired technology if they can absorb and adapt such technology.

Meanwhile, many Third World countries have expressed concern not only over their dependence on Northern technology but also on importing technology which is unsuitable for local conditions. This has led to the demand for appropriate technology.

Third World
Conventionally used to refer to those countries (practically all former colonial territories) which do not belong to either of the former major power blocs – the industrialized market economies of the 'First World' or the then-socialist centrally-planned economies of the 'Second World'. In practice, 'Third World' countries are also known as the 'South' or as 'developing countries', and on occasion the term is also used as a synonym for 'Non-Aligned' nations.

The Third World, the countries of which are characterized by greater or lesser degrees of economic underdevelopment, contain 3.5 billion people, three-quarters of all humanity, and cover more than two-thirds of the Earth's land surface area. The socio-economic development of Third World countries is heavily conditioned by the external environment, primarily the economic interests of the industrialized North.

The South Commission Report notes that Third World countries 'vary greatly in size, in natural resource endowment, in the level of economic, social and technological development. They also differ in their cultures, in their political systems, and in the ideologies they profess.' But, argues the report, what the Third World countries 'have in common transcends their differences; it gives them a shared identity'.

Trade and Development Board
The permanent executive body of the UN Conference on Trade and Development (UNCTAD), which is based in Geneva and normally meets twice a year. It receives reports and recommendations from a number of permanent committees on specific trade areas, including commodities, Economic Cooperation among Developing Countries (ECDC), invisibles and financing, manufacturing, shipping, transfer of technology and trade preferences.

Trade liberalization
The attempt to open up the international trade system, primarily with the aim of benefiting Third World country exporters, by reducing tariff and non-tariff restrictions on imports, mostly imposed by the industrialized market economies of the North.

Transnational corporations (TNCs)
Also often referred to as 'multinational corporations', TNCs are defined by the United Nations as 'corporations that possess or control the means of production or services outside the country where they are established'. TNCs are concentrated in the industrialized countries of the North and, though they vary in size and influence, share two aspects in common:

- Individually, they are decision-making centres, controlling the production process in more than one country and managing investments, production, commercialization, finance and prices across international boundaries.
- Collectively, they are the main components of world capital and the most powerful agent in the transnationalization of production, finance, trade, information and the values of market capitalism.

As such, they subordinate national states' and private capital to their own interests. The Brandt Commission Report notes that TNCs 'are now major actors in the world's political economy. They control between a quarter and a third of all world production.' A major concern for Third World countries is that much of the international trade conducted by TNCs is within themselves, between parent companies and affiliates.

The Brandt Report estimated that such 'intra-firm trade' accounts for over 30 per cent of all world trade. At the same time, argues the report, TNCs manipulate financial flows by the use of artificial transfer prices, shifting profits from high to low tax countries or to get around exchange or price controls or customs duties.

TNCs have also been criticized for imposing restrictive trade practices (such as allocation of markets) that hinder development in host countries, and for engaging in unethical political and commercial activities in many Third World countries, which has encouraged corruption in the ranks of local elites. International concern with the activities of TNCs led to the setting up of the UN Centre on Transnational Corporations. There has also been pressure for agreeing international codes of conduct for TNCs.

UN Centre on Transnational Corporations
The Centre on Transnational Corporations (TNCs) is an autonomous body within the United Nations Secretariat and serves the Commission on Transnational Corporations, a subsidiary of the UN Economic and Social Council (ECOSOC). Its role is to promote understanding of transnational corporations (TNCs) and their political, socio-economic and legal effects on home and host countries, and in international relations (particularly between industrialized and Third World countries).

The centre also aims to increase the contribution of TNCs to national development goals and strength of the world economy while controlling and eliminating their negative effects, and to strengthen the negotiating capacity of developing host countries in particular in their dealings with TNCs.

UN Charter
The United Nations Charter was drawn up in 1945 by representatives of 50 countries on the basis of proposals worked out by representatives of Britain, China, Soviet

Union and United States at Dumbarton Oaks, Washington in 1944. The Charter was signed on 26 June 1945 and the United Nations officially came into existence on 24 October 1945 when the Charter had been ratified by Britain, China, France, Soviet Union and United States, and by a majority of other signatories. October 24 is celebrated each year as United Nations Day.

Preamble to the United Nations Charter
The Preamble to the Charter expresses the ideals and common aims of all the peoples whose governments joined together to form the United Nations:

We the peoples of the United Nations, determined

to save succeeding generations from the scourge of war, which twice in our lifetime has brought untold sorrow to mankind, and to reaffirm faith in fundamental human rights, in the dignity and worth of the human person, in the equal rights of men and women and of nations large and small, and

to establish conditions under which justice and respect for the obligations arising from treaties and other sources of international law can be maintained, and

to promote social progress and better standards of life in larger freedom,

and for these ends

to practise tolerance and live together in peace with one another as good neighbours, and

to unite our strength to maintain international peace and security, and

to ensure, by the acceptance of principles and the institution of methods, that armed force shall not be used, save in the common interest, and

to employ international machinery for the promotion of the economic and social advancement of all peoples,

have resolved to combine our efforts to accomplish these aims

Accordingly, our respective Governments, through representatives assembled in the city of San Francisco, who have exhibited their full powers found to be in good and due form, have agreed to the present Charter of the United Nations and do hereby establish an international organization to be known as the United Nations.

UN Commission on Human Rights (UNCHR)
Set up by the United Nations to receive reports submitted by member states of the UN General Assembly's International Convention on Civil and Political Rights. The commission is entitled to address general comments to these states and to the UN Economic and Social Council (ECOSOC). A Facultative Protocol (1976) on the convention gave the commission the power to examine claims from individuals of violation of any of the rights specified in the convention by a member state, provided that such individuals have exhausted all available means under domestic jurisdiction.

UN Conference on Trade and Development (UNCTAD)
Held in Geneva in 1964, the first UN Conference on Trade and Development (UNCTAD-I) led to the setting up of UNCTAD as a permanent UN body, with a secretariat in Geneva. The conference grew out of the increasing dissatisfaction of Third World countries with the failure to close the gap between their economies and those of the industrialized world. UNCTAD-I saw the creation of the Third World Group of 77 (G77).

A major concern of UNCTAD is to negotiate and adopt multilateral legal instruments to govern the conduct of international trade, and it is also concerned with implementing programmes aimed at securing remunerative, equitable and stable prices for the primary commodities on which Third World countries depend for export earnings. Such programmes are negotiated under the umbrella of UNCTAD's Integrated Programme for Commodities, a central element of which is the Common Fund that came into existence in 1989. Key fixed-term agreements on specific commodities include those concerning natural rubber (1987), cocoa (1986) and olive oil (1986). Other significant UNCTAD initiatives include fixing levels for aid targets, and setting up the Generalized System of Preferences scheme for exports of manufactured goods from the Third World. Major multilateral agreements negotiated by UNCTAD in the field of international trade include:

> *Convention on a Code of Conduct for Liner Conferences* (1974), which establishes rules concerning the operation of liner shipping;
> *Set of Multilaterally Agreed Equitable Principles and Rules for the Control of Restrictive Business Practices* (1980), which established for the first time international means for controlling restrictive business practices, including those of transnational corporations (TNCs), adversely affecting the trade and economic development of Third World countries in particular;
> *United Nations Convention on International Multimodal Transport of Goods* (1980), which established a legal regime for the contract of such goods;
> *United Nations Convention on Conditions for Registration of Ships* (1986), which introduced new standards of responsibility and accountability in world shipping.

Negotiations have been under way since 1978 on an International Code of Conduct on the Transfer of Technology.

In the early 1980s, UNCTAD launched a 'Substantial New Programme of Action for the 1980s' for the least developed countries, with a view to transforming their economies by ushering in self-sustained development and minimum standards of nutrition, health, transport and communications, housing, education and job opportunities. The executive organ of UNCTAD is the Trade and Development Board, which normally meets twice a year.

UN Development Decades

In the 1960s, 1970s and 1980s, the UN General Assembly proclaimed Development Decades geared to promoting the implementation of an International Development Strategy to benefit the countries of the South. The first UN Development Decade (1961–70) was declared by the UN General Assembly in December 1961, the second (1971–80) in October 1970 and the third (1981–90) in December 1980. These initiatives are widely recognized as having failed, as the gap between North and South has widened.

The Third UN Development Decade pledged governments 'to fulfil their commitment to establish a new international economic order based on justice and equity' but the Preamble to the International Development Strategy recognized the failure of the preceding two decades and warned that the inequities and imbalances in international economic relations 'are widening the gap between developed and developing countries', constitute a 'major obstacle to the development of the developing countries' and 'adversely affect international relations and the promotion of world peace and security'.

UN Development Programme (UNDP)

Set up by the United Nations in 1965 through the merger of the UN Special Fund and the Expanded Programme of Technical Assistance to coordinate the various types of technical cooperation programmes being carried out within the UN system. The New York-based UNDP, the world's largest channel for multilateral technical and pre-investment cooperation, is active in more than 150 Third World countries and aims to help build more productive societies and economies in low-income nations by developing natural resources and human capacity.

Aid is administered through five-year 'country programmes' that fund projects in the sectors of attracting development capital, training skilled manpower, and providing the technologies necessary for expanding commerce, industry and communication. The aim is to help developing countries make better use of their human and natural resources, improve living standards and expand productivity. UNDP also tries to act as a catalyst in helping mobilize the capital investments required.

UN Economic and Social Council (ECOSOC)

The Economic and Social Council was set up under the Charter of the United Nations as the main body for coordinating economic and social issues of a global or interdisciplinary nature within the United Nations and its specialized agencies and institutions. It also formulates policy recommendations on such issues. The council has 54 members each of whom serves for three years, 18 being replaced each year. Voting is by simple majority, with each member having one vote. The New York-based ECOSOC has various subsidiary bodies:

- Six *functional commissions* on Statistics, Population, Social Development, Human Rights, Status of Women, and Narcotic Drugs;
- Five *regional commissions*
  Economic Commission for Africa (ECA), based in Addis Ababa, Ethiopia
  Economic and Social Commission for Asia and the Pacific (ESCAP), based in Bangkok, Thailand
  Economic Commission for Europe (ECE), based in Geneva, Switzerland
  Economic Commission for Latin America and the Caribbean (ECLAC), based in Santiago, Chile
  Economic and Social Commission for Western Asia (ESCWA), based in Baghdad, Iraq
- Six *standing committees* on Programme and Coordination, Natural Resources, Non-Governmental Organizations, Negotiations with Inter-Governmental Agencies, Transnational Corporations, and Human Settlements.

UN Economic Commission for Africa (ECA)

Set up by the United Nations in 1958 with headquarters in Addis Ababa, the commission carries out research and provides advice on economic and technological development in Africa.

UN Educational, Scientific and Cultural Organization (UNESCO)

The specialized UN agency created in 1946 to contribute to world peace by promoting international cooperation in the fields of education, science, culture and communication. The Paris-based agency attempts to assist the national efforts of member states in the elimination of illiteracy and the extension of free education. It also seeks to encourage the free exchange of ideas and knowledge among peoples and nations by providing exchange services.

In the social sciences sector, UNESCO has commissioned studies on issues ranging from tensions leading to war and racism, through the socio-economic factors of development to the relationship between humans and their environment. The agency's cultural activities are mainly concerned with stimulating artistic creativity, conservation of the world's inheritance of books, works of arts and monuments, and the preservation of cultural identities and oral traditions.

In communications, UNESCO has created the International Programme for the Development of Communication (IPDC) to provide finance for setting up infrastructures in this sector, primarily in the Third World. UNESCO came under fire in the 1970s and 1980s from Western nations for supporting Third World calls for a New World Information and Communication Order (NWICO). The West claimed that its support for adjusting imbalances in the international information order masked an attempt to legitimize suppression of press freedom. UNESCO came under particularly fierce attack in 1978 for adopting the 'Declaration on Fundamental Principles concerning the contribution of the Mass Media to strengthening Peace and International Understanding, to the Promotion of Human Rights and to countering Racialism, Apartheid and Incitement to War'. The United States and Britain both withdrew from UNESCO in 1985 on the grounds that the then Secretary-General, Amadou Mahtar M'Bow of Senegal, had 'over-politicized' the agency.

United Nations (UN)

Officially established by Charter (see UN Charter) on 24 October 1945 with the aims of:

- maintaining international peace and security;
- developing friendly relations among nations on the principle of equal rights and self-determination;
- encouraging international cooperation in solving international economic, social, cultural and humanitarian problems.

The United Nations comprises six main organs:

1. The *UN General Assembly* – includes representatives of all members of the United Nations, each nation having one vote. Decisions are reached either by majority or two-thirds vote depending on the issue.
2. The *UN Security Council* – comprises five permanent members (Britain, China, France, Soviet Union and United States) and ten non-permanent members on a one-month rotating basis. Nine votes are sufficient to carry a Security Council decision but any permanent member may exercise a veto.
3. The *UN Economic and Social Council* – comprises 27 members elected for three years by the UN General Assembly. It is mainly concerned with management of the United Nations' social, economic, cultural and humanitarian activities.
4. The *UN Trusteeship Council* – handles the affairs of trust territories placed under the care of a country by the United Nations. Members are elected by the UN General Assembly for a three-year term on the basis of need, depending on the number of trusteeships.
5. The *UN International Court of Justice* – also known as the 'World Court', it is located in The Hague and is the main judicial branch of the United Nations, comprising 15 judges elected for nine-year terms by both the UN General Assembly and the UN Security Council.

6. The *UN Secretariat* – the administrative department of the United Nations, headed by the Secretary-General, who is appointed by both the UN General Assembly and the UN Security Council.

Current Secretary-General
Boutros Boutros-Ghali Egypt (1992–   )

Former Secretaries-General
Javier Pérez de Cuellar, Peru (1982–91)
Kurt Waldheim, Austria (1972–81)
U Thant, Burma (1962–71)
Dag Hammarskjöld, Sweden (1953–61)
Trygve Lie, Norway (1946–53)

UN Security Council
One of the six major organs of the United Nations, the Security Council comprises five permanent members (Britain, China, France, Soviet Union and United States) and ten non-permanent members on a one-month rotating basis. Nine votes are sufficient to carry a Security Council decision but any permanent member may exercise a veto.

Universal Declaration of Human Rights
Adopted and proclaimed by the UN General Assembly under General Resolution 217 A (III) of 10 December 1948, the Declaration sets out internationally agreed standards on the rights to be enjoyed by and protected for all peoples and nations.

Universal Postal Union (UPU)
Set up in 1875 when the Universal Postal Convention came into force. The Berne-based organization aims to ensure the organization and perfection of the postal services of member countries, which are united in a single postal territory for the reciprocal exchange of correspondence.

Warsaw Pact
Formally the Warsaw Treaty of Friendship, Cooperation and Mutual Assistance, the pact was a treaty signed in 1955 establishing a mutual defence organization comprising Bulgaria, Czechoslovakia, German Democratic Republic, Hungary, Poland, Romania and the Soviet Union. Albania withdrew in 1968. The pact, which was dissolved in 1991 following the collapse of communism in Eastern Europe, was set up in reaction to the admission of the then Federal Republic of Germany to the North Atlantic Treaty Organization (NATO).

West Asia (see Middle East)

World Bank
The World Bank (officially known as the International Bank for Reconstruction and Development – IBRD), set up in 1945 and owned by the governments of 179 countries, has the declared aim of raising living standards in developing countries through the provision of loans that stimulate economic growth.
   The Bank's capital is subscribed by member countries, and it finances its lending operations primarily from its own borrowings in the world capital markets. World Bank loans, which are made to governments and must be guaranteed by the

governments concerned, normally carry a five-year grace period and are repayable over 15 years or less.

Together with the International Monetary Fund (IMF), the World Bank is widely known as a Bretton Woods institution, after the name of the US town in which the 1944 UN monetary and financial conference that led to their creation took place.

World Commission on Environment and Development (WCED) (see Brundtland Commission)

World Intellectual Property Organization (WIPO)
The Geneva-based World Intellectual Property Organization became a specialized UN agency in 1974. It had its origins in the 1883 Paris Convention for the Protection of Industrial Property and the 1886 Berne Convention for the Protection of Literary and Artistic Works. The convention establishing WIPO was signed in 1967 and entered into force in 1970. WIPO's main objectives are to maintain and increase respect for intellectual property throughout the world, and to promote industrial and cultural development by stimulating creative activity and facilitating the transfer of technology and dissemination of literary and artistic works. Intellectual property comprises industrial property (inventions, trade marks and design) and copyright. (See also Intellectual Property Rights.)

World Trade Organization (WTO)
The World Trade Organization (WTO) is the embodiment of the results of the Uruguay Round of trade negotiations and the successor to the General Agreement on Tariffs and Trade (GATT). Established on 1 January 1995, it is the legal and institutional foundation of the multilateral trading system. It provides the principal contractual obligations determining how governments frame and implement domestic trade legislation and regulations. And it is the platform on which trade relations among countries evolve through collective debate, negotiation and adjudication.

References

Abel, E. (1982) 'Global Information: The New Battleground', *Political Communication and Persuasion* 1: 347–57.

Adams, N. (1994) 'The UN's Neglected Briefs "The advancement of all peoples"?' in Childers, E. (ed.), *Challenges to the United Nations*. London: St. Martin's Press. pp. 26–50.

Adorno, T. and Horkheimer, M. (1972) *Dialectic of Enlightenment*. New York: Seabury Press.

Ajayi, J.F.A. (1969) 'Colonialism: An Episode' in Gann, L.H. and Duignan, P. (eds) *Colonialism in Africa 1870–1960: Vol One – The History and Politics of Colonialism, 1870–1914*. Cambridge: Cambridge University Press. pp. 497–509.

Alavi, B. (1972) 'The State in Post-Colonial Societies: Pakistan and Bangladesh', *New Left Review*, 74: 59–81.

Altbach, P. (1987) *Higher Education in the Third World*. New York: Advent Books.

Altbach, P., Arboleda, A. and Gopinatham, S. (eds) (1985) *Publishing in the Third World*. London: Heinemann.

Altbach, P., Altbach, G. and Kelly, G.P. (1988) *Textbooks in the Third World*. New York and London: Garland Publishing.

Althusser, L. (1971) 'Ideology and Ideological State Apparatuses', in Althusser, L. *Lenin and Philosophy and Other Essays*. New York: Monthly Review Press. pp. 121–73.

Alvares, C.A. (1979) *Homo Faber: Technology and Culture in India, China and the West 1500–1972*. Bombay: Allied Publishers.

Amin, S. (1976) 'The Third World and the New Economic Order', *Cultures*, 3: 4. Paris: UNESCO.

Amin, S. (1977a) *Imperialism and Unequal Development*. Brighton: Harvester Press.

Amin, S. (1977b) 'Self-Reliance and the New International Economic Order', *Monthly Review*, 29: 3.

Amin, S. (1989) *Eurocentrism*. New York: Monthly Review Press.

Amin, S. (1990a) *Maldevelopment: Anatomy of a Global Failure*. London: Zed Press.

Amin, S. (1990b) *Delinking: Towards a Polycentric World*. London: Zed Press.

Amin, S. (1990c) *The Future of Socialism*. Southern Africa Political Economy. Series 5. Zimbabwe: Southern Africa Printing and Publishing House.

Amin, S., Arrighi, G., Frank, A.G. and Wallerstein, I. (1990) *Transforming the Revolution: Social Movements and the World System*. New York: Monthly Review Press.

Anderson, P. (1974) *Lineages of the Absolutist State*. London: Verso.

Ansah, P. (1985) 'African Responses to the NWICO Debate', in Lee, P. (ed.) *Communication For All: New World Information and Communication Order*. New York: Orbis Books. pp. 57–69.

Ansah, P. (1986) 'The Struggle for Rights and Values in Communication', in Traber,

M. (ed.) *The Myth of the Information Revolution: Social and Ethical Implications of Communication Technology*. London: Sage Publications. pp. 64–83.

Apels, K. (1992) 'The Moral Imperative', *The UNESCO Courier*, July/August: 13–17.

Appadurai, A. (1990) 'Disjuncture and Difference in the Global Cultural Economy', *Public Culture*, 2 (2): 2–23.

Arnold, D. (1988) *Imperial Medicine and Indigenous Societies*. Manchester: Manchester University Press.

Ascher, F. (1985) *Transnational Corporations and Cultural Identities*. Paris: UNESCO.

Atwood, L.E. and Bullion, S.J. (1982) 'News Maps of the World: A View from Asia', in Atwood, L.E., Bullion, S.J. and Murphy, S.M. (eds) *International Perspectives on News*. Carbondale: South Illinois University Press.

Avinieri, S. (1969) *Karl Marx on Colonialism and Modernization*. New York: Anchor Doubleday.

Ayling, S. (1988) *Edmund Burke: His Life and Opinions*. London: John Murray.

Bailey, G. (1994) 'Trends in Media Literacy: Hawaii, the United States and Global', MA Thesis, University of Hawaii-Manoa.

Barnet, S.W. and Fairbank, J.K. (eds) (1985) *Christianity in China: Early Protestant Missionary Writings*. Harvard Studies in American East Asian Relations 9. Cambridge, MA: Harvard University Press.

Barnett, T. and Abdelkarim, A. (eds) (1988) *Sudan: State, Capital and Transformation*. London: Croom Helm.

Baxi, U. (1991) 'Complicity and Struggle: Theory and Society', *Social Scientist*, 19 (9–10): 19–26.

Bayart, J.F. (1985) 'L'etat au Cameroon', quoted by John Mope Simo in PhD Thesis, 'Gender Relations and Rural Change in Cameroon', School of Development Studies, University of East Anglia, 1991.

Beaud, M. (1989) *L'économie mondaile dans les années quatre-vingt*. Paris: La Dicouverte.

Becker, J. (1986) 'From Prejudice to Dependency: Conflicts on the Way to a New International Information Order', *Law and State*, 33: 44–65.

Beckman, B. (1982) 'State and Capitalist Development in Nigeria', *Review of African Political Economy*, 23.

Bell, D. (1973) *The Coming of Post-Industrial Society*. New York: Basic Books.

Beltrán, L.R. (1974) *Las politicas nacionales de comunicación en America Latina: los primeros pasos*. Paris: UNESCO (mimeograph).

Beltrán, L.R. (1976) 'Alien Premises, Objects and Methods in Latin American Communications Research', in Rogers, E. (ed.) 'Communication and Development: Critical Perspectives', *Communications Research*, 3 (2), April: 107–34.

Beltrán, L.R. and de Cardona, E.F. (1979) 'Latin America and the United States: Flaws in the Free Flow of Information', in Nordenstreng, K. and Schiller, H.I. (eds) *National Sovereignty and International Communication*. Norwood, NJ: Ablex Publishing Corporation. pp. 33–64.

Berman, M. (1988) *All That is Solid Melts into Air: The Experience of Modernity*. Harmondsworth: Penguin.

Bernstein, V. and Gordon, J. (1967) 'The Press and the Bay of Pigs', *Columbia University Forum*, Fall.

Berwanger, D. (1987) *Television in the Third World, New Technology and Social Change*. Bonn: Friedrich-Ebert-Stiftung.

Billig, M. (1995) *Banal Nationalism*. London: Sage Publications.

Bordenave, J.D. (1976) 'Communication and Agricultural Innovations in Latin

America: The Need for New Models', in Rogers, E. (ed.) 'Communication and Development: Critical Perspectives', *Communications Research*, 3 (2), April: 107–34.

Bourdieu, P. (1977) *Outline of a Theory of Practice*. Cambridge: Cambridge University Press.

Bourdieu, P. and Passeron, J.C. (1977) *Reproduction in Education, Economy and Society*. London: Sage Publications.

Boyd-Barrett, O. (1977) 'Media Imperialism: Towards an International Framework for the Analysis of Media Systems', in Curran, J., Gurevitch, M. and Woolacott, J. (eds) *Mass Communication and Society*. London: Edward Arnold. pp. 116–35.

Boyd-Barrett, O. (1980) *The International News Agencies*. London: Constable.

Brandt Commission (1980) *North-South: A Programme for Survival*. London: Pan Books.

Brandt Commission (1983) 'Common Crisis, North-South: Cooperation for World Recovery', 2nd Report of The Brandt Commission.

Breman, S. (1990) 'Trade and Information Policy', *Media, Culture and Society*, 12 (3): 361–85.

Brown, M.B. (1993) *Fair Trade*. London: Zed Books.

Bruck, A. (1979) 'The International Information Order: Consequences for Development Co-operation', in Bielenstein, D. (ed.) *Toward a New Information Order: Consequences for Development Policy*. Bonn: Institute for International Relations/ Friedrich-Ebert-Stiftung. pp. 65–72.

Canadian Commission for UNESCO (1986) 'The New World Information and Communication Order: A Failure to Communicate?', *Bulletin*, 5 (December).

Canadian Delegate to UNESCO's General Conference (1989) 'Statement at Commission IV of the 25th General Conference of UNESCO', Paris: 6 November (mimeograph).

Carnoy, M. (1974) *Education as Cultural Imperialism*. New York: David McKay.

Carr, E.H. (1966) *The Bolshevik Revolution 1917-1923, Volume 3*. Harmondsworth: Penguin.

Cassirer, E. (1946) *The Myth of the State*. New Haven and London: Yale University Press.

Chazan, N., Mortimer, R., Ravenhill, J. and Rothchild, D. (1988) *Politics and Society in Contemporary Africa*. London: Macmillan.

Chomsky, N. (1994) *World Orders, Old and New*. London: Pluto Press.

Churchill, E.M. (1991) 'The Mass Media and Regional Integration in Africa', *Africa Media Review*, 5 (1): 17–35.

Clarke, R. (1985) *Science and Technology in World Development*. Oxford University Press/UNESCO.

Clay, E. and Schaffer, B. (1984) *Room for Manoeuvre*. London: Heinemann.

Cleverdon, R. (1993) 'Global Tourism Trends: Influences, Determinants and Directional Flows', in *World Travel and Tourism Review 1993*. Wallingford: CAB International.

Clignet, R. (1971) 'Damned if You Do, Damned if You Don't. The Dilemmas of Colonizer–Colonized Relations', *Comparative Education Review*, October: 296–312.

Clymer, K.J. (1986) *Protestant Missionaries in the Philippines: 1898-1916: An Inquiry into the American Colonial Mentality*. Urbana: University of Illinois Press.

Coates, R.A. (1988) *Unilateralism, Ideology and US Foreign Policy: The United States in and out of UNESCO*. Boulder, CO: Lynne Rienner.

Collins, R. (1986) 'Broadband Black Death Cuts Queues. The Information Society and the UK', in Collins, R., Curran, J., Garnham, N., Scannel, P., Schlesinger, P. and Sparks, C. (eds) *Media, Culture and Society: A Critical Reader*. London: Sage Publications. pp. 287–308.

Committee on Government Operations (1980) *International Information Flow: Forging a New Framework*. Report to the 96th Congress, 2nd Session, House Report No. 96–1535, 11 December. Washington, DC: US Government Printing Office.

Compaine, B.M. (ed.) (1979) *Who Owns the Media? Concentration of Ownership in the Mass Communications Industry*. New York: Harmony Books.

The Conference Board (1972) *Information Technology Initiatives for Today – Decisions That Cannot Wait and Information Technology: Some Critical Implications for Decision Makers*. New York: The Conference Board. Quoted in Mosco (1982).

The Conference Board (1984) 'UNESCO: Who Needs It?', *Across the Board*, September.

Coquery-Vidrovitch, C. (1969) 'French Colonization in Africa to 1920 – Administration and Economic Development' in Gann, L.H. and Duignan, P. (eds) *Colonisation in Africa 1870–1960: Volume One – The History and Politics of Colonialism, 1870–1914*. Cambridge: Cambridge University Press. pp. 165–98.

Corrigan, P. and Sayer, D. (1985) *The Great Arch: English State Formation as Cultural Revolution*. Oxford: Basil Blackwell.

Curry, R.O. (ed.) (1988) *Freedom at Risk. Secrecy, Censorship and Repression in the 1980s*. Philadelphia: Temple University Press.

Cushman, D.P. and Kincaid, D.L. (1987) 'Introduction and Initial Insights', in Kincaid, D.L., *Communication Theory: Eastern and Western Perspectives*. London: Academic Press. pp. 1–10.

Cuthbert, M. (1980) 'Reaction to International News Agencies: 1930s and 70s Compared', *Gazette*, 26.

Das, V. (ed.) (1990) *Mirrors of Violence: Communities, Riots and Survivors in South Asia*. New Delhi: Oxford University Press.

Davidian, Z.N. (1994) *Economic Disparities Among Nations*. Calcutta: Oxford University Press.

Davis, D. (1994) 'Gendered Applications of Telecommunication Technologies: Empowerment or Entrenchment?'. Paper presented at the 6th MacBride Round Table, Honolulu, 23 January.

Delavignette, R.L. (1970) 'French Colonial Policy in Black Africa', in Gann. L.H. and Duignan, P. (eds) *Colonialism in Africa 1870–1960: Volume Two – The History and Politics of Colonialism 1914–1960*. Cambridge: Cambridge University Press. pp. 251–86.

Demac, D.A. (1988) *Liberty Denied. The Current Rise of Censorship in America*. New York: PEN American Centre.

Devèze, J. (1990) 'La place des images provenant de l'étranger dans la télévision française'. Paper presented at the Biannual Conference of the International Association for Mass Communication Research (IAMCR), Bled, Yugoslavia: 26–31 August.

Dworkin, R. (1981) 'What is Equity? Part I: Equity of Welfare; Part II: Equity of Resources', *Philosophy and Public Affairs*, 10 (3–4): 185–246, 283–345.

Dworkin, R. (1985) *A Matter of Principle*. Cambridge and London: Harvard University Press.

Editor and Publisher (1994) 'Group Urges US To Rejoin UNESCO', 12 March: 23.

Eger, J. (1978) 'Transnational Data Flow: The Need For Action', *Computerworld*, 13 February.

Engels, F. (1973) *Ludwig Feuerbach and the End of Classical German Philosophy*. London: Central Books.

English, J.W. (1982) 'Asian News', *Gazette*, 30: 177–187.

Enloe, C. (1990) *Bananas, Beaches and Bases*. Berkeley: University of California Press.

Fairbanks, J.K. (ed.) (1974) *The Missionary Enterprise in China and America*. Cambridge, MA: Harvard University Press.

Fanon, F. (1967) *The Wretched of the Earth*. Harmondsworth: Penguin.

Fanon, F. (1973) *Black Skins, White Masks*. London: Paladin.

Farer, T.J. (1975) 'The United States and the Third World: A Basis for Accommodation', *Foreign Policy*, 54 (1): 79–97.

Federal Ministry for Economic Cooperation (1978) 'Prospects of Cooperation between the Federal Republic of Germany and the Developing Countries in the Field of Communications'. Working Paper for International Conference: Towards a New World Information Order: Consequences for Development Policy, Bonn: 4–6 December.

Fejes, F. (1981) 'Media Imperialism: An Assessment', *Media, Culture and Society*, 3 (3): 281–9.

Fichte, J.G. (1909) *Fichte redem am die deutsche nation – engeleitet von Rudolf Eucken*. Leipzig: Insel-Verlag.

Fox Piven, F. (1995) 'Is it Global Economics or Neo-Laissez-Faire?', *New Left Review*, 213 (September/October): 107–114.

Frederick, H.H. (1992) *Global Communication & International Relations*. Belmont, CA: Wadsworth Publishing Co.

Friedman, A. (1995) 'G-7 Nations in Deep Split over Plunge of the Dollar', *International Herald Tribune*, 26 April: 1.

Fromkin, D. (1989) *A Peace to End All Peace*. New York: Avon.

Fukuyama, F. (1992) *The End of History and the Last Man*. New York: Avon Books.

Galtung, J. (1985) 'Social Communication and Global Problems', in Lee, P. (ed.) *Communication for All: New World and Communication Order*. New York: Orbis Books.

Galtung, J. and Vincent, R.C. (1992) *Global Glastnost; Toward a New World Information and Communication Order?* Italian translation by Edizioni Gruppo Abele, Torino, Italy. Cresskill, NJ: Hampton Press.

Galtung, J.V. and Vincent, R.C. (1996) *US Glasnost: Missing Political Themes in US Media Discourse*. Cresskill, NJ: Hampton Press.

Gann, L.H. and Duignan, P. (eds) (1970) *Colonialism in Africa 1870–1960: Volume One – The History and Politics of Colonialism, 1870–1914*. Cambridge: Cambridge University Press.

Garbo, G. (1983) 'The Role of the IPDC in the Implementation of the New World Information and Communication Order'. Presentation at conference of NAMEDIA, New Delhi, 9–12 December.

Garofalo, R. (1993) 'Whose World, What Beat: The Transnational Music Industry, Identity, and Cultural Imperialism', *The World of Music*, 35(2): 16–22.

Giffard, A.C. (1983) 'Inter Press Service News from the Third World'. Paper presented to the Association for Education in Journalism and Mass Communication at the annual convention, Corvallis, Oregon, August. Comments at the biannual meeting of the International Association for Mass Communication Research, Guaruja (São Paulo), Brazil, 16–21 August 1992.

Giffard, A.C. (1989) *UNESCO and the Media*. New York: Longman.

Giffard, A.C. (1992) 'Inter Press Service', *Gazette*, 50.
Gilbert, I. (1972) 'The Indian Academic Profession: The Origins of a Tradition of Subservience', *Minerva*, 10 July: 384–411.
Gitlin, T. (1987) *The Sixties: Years of Hope, Days of Rage*. New York: Bantam.
Gobineau, A. (1933) *Essai sur l'inégalité des races humaines*. Paris: Firmin-Didot.
Golding, P. (1974) 'Media Role in National Development', *Journal of Communication*, 24 (3), Summer: 39–53.
Golding, P. (1977) 'Media Professionalism in the Third World: The Transfer of an Ideology', in Curran, J., Gurevitch, M. and Woollacott, J. (eds) *Mass Communication and Society*. London: Edward Arnold.
Golding, P. (1990) 'Whose World; What Information; Which Order? – Rethinking NWICO in the 1990s'. Working Paper for WACC Colloquium on NWICO, London, 24–25 September.
Golding, P. (1994) 'The Communication Paradox: Inequity at the National and International Levels', *Media Development*, 4: 7–9.
Golding, P. and Elliot, P. (1979) *Making the News*. London: Longman.
Gonzalez-Manet, E. (1988) *The Hidden War of Information*. Translated by Laurien Alexandre. Norwood, NJ: Ablex Publishing Corp.
Goulet, D. (1975) *The Cruel Choice: A New Concept in the Theory of Development*. New York: University Press of America.
Greenberg, B.S. (1980) *Life on Television: Content Analyses of US TV Drama*. Norwood, NJ: Ablex Publishing Corp.
Greenberg, B.S. and D'Alessio, D. (1985) 'Quality and Quantity of Sex in the Soaps', *Journal of Broadcasting and Electronic Media*, 29 (Summer): 309–21.
Greenberg, B.S., Graef, D., Fernandez-Collado, C., Korzenny, F. and Atkin, C.K. (1980) 'Sexual Intimacy on Commercial TV During Prime Time', *Journalism Quarterly*, 57: 211–15.
Greenwood, D.J. (1977) 'Culture by the Pound: An Anthropological Perspective on Tourism as Cultural Commoditization', in Smith, V. (ed.) *Hosts and Guests*. Philadelphia: University of Pennsylvania Press. pp. 129–39.
Guha, R. (ed.) (1982–92) *Subaltern Studies. Vols. 1–7*. Delhi: Oxford University Press.
Hall, E. (1969) *The Hidden Dimension*. New York: Anchor Books.
Hall, S. (1992) '"The West and the Rest": Discourse and Power', in Hall, S. and Gieben, B. (eds) *Formations of Modernity*. Cambridge: Polity Press. pp. 275–320.
Hamelink, C.J. (ed.) (1980) *Communication in the Eighties*. Rome: IDOC.
Hamelink, C.J. (1983) *Cultural Autonomy in Global Communications*. New York and London: Longman.
Hamelink, C.J. (1984) *Finance and Information: A Study of Converging Interests*. Norwood, NJ: Ablex.
Hamelink, C.J. (1988) *The Technology Gamble*. Norwood, NJ: Ablex.
Hamelink, C.J. (1989a) 'UNESCO: The New International Information Order', in Everts, P.H. and Walraven, G. (eds) *The Politics of Persuasion. Implementation of Foreign Policy by the Netherlands*. Aldershot: Gower.
Hamelink, C.J. (1989b) 'The Relationship between Cultural Identity and Modes of Communication', in Anderson, J.A. (ed.) *Communication Yearbook 12*. London: Sage Publications. pp. 417–26.
Hamelink, C.J. (1994) *Trends in World Communication: On Disempowerment and Self-Empowerment*. Penang, Malaysia: Southbound.

Hamelink, C.J. and Mehra, A. (eds) (1990) *Communication Development and Human Rights*. Singapore: AMIC.

Harris, J.F. (1995) 'White House Opens Fire on "Backdoor Isolationism"', *International Herald Tribune*, 3 April: 29–30.

Harris, N. (1977) *The End of the Third World*. Harmondsworth: Penguin.

Harris, P. (1978) 'News Dependence: The Case for a New World Information Order'. Revised manuscript for UNESCO. Leicester Centre for Mass Communication Research.

Harris, P. (1985) 'The West African Wire Service of Reuters', in Ugboajah, F.O. (ed.) *Mass Communication, Culture and Society in West Africa*. New York: Hans Zell.

Harriss, J.C. and Mishra, S.C. (eds) (1983) *The State in South Asia*. Developmental Studies Occasional Paper 22. Norwich: University of East Anglia, School of Development Studies.

Haule, J.J. (1984) 'International Press Coverage of African Events: The Dilemma of the Future', *Gazette* 33: 107–114.

Head, S.W. (1985) *World Broadcasting Systems: A Comparative Analysis*. Belmont, CA: Wadsworth Publishing Co.

Herman, E.S. and Chomsky, N. (1988) *Manufacturing Consent*. New York: Pantheon Books.

Herzog, D. (1986) 'Some questions for Republicans', *Political Theory*, 14: 473–93.

Hill, P. (1985) *The World Their Household: The American Woman's Foreign Mission Movement and Cultural Transformation, 1879–1920*. Ann Arbor: University of Michigan Press.

Hills, J. (1992) 'Dependency Theory and its Relevance Today: International Institutions in Telecommunications and Structural Power'. Paper presented at the IAMCR Conference, Guaruja, August.

Hobbes, T. (1962) *Leviathan*. London: Fontana.

Hobsbawm, E. (1989) *Age of Empire*. New York: Vintage.

Hoskins, C. and Mirus, R. (1988) 'Reasons for the US Dominance of the International Trade in Television Programmes', *Media, Culture and Society*, 10 (4): 499–515.

Houghton, N.D. (1965) 'The Cuban Invasion of 1961 and the US Press in Retrospect', *Journalism Quarterly*, 42 (3), Summer.

Hudson, H. Zimmerman, B. (1990) Interview with Colleen Roach. 7 May.

Hudson, H. (1991) 'WARC-92: Issues and Strategies for the Developing World', in *Sharing Spectrum in the Digital World*. London: IIC.

Hveem, H. (1983) 'Selective Disassociation in Technology', in Ruggie, J.G. (ed.) *The Antinomies of Interdependence*. New York: Columbia University Press. pp. 273–316.

Hyden, G. (1983) *No Shortcuts to Progress*. London: Heinemann.

Ihonvbere, J.O. (1992) 'The Third World and the New World Order in the 1990s', *Futures*, December: 987–1002.

Information in the Non-Aligned Countries (1976) International Symposium on the Ways to Develop Information between Non-Aligned Countries, Tunis, 26–30 March.

International Commission for the Study of Communication Problems (no date) *The World of News Agencies*. Report 11. Paris: UNESCO.

International Herald Tribune (1995) 'Newts Notion: Laptops For All', 7–8 January: 30.

International Journalism Institute (1991) 'Selected Bibliography on WIICO'. Paper presented to the participants of the 3rd MacBride Round Table on Communication, 17 June, Prague; 21 June, Istanbul.

International Telecommunications Union (ITU) (1984) *The Missing Link: Report of the Independent Commission for World Wide Telecommunications Development.* Geneva: ITU.

Jacobs, S.M. (ed.) (1982) *Black Americans and the Missionary Movement in Africa.* Contributions in Afro-American and African Studies 66. Westport, CT: Greenwood Press.

Jakubowicz, K. (1985) 'Third World News Cooperation Schemes in Building a NWICO: Do they Stand a Chance?', *Gazette*, 36 (2): 81–93.

Jankowitsch, J. and Sauvant, K.P. (eds) (1978) *The Third World Without Superpowers: The Collected Documents of the Non-Aligned Countries.* Volume I. Dobbs Ferry, NY: Oceana Publications. Original document: Economic Declaration, Algiers, 5–9 September 1973. Fourth Conference of Heads of State or Government of Non-Aligned Countries. Algiers, 5–9 September 1973. Fundamental Texts, Algeria, Ministry of Foreign Affairs. pp. 61–73.

Jha, P.S. (1980) *The Political Economy of Stagnation.* Oxford and New York: Oxford University Press.

Jussawalla, M. (1979) 'The economics of telecoms for development', in Wedemeyer, D. (ed.) *Pacific Telecommunications Conference Proceedings.* Honolulu: Pacific Telecommunications Council. pp. 1D/1–1D/9.

Kane, C.H. (1986) *Ambiguous Adventure.* London: Heinemann.

Kaplún, M. (1973) *La comunicación de masas en America Latina.* Educación Hoy 5. Bogota: Asociación de Poblaciones Educativas.

Kennedy, P. (1987) *The Rise and Fall of the Great Powers.* New York: Random House.

Kharkanis, S. (1981) *Indian Politics and the Role of the Press.* New Delhi: Vikas Publishing.

Kieh, G.K. (1992) 'The Roots of Western Influence in Africa: An Analysis of the Conditioning Process', *The Social Science Journal*, 29(1): 7–19.

Kiernan, V. (1969) *The Lords of Human Kind.* London: The Cresset Library.

Kirat, M. and Weaver, D. (1985) 'Foreign News Coverage in Three Wired Services: A Study of AP, UPI and the Non-aligned News Agencies Pool', *Gazette*, 35: 31–47.

Kroloff, G. and Cohen, S. (1977) 'The New World Information Order'. Report to the Committee on Foreign Relations, US Senate, Washington, DC.

Laitin, D. (1983) 'Language Disassociation for Africa', in Ruggie, J.G. (ed.) *The Antinomies of Interdependence.* New York: Columbia University Press. pp. 317–68.

Laitin, D (1991) 'Can Language be Planned?', *Transition*, 54: 131–42.

Laszlo, E., Lozoya, J., Bhattachanya, A.K., Estevez, J., Green, R. and Raman, V. (1980) *The Obstacles to the New International Economic Order.* New York: Pergamon Press.

Lea, J. (1988) *Tourism and Development in the Third World.* London: Routledge.

Lee, C.C. (1980) *Media Imperialism Reconsidered.* Beverly Hills, CA: Sage Publications.

Lee, F.J.T. (1983) 'Dependency and Revolutionary Theory in the African Situation', in Barongo, Y. (ed.) *Political Science in Africa.* London: Zed Press.

Leiss, W. (1984) 'Under Technology's Thumb: How Not to Think about the Information Society'. Paper presented at the Biannual Conference of the IAMCR, Prague, August.

References 249

Lenin, V.I. and Service, R. (eds) (1992) *State and Revolution*. Harmondsworth: Penguin.

Lent, J.A. (1976) 'Foriegn News Content of United States and Asian Print Media: A Literature Review and Problem Analysis', *Gazette*, 22.

Lerner, D. (1958) *The Passing of Traditional Society*. New York: Free Press.

Lerner, D. (1980) Untitled book review of *National Sovereignty and International Communications*, *Public Opinion Quarterly*, Spring: 137.

Levi, W. (1974) *International Politics: Foundations of the System*. Oxford: Oxford University Press.

Lewis, N. (1988) *The Missionaries: God against the Indians*. New York: McGraw-Hill.

Leys, C. (1981) 'The "Over-Developed" Post-Colonial State: A Re-evaluation', *Review of African Political Economy*, 5: 39–62.

Locke, J. (1988) *Two Treatises of Civil Government*. London and Cambridge: Cambridge University Press.

Lugard, F. (1965) *The Dual Mandate in British Tropical Africa*. London: Frank Cass.

Lund, S. (1988) 'Satellite Television and Media Research', *European Journal of Communication*, 3 (3): 345–54.

MacCannell, D. (1976) *The Tourist: A New Theory of the Leisure Class*. New York: Schocken Books.

MacKensie, J.M. (1984) *Propaganda and Empire*. Manchester: Manchester University Press.

MacKensie, J.M. (ed.) (1986) *Imperialism and Popular Culture*. Manchester: Manchester University Press.

McPhail, T.L. (1981) *Electronic Colonialism*. Beverly Hills/London: Sage.

McPhail, T.L. (1982a) Comments at Canadian Commission for UNESCO's Round Table: Towards a Canadian Perspective on International Communication Issues. Ottawa, 26–7 August. Report.

McPhail, T.L. (1982b) 'A New World Information Order?', *International Perspective*, May/June.

Maitland, D. (1984) *The Missing Link*. Geneva: International Telecommunications Union.

Mansoori, A. (1986) 'American Missionaries in Iran, 1834–1934'. PhD dissertation, Ball State University.

Marham, J.W. (1961) 'Foreign News in the United States and South American Press', *Public Opinion Quarterly*, 25: 249–62.

Martin, P. and Musa, M. (1987) 'Recreating the Image: Regional News Agencies in Africa and the Caribbean', in *Communication Socialist Yearbook*.

Martin-Barbero, J. (1989) 'Repossessing Culture – The Quest of Popular Movements in Latin America', *Media Development*, 2: 21–4.

Martin-Barbero, J. (1993) *Communication, Culture and Hegemony: From Media to Mediations*. London: Sage Publications.

Marx, K. (1985) *The Eighteenth Brumaire of Louis Bonaparte*. London: Lawrence and Wishart.

Marx, K. and Engels, F. (1965) *The German Ideology*. London: Lawrence and Wishart.

Marx, K. and Engels, F. (1975) *Manifesto of the Communist Party*. Peking: Foreign Languages Press.

Masmoudi, M. (1979) 'The New World Information Order', *Journal of Communication*, 29 (2): 172–85.

Mattelart, A. (1974) *Mass media, idéologies et mouvement révolutionnaire*. Paris: Anthropos.

Mattelart, A. (1979) *Multinational Corporations and the Control of Culture*. Brighton: Harvester Press.

Mattelart, A. (1980) *Mass Media, Ideologies and the Revolutionary Movement*. Brighton: Harvester Press.

Mattelart, A. (1982) 'Des difficultés de conjuguer technologies et démocratie'. Plenary paper at the biannual conference of the IAMCR, Paris, August.

Mattera, P. (1990) *Prosperity Lost*. New York: Addison-Wesley.

Mazrui, A. (1975) 'The African University as a Multi-National Corporation: Problems of Penetration and Dependency', *Harvard Education Review*, 42, May.

Mazrui, A. (1977) *Africa's International Relations: The Diplomacy of Dependency and Change*. London: Heinemann.

Mead, M. (1970) *Culture and Commitment: The New Relationship between the Generations in the 1970s*. New York: Anchor Books.

Mehra, A. (1986) *Free Flow of Information: A New Paradigm*. Westport, CT: Greenwood Press.

Meisler, S. (1993) 'US Should Rejoin Controversial UN Agency, Task Force Says' *Los Angeles Times*, 31 August: 3.

Melody, W. and Samarajiwa, R. (1986) 'Canada's Contradictions on the New Information Order', in Becker, J., Hedebro, G. and Paldan, L. (eds) *Communication and Domination*. Norwood, NJ: Ablex.

Memmi, A. (1984) *Dependence*. Boston: Beacon Press.

Midgely, J. (1981) *Professional Imperialism: Social Work in the Third World*. London: Heinemann.

Mill, J.S. (1962) *Mill on Bentham and Coleridge*, ed. by F. Lewis. London: Chatto and Windus.

Mill, J.S. (1967) 'Chapters on Socialism', in *Collected Works, Vol. V*. Toronto: University of Toronto Press.

Mitra, A. (1977) *Terms of Trade and Class Relations*. London: Frank Cass.

Montgomery, H.B. (1906) *Christus Redemptor: An Outline History of the Island World of the Pacific*. Macmillan.

Moore, B. (1991) *The Social Origins of Dictatorship and Democracy: Lord and Peasant in the Making of the Modern World*. Harmondsworth: Penguin.

Mosco, V. (1979) *Broadcasting in the United States*. Norwood, NJ: Ablex.

Mosco, V. (1982) *Pushbutton Fantasies*. Norwood, NJ: Ablex.

Mosco, V. (1993) 'Free Trade in Communication: Building a World Business Order', in Nordenstreng, K. and Schiller, H. (eds) *Beyond National Sovereignty: International Communications in the 1990's*. Norwood, NJ: Ablex Publishing Corp. pp. 193–209.

Mosco, V. and McAllister, M.L. (1986) 'Canada and the International Telecommunications Union'. Report for the Department of Communication (DOC). Ottawa: DOC.

Mowlana, H. and Roach, C. (1991) 'New World Information and Communication Order since Prague: Overview of Developments and Activities'. Paper presented at the Third MacBride Round Table on Communication, 21 June, Istanbul, Turkey.

Musa, M.D. (1989) 'Confronting Western News Hegemony: A Case Study of News Agencies of Nigeria'. PhD thesis, University of Leicester.

Musa, M.D. (1990) 'News Agencies, Transnationalisation and the New Order', *Media, Culture and Society*, 12 (3): 325–42.

Nandy, A. (1987) 'Winners and Victims', *Development: Seeds of Change*, 1: 7–12.

Nandy, A. (ed.) (1988) *Science, Hegemony and Violence: A Requiem for Modernity*. Tokyo: United Nations University/Delhi: Oxford University Press.

Nash, D. (1977) 'Tourism as a Form of Imperialism', in Smith, V. (ed.) *Hosts and Guests*. Philadelphia: University of Pennsylvania Press. pp. 33–48.

Negrine, R. and Papathanasspoulos, S. (1991) 'The Internationalisation of Television', *European Journal of Communication*, 6 (1): 9–32.

New York Times (1994) 'Don't Rush Back to UNESCO', 23 February: 18.

Ngugi wa Thiong'o. (1986) *Decolonizing the Mind. The Politics of Language in Africa*. London: Heinemann.

Ngugi wa Thiong'o. (1991) 'The Language of Struggle', *Transition*, 54: 142–55.

Nicholson-Lord, D. (1990) 'Death by Tourism', *Independent on Sunday*, 5 August.

Nora, S. and Minc, A. (1980) *The Computerisation of Society*. Cambridge, MA: MIT Press.

Nordenstreng, K. (1984) *The Mass Media Declaration of UNESCO*. Norwood, NJ: Ablex.

Nordenstreng, K. (1994a) 'Monitoring Media Performance: An International Program for Content Analysis and Media Criticism'. Paper presented at the 6th annual MacBride Round Table on Communication, 22 January, Honolulu.

Nordenstreng, K. (1994b) Address at Media Flows Symposium, University of Tampere, Finland, 4–6 September.

Nordenstreng, K. and Schiller, H. (eds) (1979) *National Sovereignty and International Communications*. Norwood, NJ: Ablex.

Nyamnjoh, F.B. (1988) 'Broadcasting in Francophone Africa: Crusading for French Culture', *Gazette*, 42.

OECD [Organization for Economic Co-operation and Development] (1990) *Development Cooperation in the 1990s*. Paris: OECD.

OECD/ITU [International Telecommunication Union] (1983) *Telecommunications for Development*. Geneva: ITU.

Ogan, C.L. and Fair, J.E. (1984) 'A Little Good News: The Treatment of Development News in Selected Third World Newspapers', *Gazette*, 33: 173–91.

O'Siochru, S. (1993) *Global Perspectives 2010 – Tasks for Science and Technology, Vol. 14: Global Stability, Telecommunications and Science and Technology Policy –* for the Forecasting and Assessment in Sciences and Technology Program. Dublin: NEXUS Research Corporation.

Paquet-Sévigny, T. (1990) 'Reflections on Information Issues in the 1990s', *The Democratic Journalist*, 37 (12), December. pp. 14–17.

Parboni, R. (1985) *The Dollar and Its Rivals. Inflation and International Finance*. Routledge/Chapman and Hall.

Pasquali, A. (1963) *Comunicación y cultura de masas*. Caracas: Monte Avila Editores.

Pasquali, A. (1967) *El aparato singular: un dia de television en Caracas*. Caracas: Universidad Central de Venezuela, Facultad de Economia.

Patnaik, P. (1979) 'Industrial Development in India since Independence', *Social Scientist*, 83.

Pendakur, M. (1983) 'The New International Information Order after the MacBride Commission Report: An International Powerplay between the Core and Periphery Countries', *Media, Culture and Society*, 5 (3/4): 395–412.

Pendakur, M. (1984) 'United States–Canada Relations: Cultural Dependence and Conflict', in Mosco, V. and Wasko, J. (eds) *The Critical Communications Reader, Vol. 2*. Norwood, NJ: Ablex.

Pendakur, M. (1991) *Canadian Dreams and American Control: The Political Economy of the Canadian Film Industry*. Detroit, MI: Wayne State University Press.

Petras, J. (1993) 'Cultural Imperialism in the Late 20th Century', *Journal of Contemporary Asia*, 23(2): 139–48.

Phillipson, R. (1992) *Linguistic Imperialism*. Oxford: Oxford University Press.

Pinney, T. (ed.) (1986) *Kipling's India: Uncollected Sketches, 1884–88*. London: Macmillan.

Plafker, T. (1995) 'China Fights the "Brain Drain"', *International Herald Tribune*, April, 24: 23.

Poikal, J.G. (1970) 'Racist Assumptions of the 19th Century Missionary Movement', *International Review of Missions*, July: 271–84.

Pool, I. de Sola (1979a) 'The Influence of International Communication on Development', *Media Asia*, 6 (3): 149–56.

Pool, I. de Sola (1979b) 'Direct Broadcast Satellites and the Integrity of National Cultures', in Nordenstreng, K. and Schiller, H.I. (eds) *National Sovereignty and International Communication*. Norwood, NJ: Ablex Publishing Corp. pp. 120–53.

Porat, M. (1976) *The Information Economy*. Palo Alto, CA: Stanford University, Washington, DC: US Government Printing Office.

Poulantzas, N. (1968) *Pouvoir politique et classes sociales*. Paris: Maspero. Published in English in 1978 as *Political Power and Social Classes*. London: Verso.

Power, S.G. (1982) Prepared Statement before the Subcommittees on International Operations and on Human Rights and International Organizations of the Committee on Foreign Affairs, House of Representatives, in *Review of US Participation in UNESCO*, 10 March, 9 and 16 July 1981. Washington, DC: US Government Printing Office.

Preston, P. (1994) 'Universal Truths? The Links Between Technological Innovation and the Neo-Liberal Regulatory Concepts: The EU's Approach to the Audiovisual Sector', Conference on a Turbulent Europe: Conflict, Identity and Culture, EFTSC, London, 19–22 July.

Preston, W.E., Herman, E.S. and Schiller, H. (1989) *Hope and Folly: The United States and UNESCO: 1945–1985*. Minneapolis: University of Minnesota Press.

Proceedings of the Symposium on 'Media Accountability under International Law' (1989) Berkeley, CA, Union for Democratic Communications and the National Lawyers Guild, 14 June.

Raj, K.N. (1973) 'The Politics and Economics of "Intermediate Regimes"', *Economic and Political Weekly*, 7 July.

Rao, A. and Rao, B.G. (eds) (1977) *The Press She Could Not Whip*. Bombay: Popular Prakashan.

Rawls, J. (1971) *A Theory of Justice*. Oxford: Oxford University Press.

Reddi, U.V. (1986) 'Leapfrogging the Industrial Revolution', in Traber, M. (ed.) *The Myth of the Information Revolution*. London: Sage Publications. pp. 84–98.

Richter, W. (1991) 'Rural Telecommunications as a Vehicle for Growth'. Paper presented at the International Telecommunications Futures Symposium, Omaha, Nebraska.

Righter, R. (1978) *Whose News? Politics, the Press and the Third World*. London: Burnett Books.

Roach, C. (1979) 'The Reaction of the French Press to the UNESCO Mass Media Declaration'. Unpublished Study Commissioned by UNESCO. Paris: UNESCO.

Roach, C. (1981) 'French Press Coverage of the Belgrade UNESCO Conference', *Journal of Communication*, 31 (4): 175–87.

Roach, C. (1983) 'La Table Ronde ONU/UNESCO sur le nouvel ordre mondial de l'information et de la communication, Igls, Austria'. Unpublished article.

Roach, C. (1986) 'Select Annotated Bibliography on a New World Information and Communication Order', in Lee, P. (ed.) *Communication for All: New World Information and Communication Order*. New York: Orbis.

Roach, C. (1987) 'The US Position on the New World Information and Communication Order', *Journal of Communication*, 34 (4): 36–51.

Roach, C. (1990) 'The Movement for a New World Information and Communication Order: A Second Wave?', *Media, Culture and Society*, 12 (3): 283–307.

Rodney, W. (1972) *How Europe Underdeveloped Africa*. London: Bogle-l'Ouverture.

Roth, D. (1982) 'The "Black Man's Burden": The Racial Background of Afro-American Missionaries and Africa', in Jacobs, S. (ed.) *Black Americans and the Missionary Movement in Africa*. Contributions in Afro-American and African Studies 66. Westport, CT: Greenwood Press.

Rousseau, J.J. (1969) *The Social Contract*. Harmondsworth: Penguin.

Rowe, W. and Schelling, V. (1991) *Memory and Modernity: Popular Culture in Latin America*. London and New York: Verso.

Ruggie, J.G. (ed.) (1983) *The Antinomies of Interdependence*. New York: Columbia University Press.

Said, E. (1993) *Culture and Imperialism*. London: Chatto and Windus.

Samarajiwa, R. (1984) 'Third World Entry to the World Market in News: Problems and Possible Solutions', *Media, Culture and Society*. 6 (1): 119–36.

Sanchez, R. (1995) 'For College Freshmen, Politics More Boring Than Ever', *International Herald Tribune*, January 10: 3.

Sandel, M. (1984) 'Morality and the Liberal Ideal', *New Republic*, 7 May, 190: 15–17.

Sapru, S. (1982) 'A National Agency's Partnership with a Transnational News Agency (an Indian Experience)', *Gazette*, 29: 57–63.

Saul, J. (1974) 'The State in Post-Colonial Societies: Tanzania', in Milliband, R. and Saville, J. (eds) *The Socialist Register 1974*. London: Merlin Press; extracted in Golbourne, H. (ed.) (1979) *Politics and the State and the Third World*. London: Macmillan.

Sayer, D. (1983) *Marx's Method: Ideology, Science and Critique in 'Capital'*. New York: Harvester.

Schiller, H. (1969) *Mass Communication and American Empire*. New York: August M. Kelley.

Schiller, H. (1976) *Communication and Cultural Domination*. New York: International Arts and Science Press.

Schiller, H. (1980) 'Whose New International Economic Information Order?', *Communication*, 5 (2): 299–314.

Schramm, W. (1964) *Mass Media and National Development*. Paris: UNESCO; Stanford, CA: Stanford University Press.

Schwartz, C. (1973) *Gershwin: His Life and Music*. New York: Da Capo Press.

Servan-Schreiber, J.J. (1980) *Le Défi mondial*. Paris: Fayard.

Shivji, I. (1975) *The Class Struggle in Tanzania*. Dar es Salaam: Tanzania Publishing House.

Shivji, I. (1979) 'The Post-Mwongozo Proletarian Struggles in Tanzania', in Golbourne, H. (ed.) *Politics and the State in the Third World*. London: Macmillan.

Sieghart, P. (1991) 'International Human Rights Law: Some Current Problems', in Blackburn, R. and Taylor, J. (eds) *Human Rights for the 1990s*. London: Manshell. pp. 24–42.

Silk, L. (1973) 'Data Technology Impact', *New York Times*, 19 July.

Sinclair, J. (1990) 'Neither West nor Third World: The Mexican Television Industry within the NWIO Debate', *Media, Culture and Society*, 12 (3): 343–60.

Singham, A. and Hune, S. (1986) *Non-Alignment in an Age of Alignment*. New York: Lawrence Hill.

Smith, A. (1980) *The Geopolitics of Information*. London: Faber and Faber.

Smythe, D. (1981) *Dependency Road: Communications, Capitalism, Consciousness and Canada*. Norwood, NJ: Ablex.

Sonaike, S.A. (1988) 'Communication and Third World Development: A Dead End', *Gazette*, 41: 104.

South Commission (1990) *The Challenge of the South*. Oxford: Oxford University Press.

Sparks, C. and Roach, C. (1990) 'Farewell to NWICO?' (editorial), *Media, Culture and Society*, 12 (3): 275–81.

Sparks, C., Schlesinger, P. and Kondopolou, Y. (1993) 'British Press Reporting of the New World Information and Communication Order Debate, 1980–1981'. Report available from PCL School of Communication, London.

Spencer, H. (1967) *The Evolution of Society: Selections from Herbert Spencer's Principles of Sociology*. Chicago and London: University of Chicago Press.

Sreberny-Mohammadi, A. (1991) 'The Global and the Local in International Communications', in Curran, J. and Gurevitch, M. (eds) *Mass Media and Society*. London: Edward Arnold. pp. 118–38.

Sreberny-Mohammadi, A. (1994) Media Flows Symposium; University of Tampere, Finland, 4–6 September; *IAMCR Newsletter* (International Association for Mass Communication Research), 4 (3): 4–5.

Sreberny-Mohammadi, A., with Nordenstreng, K., Stevenson, R.L. and Ugboajah, F. (1984) *Foreign News in the Media: International Reporting in Twenty-nine Countries*. Reports and Papers on Mass Communication, no. 93. Paris: UNESCO.

State of California (1994) AB2524, Legislation, State of California.

Steinbruner, J. (1991) 'The Rule of Law', *The Bulletin of the Atomic Scientists*, 47 (5): 20.

Steven, R. (1994) 'New World Order: A New Imperialism', *Journal of Contemporary Asia*, 24 (3): 271–96.

Stevenson, R.L. (1990) 'Communication and Third World Growth, 1965–1985'. Paper presented at biannual conference of the IAMCR, Bled, Yugoslavia, August.

Stevenson, R.L. and Cole, R. (1984) 'Pattern of Foreign News', in Stevenson, R. and Shaw, D.L. (eds) *Foreign News and the NIIO*. Ames: Iowa State University Press.

Sussman, G. and Lent, J.A. (eds) (1991) *Transnational Communications: Wiring the Third World*. Newbury Park, CA and London: Sage.

Svendsen, K.D.G. (1994) 'International Law and the Human Right to Communicate'. Paper presented at biannual meeting of the International Association for Mass Communication Research, Seoul, Korea, 3–8 July.

Szcylowitcz, J. (1973) *Education and Modernization in the Middle East*. Ithaca, NY: Cornell University Press.

Taylor, C. (1986) 'Alternative Futures: Legitimacy, Identity and Alienation in late Twentieth Century Canada', in Cairns, A. and Williams, C. (eds) *Constitutionalism, Citizenship and Society in Canada*. Toronto: University of Toronto Press.

Taylor, P. (1989) *Political Geography* (2nd edn). London: Longman.

Tehranian, M. (1990) *Technologies of Power: Information Machines and Democratic Prospects*. Norwood, NJ: Ablex Publishing Corporation.

Thomas, N. (1994) *Colonialism's Culture: Anthropology, Travel and Government.* Cambridge: Polity Press.

Tomlinson, J. (1991) *Cultural Imperialism.* Baltimore, MD: Johns Hopkins University Press.

Tunstall, J. (1977) *The Media are American: Anglo-American Media in the World.* London: Constable.

Turner, L. and Ash, J. (1976) *The Golden Hordes: International Tourism and the Pleasure Principle.* New York: St Martin's Press.

UNA (United Nations Association of the United States) (1989) *A Forum in Restoration: International Intellectual Cooperation and America's Interests.* New York: UNA.

UNESCO (1978) *Mass Media Declaration.*

UNESCO (1980a) *Many Voices, One World.* Paris: International Commission for the Study of Communication Problems, UNESCO.

UNESCO (1980b) Resolution adopted by the General Conference of UNESCO at its Twenty-First Session, Belgrade, September–October, Section 4/19 of the Annex.

UNESCO (1989) *World Communication Report.* Paris: UNESCO.

UNESCO (1990) Resolution 21 C/4.19, General Conference of UNESCO, September–October, Belgrade.

UNESCO (1991a) *Statistical Yearbook 1991.* Paris: UNESCO.

UNESCO (1991b) 'Budget for 1991, including Financial Position of the Special Account', IPDC 12th Session, Paris: 11–18 February, CII–91/CONF.214/2 (no pagination).

Union for Democratic Communications and the National Lawyers Guild (1989) *Proceedings of the Symposium on 'Media Accountability under International Lawyers'.* Berkeley, CA: the Union for Democratic Communications and the National Lawyers Guild, 14 June.

United Nations (1948) Article 19, Universal Declaration of Human Rights, United Nations General Assembly.

US Congress (1983) *Long-Range Goals in International Telecommunications and Information: An Outline for United States Policy.* Washington, DC: US Government Printing Office.

Varis, T. (1973) *International Inventory of Television Programme Structure and the Flow of Television Programmes Between Nations.* University of Tampere, Finland.

Vincent, R.C. (1989) 'Clio's Consciousness Raised? The Portrayal of Women in Rock Videos Reexamined', *Journalism Quarterly,* 66: 155–60.

Vincent, R.C. (1992) 'New World Order? Changes in Global Hierarchy: Implications for the NWICO Concept'. A paper presented at the annual meeting of the International Association for Mass Communication Research, Guarujá (São Paulo), Brazil, 16–21 August.

Vincent, R.C. (1994) 'New Order or Old? World Distribution of Communication Technologies'. Paper presented to the biannual meeting of the International Association for Mass Communication Research (IAMCR), Seoul, Korea, 3–8 July.

Vincent, R.C. and Riaz, A. (1990) 'Foreign News on Bangladesh Television: An Analysis of News Content and Selection'. Paper presented at the 40th annual meeting of the International Communication Association, Dublin, Ireland, 27 June.

Vincent, R.C., Davis, D.K. and Boruszkowski, L.A. (1987) 'Sexism on MTV: The Portrayal of Women in Rock Videos', *Journalism Quarterly,* 64: 750–6, 941.

Voices of Freedom: A World Conference of Independent News Media (1981) Talloires, France: 15–17 May. Published proceedings. Medford, Massachusetts: Edward R. Murrow Centre of Public Diplomacy.

Wallis, R. and Malm, K. (1984) *Big Sounds from Small People. The Music Industry in Small Countries*. London: Constable.

Wardhaugh, R. (1987) *Languages in Competition*. Oxford: Basil Blackwell.

Warren, B. (1980) *Imperialism: Pioneer of Capitalism*. London: Verso.

Warren, G. (1980) 'Statement at the 21st General Conference of UNESCO', Paris, 13 October.

Washington Post (1993) 'Why UNESCO?', 19 April: 22.

Waters, M. (1995) *Globalization*. London and New York: Routledge.

Williams, R. (1961) *Culture and Society*. London: Penguin Books.

Williams, R. (1983) *Keywords*. London: Fontana.

Williams, W. (1982) *Black Americans and the Evangelization of Africa 1877–1900*. Madison: University of Winsconsin Press.

Winsbury, R. (1990) 'Television in Kenya', *Intermedia*, 18 (1): 36.

Wood, R.E. (1986) *From Marshall Plan to Debt Crisis: Foreign Aid and Development Choices in the World Economy*. Berkeley: University of California Press.

World Commission on Environment and Development (1987) *Our Common Future*. Oxford: Oxford University Press.

Worsley, P. (1984) *The Three Worlds: Culture and World Development*. London: Weidenfield and Nicholson.

Zirinsky, M. (1993) 'A Panacea for the Ills of the Country: American Presbyterian Education in Inter-War Iran', *Iranian Studies*, 26 (1–2): 119–28.

Index